Start a Business in Pennsylvania

Fourth Edition

Desiree A. Petrus
Mark Warda

Attorneys at Law

SPHINX® PUBLISHING
AN IMPRINT OF SOURCEBOOKS, INC.®
NAPERVILLE, ILLINOIS
www.SphinxLegal.com

Fourth Edition: 2006

Published by: **Sphinx® Publishing, An Imprint of Sourcebooks, Inc.®**

Naperville Office
P.O. Box 4410
Naperville, Illinois 60567-4410
630-961-3900
Fax: 630-961-2168
www.sourcebooks.com
www.SphinxLegal.com

This publication is designed to provide accurate and authoritative information in regard to the subject matter covered. It is sold with the understanding that the publisher is not engaged in rendering legal, accounting, or other professional service. If legal advice or other expert assistance is required, the services of a competent professional person should be sought.

From a Declaration of Principles Jointly Adopted by a Committee of the American Bar Association and a Committee of Publishers and Associations

This product is not a substitute for legal advice.

Disclaimer required by Texas statutes.

Library of Congress Cataloging-in-Publication Data
Petrus, Desiree A., 1964-
    Start a business in Pennsylvania / by Desiree A. Petrus and Mark Warda. -- 4th ed.
       p. cm.
    Rev. ed. of: How to start a business in Pennsylvania. 3rd ed. 2003.
    Includes index.
    ISBN-13: 978-1-57248-561-7 (pbk. : alk. paper)
    ISBN-10: 1-57248-561-2 (pbk. : alk. paper)
    1. Business enterprises--Law and legislation--Pennsylvania--Popular works. 2. Business law--Pennsylvania.   I. Warda, Mark.
II. Petrus, Desiree A., 1964-   . How to start a business in Pennsylvania. III. Title.
KFP205.Z9P48 2006
346.748'065--dc22
                                                                                          2006022330

Printed and bound in the United States of America.
SB — 10 9 8 7 6 5 4 3 2 1

Contents

Using Self-Help Law Books

Before using a self-help law book, you should realize the advantages and disadvantages of doing your own legal work and understand the challenges and diligence that this requires.

The Growing Trend

Rest assured that you will not be the first or only person handling your own legal matter. For example, in some states, more than 75% of the people in divorces and other cases represent themselves. Because of the high cost of legal services, this is a major trend, and many courts are struggling to make it easier for people to represent themselves. However, some courts are not happy with people who do not use attorneys and refuse to help them in any way. For some, the attitude is, "Go to the law library and figure it out for yourself."

We write and publish self-help law books to give people an alternative to the often complicated and confusing legal books found in most law libraries. We have made the explanations of the law as simple and easy to understand as possible. Of course, unlike an attorney advising an individual client, we cannot cover every conceivable possibility.

Cost/Value Analysis

Whenever you shop for a product or service, you are faced with various levels of quality and price. In deciding what product or service to buy, you make a cost/value analysis on the basis of your willingness to pay and the quality you desire.

When buying a car, you decide whether you want transportation, comfort, status, or sex appeal. Accordingly, you decide among choices such as a Neon, a Lincoln, a Rolls Royce, or a Porsche. Before making a decision, you usually weigh the merits of each option against the cost.

When you get a headache, you can take a pain reliever (such as aspirin) or visit a medical specialist for a neurological examination. Given this choice, most people, of course, take a pain reliever, since it costs only pennies; whereas a medical examination costs hundreds of dollars and takes a lot of time. This is usually a logical choice because it is rare to need anything more than a pain reliever for a headache. But in some cases, a headache may indicate a brain tumor, and failing to see a specialist right away can result in complications. Should everyone with a headache go to a specialist? Of course not, but people treating their own illnesses must realize that they are betting, on the basis of their cost/value analysis of the situation, that they are taking the most logical option.

The same cost/value analysis must be made when deciding to do one's own legal work. Many legal situations are very straightforward, requiring a simple form and no complicated analysis. Anyone with a little intelligence and a book of instructions can handle the matter without outside help.

But there is always the chance that complications are involved that only an attorney would notice. To simplify the law into a book like this, several legal cases often must be condensed into a single sentence or paragraph. Otherwise, the book would be several hundred pages long and too complicated for most people. However, this simplification necessarily leaves out many details and nuances that would apply to special or unusual situations. Also, there are many ways to interpret most legal questions. Your case may come before a judge who disagrees with the analysis of our authors.

Therefore, in deciding to use a self-help law book and to do your own legal work, you must realize that you are making a cost/value analysis. You have decided that the money you will save in doing it yourself outweighs the chance that your case will not turn out to your satisfaction. Most people handling their own simple legal matters never have a problem, but occasionally people find that it ended up costing them more to have an attorney straighten out the situation than it would have if they had hired an attorney in the beginning. Keep this in mind while handling your case, and be sure to consult an attorney if you feel you might need further guidance.

Local Rules   The next thing to remember is that a book which covers the law for the entire nation, or even for an entire state, cannot possibly include every procedural difference of every jurisdiction. Whenever possible, we provide the exact form needed; however, in some areas, each county, or even each judge, may require unique forms and procedures. In our state books, our forms usually cover the majority of counties in the state or provide examples of the type of form that will be required. In our national books, our forms are sometimes even more general in nature but are designed to give a good idea of the type of form that will be needed in most locations. Nonetheless, keep in mind that your state, county, or judge may have a requirement, or use a form, that is not included in this book.

You should not necessarily expect to be able to get all of the information and resources you need solely from within the pages of this book. This book will serve as your guide, giving you specific information whenever possible and helping you to find out what else you will need to know. This is just like if you decided to build your own backyard deck. You might purchase a book on how to build decks. However, such a book would not include the building codes and permit requirements of every city, town, county, and township in the nation; nor would it include the lumber, nails, saws, hammers, and other materials and tools you would need to actually build the deck. You would use the book as your guide, and then do some work and research involving such matters as whether you need a permit of some kind, what type and grade of wood is available in your area, whether to use hand tools or power tools, and how to use those tools.

Before using the forms in a book like this, you should check with your court clerk to see if there are any local rules of which you should be aware or local forms you will need to use. Often, such forms will require the same information as the forms in the book but are merely laid out differently or use slightly different language. They will sometimes require additional information.

Changes in the Law

Besides being subject to local rules and practices, the law is subject to change at any time. The courts and the legislatures of all fifty states are constantly revising the laws. It is possible that while you are reading this book, some aspect of the law is being changed.

In most cases, the change will be of minimal significance. A form will be redesigned, additional information will be required, or a waiting period will be extended. As a result, you might need to revise a form, file an extra form, or wait out a longer time period. These types of changes will not usually affect the outcome of your case. On the other hand, sometimes a major part of the law is changed, the entire law in a particular area is rewritten, or a case that was the basis of a central legal point is overruled. In such instances, your entire ability to pursue your case may be impaired.

Introduction

There has never been a better time to start a business in Pennsylvania than now. Pennsylvania is a booming state due to the low cost of living and the clean environment. Also, the state government has developed a new attitude to help attract businesses by providing quick access to forms and clearly stating the requirements to start a business in Pennsylvania.

Pennsylvania ranks sixth in the nation for new and expanding business sites, fifth for affordable housing, eighth for quality health care, and ninth for expenditure per pupils for schools. A flat personal income tax of 2.8% (one of the lowest in the nation) and a highly skilled work-force make Pennsylvania attractive for starting and maintaining a successful business.

The best way to take part in this booming and rich atmosphere is to run your own business. Be your own boss and be as successful as you dare to be. However, be aware that if you do not follow the laws of the state, your progress can be slowed or stopped by government fines, civil judgments, or even criminal penalties.

This book gives you the framework for legally opening a business in Pennsylvania. It also includes information on where to find special rules for each type of business. If you have problems that are not covered by this book, you should seek an attorney who can be available for your ongoing needs.

In order to cover all of the aspects of any business you are thinking of starting, you should read through this entire book, rather than skipping to the parts that look most important. There are many laws that may not sound as if they apply to you, but they do have provisions that will affect your business.

You will find new forms that you will need to start your business within this book. In almost all cases, these forms should be submitted electronically. The forms in this book were the most recent at the time of publication. They may have been revised by the time you read this book, but most of the information requested will be the same. You are advised to check the websites where these forms can be downloaded before submitting them to the required agency.

Finally, a helpful Business Start-Up Checklist, found in Appendix A, sums up each chapter and makes it easy for you to remember each step in establishing your new business.

Deciding to Start a Business

If you are reading this book, then you have probably made a serious decision to take the plunge and start your own business. Hundreds of thousands of people make the same decision each year, and many of them become very successful. A lot of them also fail. Knowledge can only help your chances of success. You need to know why some businesses succeed while others fail. Some of what follows may seem obvious, but to someone wrapped up in a new business idea, some of this information is occasionally overlooked.

KNOW YOUR STRENGTHS

The last thing a budding entrepreneur wants to hear is that he or she is not cut out for running a business. You might avoid those *do you have what it takes* quizzes because you are not sure you want hear the answer. However, you can be successful if you know where to get the skills you lack.

You should consider all of the skills and knowledge that running a successful business requires, and decide whether you have what it takes. If you do not, it does not necessarily mean you are doomed to be an employee all your life. Perhaps you just need a partner who has the skills you lack. Perhaps you can hire someone with the skills you need, or you can structure your business to avoid areas where you are weak. If those tactics do not work, maybe you can learn the skills.

For example, if managing employees is not your strong suit, you can:

- handle product development yourself, and have a partner or manager deal with employees;

- take seminars in employee management; or,

- structure your business so that you do not need employees (use independent contractors or set yourself up as an independent contractor).

When planning your business, consider the following factors.

- *If it takes months or years before your business turns a profit, do you have the resources to hold out?* Businesses have gone under or have been sold just before they were about to take off. Staying power is an important ingredient to success.

- *Are you willing to put in a lot of overtime to make your business a success?* Owners of businesses do not set their own hours—the business sets hours for the owner. Many business owners work long hours seven days a week. You have to enjoy running your business and be willing to make some personal time sacrifices.

- *Are you willing to do the dirtiest or most unpleasant work of the business?* Emergencies come up and employees are not always dependable. You might need to mop up a flooded room, spend a weekend stuffing 10,000 envelopes, or work Christmas if someone calls in sick.

- *Do you know enough about the product or service?* Are you aware of the trends in the industry and what changes new technology might bring? Think of the people who started typesetting or printing businesses just before type was replaced by laser printers.

✪ *Do you know enough about accounting and inventory to manage the business?* Do you have a good head for business? Some people naturally know how to save money and do things profitably. Others are in the habit of buying the best or the most expensive of everything. The latter can be fatal to a struggling new business.

✪ *Are you good at managing employees?* If your business has employees (or will have in the future), managing them is an unavoidable part of running the business.

✪ *Do you know how to sell your product or service?* You can have the best product on the market, but people will not know about it unless you tell them about it. If you are a wholesaler, shelf space in major stores is hard to get, especially for a new company without a record, a large line of products, or a large advertising budget.

✪ *Do you know enough about getting publicity?* The media receives thousands of press releases and announcements each day, and most are thrown away. Do not count on free publicity to put your name in front of the public.

KNOW YOUR BUSINESS

Not only do you need to know the concept of a business, but you need the experience of working in a business. Maybe you always dreamed of running a bed and breakfast or having your own pizza place. Have you ever worked in such a business? If not, you may have no idea of the day-to-day headaches and problems of the business. For example, do you really know how much to allow for theft, spoilage, and unhappy customers?

You might feel silly taking an entry-level job at a pizza place when you would rather start your own, but it might be the most valuable preparation you do. A few weeks of seeing how a business operates could mean the difference between success and failure.

Working in a business as an employee is one of the best ways to be a success at running such a business. People with new ideas can revolutionize established industries with obvious improvements that no one before dared to try.

SOURCES OF FURTHER GUIDANCE

The following offices offer free or low-cost guidance for new businesses.

SCORE The *Service Corps of Retired Executives* (SCORE) is a group of retired, former executives who will give advice to new businesses at no charge. Following is a list of local Pennsylvania SCORE offices.

Altoona
3900 Industrial Drive #6
Altoona, PA 16602
814-942-9054

Bethlehem
621 Taylor Street
Bethlehem, PA 18015
610-758-4496

Chambersburg
100 Lincoln Way East
Chambersburg, PA 17201
717-264-7101

Erie
120 West Ninth Street
Erie, PA 16501
814-871-5650

Fairless Hills
409 Hood Boulevard
Fairless Hills, PA 19030
215-943-8850

Harrisburg
349 Wiconisco Street
Suite 237
Harrisburg, PA 17110
717-213-0435

Jenkintown
1653 The Fairway #204
Jenkintown, PA 19046
215-885-3027

Lancaster
312 West Liberty Street
Lancaster, PA 17603
717-397-3092

Latrobe
300 Fraser Purchase Road
Latrobe, PA 15650
724-539-7505

Monroe-Stroudsburg
556 Main Street
Stroudsburg, PA 18360
570-421-4433

Pittsburgh
411 Seventh Avenue
Suite 1450
Pittsburgh, PA 15219
412-395-6560

Pottstown
244 High Street
Suite 302
Pottstown, PA 19464
610-327-2673

Reading
645 Penn Street
Reading, PA 19603
610-376-6766

State College
200 Innovation Boulevard #242B
State College, PA 16803
814-234-9415

Uniontown
140 North Beeson Avenue
Uniontown, PA 15401
724-437-4222

West Chester
601 Westtown Road, #281
West Chester, PA 19380
610-344-6910

Wilkes-Barre
7 North Wilkes-Barre Boulevard #407
Wilkes-Barre, PA 18702
570-826-6502

Small Business Development Centers

Educational programs for small businesses are offered through the Small Business Development Centers at many Pennsylvania colleges and universities. You should see if they have any that could help you in any areas in which you are weak.

Bucknell University
112 Dana English Building
Lewisburg, PA 17837
570-577-1249

Clarion University
102 Dana Still Building
Clarion, PA 16214
814-393-2060

Duquesne University
600 Forbes Avenue
Pittsburgh, PA 15282
412-396-6233

Gannon University
120 West 9th Street
Erie, PA 16501
814-871-7232

Indiana University of Pennsylvania
108 Eberly College of Business
Indiana, PA 15705
724-357-7915

start a business in pennsylvania   6

Kutztown University
3211 North Front Street
Harrisburg, PA 17110
717-232-3770

Lehigh University
621 Taylor Street
Bethlehem, PA 18015
610-758-3980

Penn State University
117 Technology Center
University Park, PA 16802
814-863-4293

Saint Francis College
P.O. Box 600
Loretto, PA 15940
814-472-3200

Saint Vincent College
300 Fraser Purchase Road
Latrobe, PA 15650
724-537-4572

Temple University
1510 Cecil B. Moore Avenue
Philadelphia, PA 19121
215-204-7282

University of Pittsburgh
230 South Bouquet Street
First Floor
Pittsburgh, PA 15213
412-648-1542

University of Scranton
800 Monroe Avenue
Scranton, PA 18510
570-941-7588

Wilkes University
7 South Main Street
Wilkes-Barre, PA 18701
570-408-4340

Choosing the Form of Your Business

The five most popular forms for a business in Pennsylvania are proprietorship, partnership, corporation, limited partnership, limited liability company, and limited liability partnership. The characteristics, advantages, and disadvantages of each are discussed in this chapter.

PROPRIETORSHIP

A *proprietorship* is one person doing business in his or her own name or under a fictitious name.

Advantages A sole proprietorship is the easiest and simplest form. There is virtually no organizational expense, and the only licenses and certificates required are those necessary for the particular service. For example, if you are opening a nail salon, you will need a cosmetologist license. The sole proprietorship allows the greatest freedom from regulation of all the business forms. There are also possible tax advantages to discuss with an accountant—the sole proprietor is taxed at the individual rate and losses may be deductible from an individual tax return. Another advantage to beginning your business as a sole proprietorship is that as your business grows, you can upgrade to another form of business entity, such as a partnership or corporation.

Disadvantages   You must carefully weigh the decision to operate as a sole proprietorship, because even though it is the easiest form in which to operate, there are disadvantages. The sole proprietor is personally liable for all debts and obligations of the business, and all profits are directly taxable as personal income. You may even be responsible for a self-employment tax. Therefore, it is very important to consult a tax professional to decide if this is an obligation you are willing to take. Also, your ability to raise and borrow money is limited by your personal credit history.

GENERAL PARTNERSHIP

A *general partnership* involves two or more people carrying on a business together, sharing the profits and losses. The rights and privileges of the partnership are defined by the partnership agreement and state law, so it is important to put the partners' agreement in writing. Laws covering partnerships are found in Title 15 of the Pennsylvania Consolidated Statutes (Pa.C.S.), Sections 8101 et seq. and 8301 et seq.

Advantages   Partnerships, which combine the assets and expertise of each partner for the health of the business, are easily created. The tax advantages and organizational costs are the same as the sole proprietorship.

Disadvantages   A number of the disadvantages of partnerships are similar to those of sole proprietorships. Each partner is personally liable for the debts and obligations of the partnership, because there is unlimited liability for the acts of the other partner. Also, one partner can commit the partnership to any obligation and all partners can be held responsible. For example, if your partner makes a promise to provide a service and fails to provide that service, you can be held liable even if the partner makes the promise without your knowledge. Weigh your choice of partner carefully, because it is often hard to get rid of a bad partner once you are committed.

CORPORATION

A *corporation* is an artificial person that carries on a business through its officers for its shareholders. In Pennsylvania, one person may form a corporation and be the sole shareholder and officer. Laws covering corporations are contained in Title 15, Sec. 1101 through Sec. 1110, Sec. 1301 through Sec. 1311, and Sec. 1501 through Sec. 1511.

An *S corporation*, formerly known as a *Subchapter S Corporation*, is a corporation that has filed IRS Form 2553, thus choosing to have all profits taxed to the shareholders, rather than to the corporation. An S corporation files a tax return, but pays no federal or state tax. The profit shown on the S corporation tax return is reported on the owner's tax returns.

An S corporation has no more than seventy-five shareholders, and its income is taxed to the shareholders as if the corporation were a partnership. The shareholders are then able to deduct S corporation losses on their personal income tax returns. Do note that a specific portion of the corporation's receipts must come from active business rather than passive investment.

A *C corporation* is a business corporation that has not elected to be taxed as an S corporation. A C corporation pays taxes on its profits. The effect of this is that when the corporation pays dividends to its shareholders, there is double taxation—once at the corporate level and again when the shareholders receive them.

A *professional corporation* is a type of corporation where people in regulated professions can practice their professions within a corporate structure. A *profession* is any kind of personal service that requires a license, admission to practice, or other legal authorization. A professional remains personally liable for any wrongdoing in performing personal services.

A *nonprofit corporation* is usually used for such organizations as churches, civic groups, and condominium associations. However, with careful planning, some types of businesses can be set up as nonprofit corporations and save a fortune in taxes. While a nonprofit corporation cannot pay dividends, it can pay its officers and employees fair salaries. Some of the major American nonprofit organizations pay their officers well over $100,000 a year. Pennsylvania's rules for nonprofit corporations are included in 15 Pa.C.S. Sec. 5101 et. seq.

Advantages

Forming a corporation is an advantageous way to do business. Unlike a sole proprietorship or partnership, liability for the debts of the corporation is limited to the amount invested in the corporation. Also, shareholders in the corporation have no liability for corporate debts and lawsuits, and except for certain limited situations, no personal liability for their corporate acts or the corporate acts of other shareholders. The corporate tax rate may be advantageous—it might be possible for an individual to only be taxed on dividends received from the corporation. Ownership of a corporation is prestigious and can be easily transferred. Unlike a sole proprietorship, ownership of a corporation may be transferred upon death. A small corporation may set up as an S corporation to avoid some corporate taxes but still retain corporate advantages. Some types of businesses may be set up as a nonprofit corporation, which can also provide significant tax savings.

Disadvantages

Corporations are more difficult to set up than other business types, but this should not dissuade you from considering this form of business. Forms must be submitted to the Department of State to create and maintain corporate status and there are costs involved to submitting the forms. Corporations are somewhat closely regulated, since they are governed by state law. Therefore, records must be kept and annual reports on capital stock tax, loans tax, and corporate net income tax must be made to the Department of Revenue. Lastly, it is important that you carefully determine what your business activities are, because corporate status limits you to those business activities listed on your incorporation papers.

LIMITED PARTNERSHIP

A *limited partnership* has characteristics similar to both a corporation and a partnership. *General partners* have the control and liability, and *limited partners* only put up money and have liability limited to what they paid for their share of the partnership (like corporate stock). Laws governing limited partnerships are found in 15 Pa.C.S. Sections 8511 et seq.

Advantages   It is easier to raise capital in a limited partnership than in a general partnership. Capital can be contributed to the partnership by limited partners who have no control of the business or have no liability for its debts beyond the amount of money they invested.

Disadvantages   General partners are personally liable for partnership debts and for the acts of each other; therefore, an extensive partnership agreement is required. Each year, an annual assessment fee must be paid to the Department of State. This assessment fee is at least $250 and is increased every three years.

LIMITED LIABILITY COMPANY

A *limited liability company* (LLC) is like a limited partnership without general partners. It has characteristics of both a corporation and a partnership—none of the partners have liability and all can have some control.

Advantages   The limited liability company offers the tax benefits of a partnership with the protection from liability of a corporation. It offers more tax benefits than an S corporation, because it may pass through more depreciation and deductions. It may have different classes of ownership and an unlimited number of members. According to recent changes in the limited liability company law, a minimum level of insurance is no longer mandatory. This change was made to stimulate the creation of limited liability companies in Pennsylvania, because fewer than one-third of the states have such a minimum insurance coverage requirement, and no other form of business is required by law to maintain insurance coverage.

Disadvantages   Like a corporation, the limited liability company must pay corporate net income tax. Also, an annual registration fee of $360 a year (as of 2003) must be made to the Department of State. As with the limited partnership annual assessment fee, this amount increases every three years.

LIMITED LIABILITY PARTNERSHIP

The *limited liability partnership* is like a general partnership, but without personal liability. It was devised to allow partnerships of lawyers and other professionals to limit their personal liability without losing their partnership structure. This was important because converting to an LLC could have tax consequences, and some states do not allow professionals to operate as LLCs. Both general and limited partnerships can register as LLPs.

Advantages   The limited liability partnership offers the flexibility and tax benefits of a partnership with the protection from liability of a corporation.

Disadvantages   Start-up and annual fees are higher for LLPs than for a corporation. Also, the law requires the partnership to maintain certain minimum insurance.

MAKING YOUR CHOICE

The selection of a form of doing business is best made with the advice of an accountant and an attorney. If you were selling normally harmless objects by mail, a proprietorship would be the easiest way to get started, but if you own a lawn service, it would be important to incorporate to avoid losing your personal assets if one of your employees were to injure someone in an accident where the damages could exceed your insurance. If you can expect a high cash buildup the first year, a corporation may be the best way to keep taxes low. If you expect the usual start-up losses, a proprietorship, partnership, or S corporation would probably be best.

START-UP PROCEDURES

Whatever form of business you choose, you have to follow specific start-up procedures to establish it.

Proprietorship   In a proprietorship, all accounts and licenses are registered in the name of the owner. See Chapter 3 for information about using a fictitious name.

Partnership

To form a partnership, a written agreement should be prepared to spell out rights and obligations of the parties. See Chapter 3 for using a fictitious name. Accounts and licenses are usually registered in the names of the partners.

Corporation

To form a corporation, *articles of incorporation* must be filed with the secretary of state in Harrisburg, along with $100 in filing fees. An organizational meeting is then held, at which officers are elected, stock is issued, and other formalities are complied with to avoid the corporate entity being set aside later. Licenses and accounts are titled in the name of the corporation.

Limited Partnership

To form a limited partnership, a written limited *partnership agreement* must be drawn up and registered with the secretary of the state in Harrisburg, and a lengthy disclosure document must be given to all prospective limited partners. Because of the complexity of securities laws and the criminal penalties for violation, it is advantageous to have an attorney organize a limited partnership.

Limited Liability Company

Two or more persons may form a limited liability company by filing *articles of organization* with the secretary of state in Harrisburg. Licenses and accounts are in the name of the company.

Limited Liability Partnership

A limited partnership is formed by one or more general partners joining with one or more limited partners. The limited partners have limited exposure to liability and are not involved in the day-to-day operations of the limited partnership. A Pennsylvania limited partnership is formed by filing a *certificate of limited partnership* on form DSCB: 15-8511, accompanied by a docketing statement in duplicate, form DSCB: 15-134A, with the Corporations Bureau of the Department of State.

Naming Your Business

Before deciding upon a name for your business, you should be sure that it is not already being used by someone else. Many business owners have spent thousands of dollars on publicity and printing, only to throw it all away because another company owned the name. A company that owns a name can take you to court and force you to stop using that name. It can also sue you if your use of the name cost it a financial loss.

If you will be running a small local shop with no plans for expansion, you may be able to get by with checking only local references, but if you plan to expand or deal nationally, you should do a thorough search of the name you choose. In either case, the potential for being sued is great, so it is advisable to check with the Corporations Bureau in Harrisburg to see if another company is using the name you have chosen or something confusingly similar. A preliminary search is free, but a report of the search with the secretary of state's seal costs $15.

To do a national search, you should check trade directories and phone books of major cities. These can be found at many libraries, and are usually reference books that cannot be checked out. The *Trade Names Directory* is a two-volume set of names compiled from many sources, published by Gale Research Company.

If you have a computer with Internet access, you can use it to search all of the Yellow Pages listings in the U.S. at a number of sites at no charge. One website, **www.infoseek.com**, offers free searches of Yellow Pages for all states at once.

To be sure that your use of the name does not violate someone else's trademark rights, you should have a trademark search done of the mark in the *United States Patent and Trademark Office* (PTO). The PTO put its trademark records online and you can now search them at **www.uspto.gov**. If you do not have access to the Internet, you might be able to do it at a public library, or have one of their employees order an online search for you for a small fee. If this is not available to you, you can have the search done through a firm. Once such firm offers searches of one hundred trade directories and 4,800 phone books.

Government Liaison Services, Inc.
P.O. Box 10648
Arlington, VA 22210
703-524-8200

The best way to make sure a name you are using is not already owned by someone else is to make one up yourself—names such as Xerox, Kodak, and Exxon were made up and did not have any meaning prior to their use by their respective companies. However, remember that there are millions of businesses, so even something you make up may already be in use. Do a search just to be sure.

FICTITIOUS NAMES

In Pennsylvania, as in most states, unless you do business in your own legal name, you must register the name you are using, called a *fictitious name*. The name must be registered with the Corporations Bureau in Harrisburg.

There is a $500 civil penalty if you fail to register a fictitious name, and you may not sue anyone for using your fictitious name unless you are registered. If someone sues you and you are not registered, the other businesses may be entitled to attorney's fees and court costs.

If your name is *John Doe* and you are operating a masonry business, you may operate your business as *John Doe, Mason* without registering it. Similarly, Doe Masonry, Doe Masonry Company, and Doe Company do not need to be registered because the proper last name of the owner is in the name of the business. Any name that does not use the last name of the owner, such as John's Masonry, must be registered as a fictitious name.

You cannot use the words "corporation," "incorporated," "corp.," or "inc." unless you are a corporation. However, corporations do not have to register the name they are using as a fictitious name unless it is different from their registered corporate name. (54 P.A.C.S. 301 et. seq.)

Attorneys and professionals licensed by the Bureau of Professional and Occupational Affairs do not have to register the names under which they practice their profession, providing that the last names of all the partners are listed.

When you use a fictitious name, you are *doing business as* (d/b/a) whatever name you are using. Legally, you would use the name "John Doe d/b/a John's Masonry."

To register a fictitious name, you must advertise that you have filed or intend to file an application to register a fictitious name in two newspapers. These newspaper ads must appear in a newspaper of general circulation and in a legal newspaper. According to the *Fictitious Name Act*, the ad must contain the following information: the name of the business; the address of the business's main office; the names and addresses of all parties involved in the registering of the business; and, a statement that you have filed or intend to file an application to register a fictitious name. The ad should usually appear in the classified section of the newspaper, and could be worded as follows.

FICTITIOUS NAME NOTICE

Notice is hereby given that an application to register the business name Acme Printing under the Fictitious Name Act has been filed with the Department of State of Pennsylvania. The principal place of business and the main office is located at 456 Main Street, Harrisburg, PA 00000. Jane Doe of 789 Back Street, Harrisburg, PA 00000 is the only individual party to this registration.

Call the classified advertising department of the newspaper and ask for rates and any other information you may need to know about advertising a fictitious name notice. Do not hesitate to contact more than one paper and shop around for the best rate. Most counties have more than one newspaper of general circulation. Also, most papers have an information sheet they can give you that explains how your ad should be worded and the cost for placing the ad. Some papers will even help you contact a local legal newspaper to place your ad there as well. The fictitious name notice need only appear once in both papers.

Before or after the ad has appeared, you must file an **APPLICATION FOR REGISTRATION OF A FICTITIOUS NAME** with the Corporations Bureau. (see form 1, p.215.) Recent changes in the law permit for a fictitious name to be used, as long as it is distinguishable from other names upon the records of the Department of State. For example, previous law forbade the use of the fictitious name Matrex Corporation, because it was similar to Matrix Corporation. According to current law, Matrex can now be used as a fictitious name because it can be distinguished on the records from Matrix. The purpose for this change in the law was to make more names available to entrepreneurs starting businesses in Pennsylvania.

However, a fictitious name search should still be conducted to make sure the name you choose is not already being used. A written report of a records search can be obtained for $12 (check or money order—the Corporations Bureau will not accept cash for any filing or service) by filing **CORPORATE CERTIFICATION AND SEARCH REQUEST FORM—COUNTER**, or by making the request on letterhead stationery. (see form 2, p.219.) Do not order business stationary, forms, stock certificates, and so on until you have obtained a written report. A phone search is considered a preliminary search and is not a guarantee of the availability of fictitious name.

Some businesses have special requirements for registration of their fictitious names. For example, a fictitious name that implies a business is a bank, trust, or educational institution, or is engaged in engineering, must obtain permission from the Department of Banking, Department of Education, or the State Registration Board of Professional Engineers, Land Surveyors, and Geologists—as appropriate. Other businesses may have similar requirements. See Chapter 7 for a list of state regulated professions and references to the laws that apply to them.

CORPORATE NAMES

A corporation does not have to register a fictitious name because it already has a legal name. The name of a corporation must contain one of the following words:

Association	Incorporated
Corporation	Inc.
Corp.	Limited
Company	Ltd.
Co.	Syndicate
Fund	

It is not advisable to use only the word "Company" or "Co.," because unincorporated businesses also use these words, so a person dealing with you might not realize you are incorporated. If this happens, you might end up with personal liability for corporate debts. You can use a combination of two of the words, such as "ABC Co., Inc."

If the name of the corporation does not contain one of the above words, it will be rejected by the secretary of state. It will also be rejected if the name used by it is already taken or is similar to the name of another corporation, or if it uses a forbidden word such as "bank" or "trust." To check on a name, you may call the name availability number in Harrisburg at 717-787-1057 from 8 a.m. to 5 p.m. Keep trying—they are usually busy.

If a name you pick is taken by another company, you may be able to change it slightly and have it accepted. For example, if there is already a Tri-City, Inc., you may be allowed to use Tri-City Upholstery, Inc. The addition of the locality is not enough to distinguish names, but the addition of a description of the business in the names usually is.

Like a fictitious name, do not have anything printed until a written report of a records search and your corporate papers are returned to you. Sometimes a name is approved over the phone but rejected when submitted.

Once you have chosen a corporate name and know it is available, you should immediately register your corporation. A name can be reserved for 120 days for $52, by filing the **Corporate Certification and Search Request Form–Counter** form or placing your request in writing and enclosing a check or money order, but it is easier just to register the corporation than to waste time and money on the name reservation.

If a corporation wants to do business under a name other than its corporate name, it can register a fictitious name, such as "Doe Corporation d/b/a Doe Industries." However, if the name used leads people to believe that the business is not a corporation, the right to limited liability may be lost. If you use such a name, be sure it is always accompanied by the corporate name.

PROFESSIONAL CORPORATIONS

Professionals can do business by creating a professional corporation. A profession is defined as any type of personal service that requires a license, admission to practice or some other legal authorization. Under Pennsylvania law, a professional corporation cannot use "Inc.," "Corp.," or "Co." in its name. Instead, it must use the words "associates," "and associates," "professional corporation," or "P.C."

TRADEMARKS

As your business builds goodwill, its name will become more valuable and you will want to protect it from others who may wish to copy it. To protect a name used to describe your goods or services, you can register it as a *trademark* (for goods) or a *service mark* (for services), with either the Corporations Bureau of the Department of State in Pennsylvania or with the United States Patent and Trademark Office.

You cannot obtain a trademark for only the name of your business, but you can trademark the name you use on your goods and services. In most cases, you use your company name on your goods as your trademark. In effect, it protects your company name. Another way to protect your company name is to incorporate. A particular corporate name can only be registered by one company in Pennsylvania.

State Registration

State registration would be useful if you only expect to use your trademark within the state of Pennsylvania. Federal registration would protect your mark anywhere in the country. The registration of a mark gives you exclusive use of the mark for the types of goods for which you register it. The only exception is people who have already been using the mark. You cannot stop people who have been using the mark prior to your registration.

The procedure for state registration is simple and the cost is $25. You should conduct a search for the mark by following the same procedure as you did for a name search. The cost is $12 for a written report. Any questions you have about filing an **APPLICATION FOR REGISTRATION OF MARK** (form 3, p.221) can be answered by calling 717-787-1057.

Before a mark can be registered, it must be used in Pennsylvania. For goods, this means it must be used on the goods themselves, or on containers, tags, labels, or displays of the goods. For services, it must be used in the sale or advertising of the services. The use must be in an actual transaction with a customer. Use on a sample mailed to a friend is not acceptable.

The $25 fee will register the mark in only one *class of goods*. If the mark is used on more than one class of goods, a separate registration must be filed. The registration is good for ten years. Six months prior to its expiration, it must be renewed.

In Appendix B is a sample filled-in form for a Pennsylvania trademark. A blank form and instructions are in Appendix C.

Federal Registration

For federal registration, the procedure is a little more complicated. There are two types of applications, depending upon whether you have already made use of the mark or whether you merely have an intention to use the mark in the future. For a trademark that has been in use, you must file an application form, along with specimens showing actual use and a drawing of the mark that complies with all of the rules of the United States Patent and Trademark Office. For an *intent to use* application, you must file two separate forms, one when you make the initial application and the other after you have made actual use of the mark, as well as the specimens and drawing. Before a mark can be entitled to federal registration, the use of the mark must be in *interstate commerce* or in commerce with another country. The fee for registration is $335, but if you file an intent to use application, there is a second fee of $100 for the filing after actual use.

DOMAIN NAMES

With the Internet changing so rapidly, all of the rules for Internet names have not yet been worked out. Originally, the first person to reserve a name owned it, and enterprising souls bought up the names of most of the Fortune 500 corporations. Then a few of the corporations went to court, and the rule was developed that if a company had a trademark for a name, that company could stop someone else from using it if the other person did not have a trademark. More recently, Congress made it illegal for cybersquatters to register the names of famous persons and companies. Once you have a valid trademark, you will be safe using it for your domain name. To find out if a domain name is available, go to **www.whois.net**.

In recent years, several new *top-level domains* (TLDs) have been created. Top-level domains are the last letters of the uniform resource locator (URL), such as ".com," ".org,"and ".net." Now you can also register names with the following TLDs.

.biz	.pro
.cc	.aero
.info	.coop
.name	.museum

One of the best places to register a domain name is **www.registerfly .com**. If your name is taken, they automatically suggest related names that might work for you, and their registration fees are lower than most other sites.

Preparing a Business Plan

Not everyone needs a business plan to start a business, but if you have one, it might help you avoid mistakes and make better decisions. For example, if you think it would be a great idea to start a candle shop in a little seaside resort, you might find out after preparing a business plan that considering the number of people who might stop by, you could never sell enough candles to pay the rent.

A business plan lets you look at the costs, expenses, and potential sales, and see whether or not your plan can be profitable. It also allows you to find alternatives that might be more profitable. In the candle shop example, you might find that if you chose a more populous location or if you sold something else in addition to the candles, you would be more likely to make a profit.

ADVANTAGES AND DISADVANTAGES OF A BUSINESS PLAN

Other than helping you figure out if your business will be profitable, a business plan would also be useful if you hope to borrow money or have investors buy into your business. Lenders and equity investors always require a business plan before they will provide money to a business.

If your idea is truly unusual, a business plan may discourage you from starting your business. A business idea might look like a failure on paper, but if in your gut you know it would work, it might be worth trying without a business plan.

Example:

When Chester Carlson invented the first photocopy machine, he went to IBM. They spent $50,000 to analyze the idea and concluded that nobody needed a photocopy machine because people already had carbon paper—which was cheaper. However, he believed in his machine and started Xerox Corporation, which became one of the biggest and hottest companies of its time.

However, even with a great concept, you need to at least do some basic calculations to see if the business can make a profit.

- ✪ If you want to start a retail shop, figure out how many people are close enough to become customers and how many other stores will be competing for those customers. Visit some of those other shops and see how busy they are. Without giving away your plans to compete, ask some general questions like "how's business?" and maybe they will share their frustrations or successes.

- ✪ Whether you sell a good or a service, do the math to find out how much profit is in it. For example, if you plan to start a house painting company, find out what you will have to pay to hire painters, what it will cost you for all of the insurance, what bonding and licensing you will need, and what the advertising will cost you. Figure out how many jobs you can do per month and what other painters are charging. In some industries, in different areas of the state there may be a large margin of profit, while in other areas there may be almost no profit.

✪   Find out if there is a demand for your product or service. Suppose you have designed a beautiful new kind of candle and your friends all say you should open a shop because everyone will want them. Before making a hundred of them and renting a store, bring a few to craft shows or flea markets and see what happens.

✪   Figure out what the income and expenses would be for a typical month of your new business. List monthly expenses, such as rent, salaries, utilities, insurance, taxes, supplies, advertising, services, and other overhead. Then, figure out how much profit you will average from each sale. Next, figure out how many sales you will need to cover your overhead and divide by the number of business days in the month. Can you reasonably expect that many sales? How will you get those sales?

Most types of businesses have trade associations, which often have figures on how profitable its members are. Some even have start-up kits for people wanting to start businesses. One good source of information on such organizations is the *Encyclopedia of Associations* published by Gale Research Inc., available in many library reference sections. Suppliers of products to the trade often give assistance to small companies getting started in an attempt to win their loyalty. Contact the largest suppliers of the products your business will be using and see if they can be of any help.

OUTLINE FOR YOUR BUSINESS PLAN

While you may believe that you do not need a business plan, conventional wisdom says you do, and it only makes good business sense to have one. A typical business plan has sections that cover topics such as:

✪   executive summary;

✪   product or service;

✪   market;

- ✪ competition;

- ✪ marketing plan;

- ✪ production plan;

- ✪ organizational plan;

- ✪ financial projections;

- ✪ management team; and,

- ✪ risks.

The following is an explanation of each.

Executive Summary

The executive summary is an overview of what the business will be and why it is expected to be successful. If the business plan will be used to lure investors, this section is the most important, since many might not read any further if they are not impressed with the summary.

Product or Service

The section on your product or service is a detailed description of what you will be selling. You should describe what is different about it, and why people would need it or want it.

Market

The market should analyze who the potential buyers of your product or service are. Describe both the physical location of the customers and their demographics. For example, a bodybuilding gym would probably mostly appeal to males in the 18 to 40 age bracket in a ten- to twenty-mile radius, depending on the location.

If you will sell things from a retail shop, you might also want to sell from mail order catalogs or over the Internet if your local customer base would not be large enough to support the business. Describe what you will be doing for those ventures.

If you are manufacturing things, you should find out who the wholesalers and distributors are, and their terms. This information should also be included in this section.

Competition

Before opening your business, you should know who and where your competitors are. If you are opening an antique shop, you might want to be near other antique shops so more customers come by your place, since antiques are unique and do not really compete with other antiques. However, if you open a florist shop, you probably do not want to be near other florist shops, since most florists sell similar products and a new shop would just dilute the customer base.

If you have a truly unique way of selling something, you might want to go near other similar businesses to grab their existing customer base and expand your market share. However, if they could easily copy your idea, you might not take away the business for long and might end up diluting the market for each business.

Marketing Plan

Many a business has closed just a few months after opening because not enough customers showed up. How do you expect customers to find out about your business? Even if you get a nice write-up in the local paper, not everyone reads the paper, many people do not read every page, and lots of people forget what they read.

Your marketing plan describes how you will advertise your business. List how much the advertising will cost, and describe how you expect people to respond to the advertising.

Production Plan

The production plan needs to address and answer questions such as the following.

- If you are manufacturing a product, do you know how you will be able to produce a large quantity of it?

- Do you know all the costs and the possible production problems that could come up?

- If Wal-Mart orders 100,000, could you get them made in a reasonable time?

The production plan needs to anticipate the normal schedule you intend to use, as well as how to handle any changes—positive or negative—to that schedule.

If you are selling a service and will need employees to perform those services, your production plan should explain how you will recruit and train those employees.

Organizational Plan

If your business will be more than a mom and pop operation, what will the organizational plan be? How many employees will you need and who will supervise whom? How much of the work will be done by employees, and how much will be hired out to other businesses and independent contractors? Will you have a sales force? Will you need manufacturing employees? Will your accounting, website maintenance, and office cleaning and maintenance be contracted out or done by employees?

Financial Projections

Tying all the previously discussed topics together is what your financial plan will discuss. You should know how much rent, utilities, insurance, taxes, marketing, product costs, and wages for labor will cost you for the first year. Besides listing known, expected expenses, you should calculate your financial well-being under a number of different possible scenarios. Some of the questions to think about and answer will be, *how long would you be in business if you have very few customers the first few months?* and *if Wal-Mart does order 100,000 of your products, could you afford to manufacture them, knowing you won't be paid for months?*

Management Team

If you will be seeking outside funding, you will need to list the experience and skills of the management of the business. Investors want to know that the people have experience and know what they are doing.

Risks

A good business plan weighs all the risks of the new enterprise. Is new technology in the works that will make the business obsolete? Would a rise in the price of a particular needed supply eliminate all your profits? What are the chances of a new competitor entering the market if you show some success, and what are you going to do about it? Part of your analysis should be to look at all of the possible things that could happen in the field you chose and to gauge the likelihood of success.

GATHERING INFORMATION

Some of the sections of your business plan require a lot of research. People sometimes take years to prepare them. Today, the Internet puts a nearly infinite amount of information at your fingertips, but you might also want to do some personal research.

Sometimes the best way to get the feel for a business is to get a job in a similar business. At a minimum, you should visit similar businesses, or perhaps sit outside of one, and see how many customers they have and how much business they do. There are startup guides for many types of businesses, which can be found at Amazon.com, your local bookstores, and the library. Your local chamber of commerce, business development office, or SCORE office might also have materials to help your research.

SAMPLE BUSINESS PLAN

The following plan is one for a simple one-person business that will use its owner's assets to start. Of course, a larger business, or one that needs financing, will need a much longer and more detailed plan.

A website with sixty sample business plans and information on business plan software is **www.bplans.com**.

Executive Summary

This is the plan for a new business, Reardon Computer Repair, LLC by Henry Reardon, to be started locally and then expanded throughout the state and perhaps further if results indicate this is feasible.

The mission of Reardon Computer Repair (RCR) is to offer fast, affordable repairs to office and home computers. The objective is to become profitable within the first three months, and to grow at a quick but manageable pace.

In order to offer customers the quickest service, RCR will rely on youthful computer whizzes who are students and have the time and expertise to provide the service. They will also have the flexibility to arrive quickly and the motivation to show off their expertise.

To reach customers, we will use limited advertising, but primarily the Internet and word of mouth from happy customers.

With nearly every business and family having several computers, and a lack of fast service currently available, it is expected this business could be successful quickly and could grow rapidly.

Product or Service

The company will offer computer repair services both at its shop and at customers' offices and homes. It will sell computer parts as necessary to complete the repairs, and it will also carry upgrades, accessories, and peripherals, which will most likely be of value to customers needing repairs.

Market

The market would be nearly every business and family at every address in the city, state, and country, since today nearly everyone has a computer. Figures show nearly 250 million computers in use in America, and that number is expected to grow to over 300 million in five years.

The market for the initial shop would be a fifteen-mile radius, which is a reasonable driving distance for our employees. The population in that area is 300,000 people, which would mean 240,000 potential customers, based on the current level of 800 computers per 1,000 people.

The market would not include new computers, which typically come with a one-year guarantee. It would also not include people who bought extended guarantees.

The growth trend for the industry is 8–10% for the next decade.

Competition

The competition would be the authorized repair shops working with the computer manufacturers. While these have the advantage of being authorized, research and experience has shown that they are slow and do not meet customers' need for an immediate repair.

There is one computer repair shop within a ten-mile radius of the proposed shop, and two more within a twenty-five-mile radius. Average wait time for a dropped off repair is one week. The two closest repair services offer no on-site repair. Shipping a computer to a dealer for repair takes one to two weeks. Most customers need their computer fixed within a day or two.

One potential source for competition would be from employees or former employees who are asked to work for customers "on the side" at a reduced rate. To discourage this, the company will have a contract with employees with a noncompete agreement that specifies that they will pay the company three times what they earn. Also, agreements with customers will include a clause that they have the option to hire away one of our employees for a one-time $2,000 fee.

Marketing Plan

The business will be marketed through networking, Internet marketing, advertising, and creative marketing.

Networking will be through the owner's contacts, as well as local computer clubs and software stores. Some local retailers do not offer service and they have already indicated that they would promote a local business that could offer fast repairs.

A website would be linked to local businesses and community groups, and to major computer repair referral sites.

Advertising would include the Yellow Pages and local computer club newsletters. Studies have shown that newspaper and television advertising would be too expensive and not cost-effective for this type of business.

Creative advertising would include vinyl lettering on the back window of owner's vehicle.

Production Plan

The company will be selling the services of computer technicians and computer parts. The owner will supply most of the services in the beginning and then add student technicians as needed.

The parts will all be purchased ready-made from the manufacturers, except for cables, which can be made on an as-needed basis much cheaper than ready-made ones.

Employees

The employees will be students who are extremely knowledgeable about computers. Some would call them computer "geeks"—in a nice way. They have extensive knowledge of the workings of computers, have lots of free time, need money, and would love to show off how knowledgeable they are.

As students, they already have health insurance and do not need full-time work. They would be available as needed. The company would pay them $12 an hour plus mileage, which is more than any other job available to students, but is not cost-prohibitive, considering the charge to customers of $50 per hour.

Financial Projections

The minimum charge for a service call will be $75 on-site and $50 in-shop, which will include one hour of service. The parts markup will be the industry standard of 20%. The average customer bill is estimated to be $100, including labor and markup.

The labor cost is estimated to be $30 per, call including time, taxes, insurance, and mileage. The owner will be estimated to handle 75% of the work the first six months and 50% the second six months.

Rent, utilities, insurance, taxes, and other fixed costs are estimated to be $3,000 per month.

Advertising and promotion expenses are expected to be $3,000 per month.

Estimated number of customers will be:

First three months:	10 per week
Second three months:	20 per week
Third three months:	35 per week
Fourth three months:	50 per week

Estimated monthly revenue:

First three months:	$4,000
Second three months:	$8,000
Third three months:	$14,000
Fourth three months:	$20,000

Monthly income and expense projection:

First three months:

Income	$4,000
Labor	$300
Fixed costs	$3,000
Advertising	$3,000
Net	$2,300 loss per month

Second 3 months:

Income	$8,000
Labor	$600
Fixed costs	$3,000
Advertising	$3,000
Net	$1,400 profit per month

Third 3 months:

Income	$14,000
Labor	$2,100
Fixed costs	$3,000
Advertising	$3,000
Net	$5,900 profit per month

Fourth 3 months:

Income	$20,000
Labor	$3,000
Fixed costs	$3,000
Advertising	$3,000
Net	$11,000 profit per month

Organization Plan

The business will start with the owner, Henry Reardon, and three students who are experts at computer repair and are available as part-time workers on an as-needed basis.

The owner will manage the business and do as many repairs as are possible with the time remaining in the week.

One of the students, Peter Galt, will work after school in the shop, and the others, Dom Roark and Howard Taggert, are willing to work on an on-call basis, either at the shop or at customers' homes.

As business grows, the company will recruit more student employees through the school job placement offices and at computer clubs.

Management Team

The owner, Henry Reardon, will be the sole manager of the company. He will use the accounting services of his accountant, Dave Burton. The owner anticipates being able to supervise up to ten employees. When there are more than ten, the company will need a manager to take over scheduling and some of other management functions.

Risks

Because the business does not require a lot of capital, there will be a low financial risk in the beginning. The biggest reason for failure would be an inability to get the word out that the company exists and can fill a need when it arises. For this reason, the most important task in the beginning will be marketing and promotion.

As the company grows, the risk will be that computers will need fewer repairs, become harder to repair, and become so cheap they are disposable. To guard against this possibility, the company will add computer consulting services as it grows, so that it will always have something to offer computer owners.

Financing Your Business

The way to finance your business is determined by how fast you want your business to grow and how much risk of failure you are able to handle. Letting the business grow with its own income is the slowest but safest way to grow. Taking out a personal loan against your house to expand quickly is the fastest but riskiest way to grow.

GROWING WITH PROFITS

Many successful businesses have started out with little money and used the profits to grow bigger and bigger. If you have another source of income to live on (such as a job or a spouse's job), you can plow all the income of your fledgling business into growth.

Some businesses start as hobbies or part-time ventures on the weekend while the entrepreneur holds down a full-time job. Many types of goods or service businesses can start this way. Even some multi-million dollar corporations, such as Apple Computer, started out this way.

This allows you to test your idea with little risk. If you find you are not good at running that type of business, or the time or location was not right for your idea, all you are out is the time you spent and your start-up capital.

However, a business can only grow so big from its own income. In many cases, as a business grows, it gets to a point where the orders are so big that money must be borrowed to produce the product to fill them. With this kind of order, there is the risk that if the customer cannot pay or goes bankrupt, the business will also go under. At such a point, a business owner should investigate the creditworthiness of the customer and weigh the risks. Some businesses have grown rapidly, some have gone under, and others have decided not to take the risk and stayed small. You can worry about that down the road.

USING YOUR SAVINGS

If you have savings you can tap to get your business started, that is the best source. You will not have to pay high interest rates and you will not have to worry about paying someone back. This section discusses some options for using your own savings to start your business, as well as potential pitfalls for each.

Home Equity

If you have owned your home for several years, it is possible that the equity has grown substantially and you can get a second mortgage to finance your business. If you have been in the home for many years and have a good record of paying your bills, some lenders will make second mortgages that exceed the equity. Just remember, if your business fails, you may lose your house.

Retirement Accounts

Be careful about borrowing from your retirement savings. There are tax penalties for borrowing from or against certain types of retirement accounts. Also, your future financial security may be lost if your business does not succeed.

Having Too Much Money

It probably does not seem possible to have too much money with which to start a business, but many businesses have failed for that reason. With plenty of start-up capital available, a business owner does not need to watch expenses and can become wasteful. Employees get used to lavish spending. Once the money runs out and the business must run on its own earnings, it fails.

Starting with the bare minimum forces a business to watch its expenses and be frugal. It necessitates finding the least expensive solutions to problems that crop up and creative ways to be productive.

BORROWING MONEY

It is extremely tempting to look to others to get the money to start a business. The risk of failure is less worrisome and the pressure is lower, but that is a problem with borrowing. If it is others' money, you do not have quite the same incentive to succeed as you do if everything you own is on the line.

Actually, you should be even more concerned when using the money of others. Your reputation is at risk, and if you do not succeed, you probably will still have to pay back the loan.

Family Depending on how much money your family can spare, it may be the most comfortable or most uncomfortable source of funds for you. If you have been assured a large inheritance and your parents have more funds than they need to live on, you may be able to borrow against your inheritance without worry. It will be your money anyway, and you need it much more now than you will ten or twenty years from now. If you lose it all, it is your own loss.

However, if you are asking your widowed mother to cash in a CD she lives on to finance your get-rich-quick scheme, you should have second thoughts about it. Stop and consider all the real reasons your business might not take off and what your mother would do without the income.

Friends Borrowing from friends is like borrowing from family members. If you know they have the funds available and could survive a loss, you may want to risk it, but if they would be loaning you their only resources, do not chance it.

Financial problems can be the worst thing for a relationship, whether it is a casual friendship or a long-term romantic involvement. Before you borrow from a friend, try to imagine what would happen if you could not pay it back and how you would feel if it caused the end of your relationship.

The ideal situation is if your friend were a co-venturer in your business and the burden would not be totally on you to see how the funds were spent. Still, realize that such a venture will put extra strain on the relationship.

Banks   In a way, a bank can be a more comfortable party from which to borrow, because you do not have a personal relationship with them as you do with a friend or family member. If you fail, they will write your loan off rather than disown you. However, a bank can also be the least comfortable party to borrow from, because they will demand realistic projections (your business plan) and be on top of you to perform. If you do not meet their expectations, they may call your loan just when you need it most.

The best thing about a bank loan is that they will require you to do your homework. You must have plans that make sense to a banker. If they approve your loan, you know that your plans are at least reasonable.

Bank loans are not cheap or easy. You will be paying a good interest rate, and you will have to put up collateral. If your business does not have equipment or receivables, the bank may require you to put up your house and other personal property to guarantee the loan.

Banks are a little easier to deal with when you get a Small Business Administration (SBA) loan. That is because the SBA guarantees that it will pay the bank if you default on the loan. These loans are obtained through local bank branches.

Credit Cards   Borrowing against a credit card is one of the fastest growing ways of financing a business, but it can be one of the most expensive ways. The rates can go higher than 20%, although many cards offer lower rates. Some people are able to get numerous cards. Some successful businesses have used credit cards to get off the ground or to weather through a cash crunch, but if the business does not begin to generate the cash to make the payments, you could soon end up in bankruptcy. A good strategy is only to use credit cards for a long-term asset, like a computer, or for something that will quickly generate cash, like buying inventory to fill an order. Do not use credit cards to pay expenses that are not generating revenue.

GETTING A RICH PARTNER

One of the best business combinations is a young entrepreneur with ideas and ambition, and a retired investor with business experience and money. Together, they can supply everything the business needs.

How to find such a partner? Be creative. You should have investigated the business you are starting and know others who have been in such businesses. Have any of them had partners retire over the last few years? Are any of the partners planning to phase out of the business?

SELLING SHARES OF YOUR BUSINESS

Silent investors are the best source of capital for your business. You retain full control of the business, and if it happens to fail, you have no obligation to them. Unfortunately, few silent investors are interested in a new business. It is only after you have proven your concept to be successful and built up a rather large enterprise that you will be able to attract such investors.

The most common way to obtain money from investors is to issue stock to them. For this, the best type of business entity is the corporation. It gives you almost unlimited flexibility in the number and kinds of shares of stock you can issue.

UNDERSTANDING SECURITIES LAWS

There is one major problem with selling stock in your business, and that is all of the federal and state regulations with which you must comply. Both the state and federal governments have long and complicated laws dealing with the sales of securities. There are also hundreds of court cases attempting to explain what these laws mean. A thorough explanation of this area of law is obviously beyond the scope of this book.

Basically, *securities* have been held to exist in any case in which a person provides money to someone with the expectation that he or she will get a profit through the efforts of that person. This can apply to any situation where someone buys stock in, or makes a loan to, your business. What the laws require is disclosure of the risks involved, and in some cases, registration of the securities with the government. There are some exemptions, such as for small amounts of money and for limited numbers of investors.

Penalties for violation of securities laws are severe, including triple damages and prison terms. You should consult a specialist in securities laws before issuing any security. You can often get an introductory consultation at a reasonable rate to learn your options.

USING THE INTERNET TO FIND CAPITAL

The Internet can also be a great resource for finding and marketing to investors. However, before attempting to market your company's shares on the Internet, be sure to get an opinion from a securities lawyer or do some serious research into securities law. The immediate accessibility of the Internet makes it very easy for you to get ahead of yourself and unintentionally violate state and federal securities laws. The Internet contains a wealth of information that can be useful in finding sources of capital. The following sites may be helpful.

America's Business Funding Directory
www.businessfinance.com

Small Business Administration
www.sba.gov

Inc. Magazine
www.inc.com

NVST
www.nvst.com

The Capital Network
www.thecapitalnetwork.com

Locating Your Business

chapter 6

The right location for your business will be determined by what type of business it is and how fast you expect it to grow. For some types of businesses, the location will not be important to your success or failure—in others, it will be crucial.

WORKING OUT OF YOUR HOME

Many small businesses get started out of the home. Chapter 7 discusses the legalities of home businesses. This section discusses the practicalities.

Starting a business out of your home can save you the rent, electricity, insurance, and other costs of setting up at another location. For some people this is ideal, and they can combine their home and work duties easily and efficiently. For other people it is a disaster. A spouse, children, neighbors, television, and household chores can be so distracting that no other work gets done.

Since residential rates are usually lower than business lines, many people use their residential telephone line or add a second residential line to conduct business. However, if you wish to be listed in the Yellow Pages, you will need to have a business line in your home. If you are running two or more types of businesses, you can probably add their names as additional listings on the original number and avoid paying for another business line.

You also should consider whether the type of business you are starting is compatible with a home office. For example, if your business mostly consists of calling clients, then the home may be an ideal place to run it. If your clients need to visit you, or you will need daily pickups and deliveries by truck, then the home may not be a good location. This is discussed in more detail in the next chapter.

CHOOSING A RETAIL SITE

For most types of retail stores, the location is of prime importance. Things to consider include how close it is to your potential customers, how visible it is to the public, and how easily accessible it is to both autos and pedestrians. The attractiveness and safety of the site should also be considered.

Location would be less important for a business that was the only one of its kind in the area. For example, if there was only one moped parts dealer or Armenian restaurant in a metropolitan area, people would have to come to wherever you are if they want your products or services. However, even with such businesses, keep in mind that there is competition. People who want moped parts can order them by mail and restaurant customers can choose another type of cuisine.

You should look up all the businesses similar to the one you plan to run in the phone book and mark them on a map. For some businesses, like a cleaners, you would want to be far from the others. However, for other businesses, like antique stores, you would want to be near the others. (Antique stores usually do not carry the same things, they do not compete, and people like to go to an antique district and visit all the shops.)

CHOOSING OFFICE, MANUFACTURING, OR WAREHOUSE SPACE

If your business will be the type where customers will not come to you, then locating it near customers is not as much of a concern and you can probably save money by locating away from the high-traffic central business districts. However, you should consider the convenience for employees, and not locate in an area that would be unattractive to them or too far from where they would likely live.

For manufacturing or warehouse operations, you should consider your proximity to a post office, trucking company, or rail line. When several sites are available, you might consider which one has the earliest or most convenient pickup schedule for the carriers you plan to use.

LEASING A SITE

A lease of space can be one of the biggest expenses of a small business, so you should do a lot of homework before signing one. There are a lot of terms in a commercial lease that can make or break your business. The most critical terms are discussed in this section.

Zoning

Before signing a lease, you should be sure that everything that your business will need to do is allowed by the zoning of the property. Check the city and county zoning regulations.

Restrictions

In some shopping centers, existing tenants have guarantees that other tenants do not compete with them. For example, if you plan to open a restaurant and bakery, you may be forbidden to sell carryout baked goods if the supermarket next door has a bakery and a non-compete clause.

Signs

Business signs are regulated by zoning laws, sign laws, and property restrictions. If you rent a hidden location with no possibility for adequate signage, your chances for success are less than with a more visible site or much larger sign.

ADA Compliance

The *Americans with Disabilities Act* (ADA) requires that reasonable accommodations be made to make businesses accessible to the disabled.

When a business is remodeled, many more changes are required than if no remodeling is done. Be sure that the space you rent complies with the law, or that the landlord will be responsible for compliance. Be aware of the full costs you will bear.

Expansion   As your business grows, you may need to expand your space. The time to find out about your options is before you sign the lease. Perhaps you can take over adjoining units when those leases expire.

Renewal   Location is a key to success for some businesses. If you spend five years building up a clientele, you do not want someone to take over your locale at the end of your lease. Therefore, you should have a renewal clause on your lease. Usually, this allows an increase in rent based on inflation.

Guarantee   Most landlords of commercial space will not rent to a small corporation without a personal guarantee of the lease. This is a very risky thing for a new business owner to do. The lifetime rent on a long-term commercial lease can be hundreds of thousands of dollars, and if your business fails, the last thing you want to do is be personally responsible for five years of rent.

Where space is scarce or a location is hot, a landlord can get the guarantees he or she demands, and there is nothing you can do about it (except perhaps set up an asset protection plan ahead of time). However, where several units are vacant or the commercial rental market is soft, often you can negotiate out of the personal guarantee. If the lease is five years, maybe you can get away with a guarantee of just the first year.

Duty to Open   Some shopping centers have rules requiring all shops to be open certain hours. If you cannot afford to staff it the whole time required, or if you have religious or other reasons that make this a problem, you should negotiate it out of the lease or find another location.

Sublease   At some point, you may decide to sell your business, and in many cases, the location is the most valuable aspect of it. For this reason, you should be sure that you have the right to either assign your lease or to sublease the property. If this is impossible, one way around a prohibition is to incorporate your business before signing the lease, and then when you sell the business, sell the stock. However, some lease clauses prohibit transfer of *any interest* in the business, so read the lease carefully.

BUYING A SITE

If you are experienced with owning rental property, you will probably be more inclined to buy a site for your business. If you have no experience with real estate, you should probably rent and not take on the extra cost and responsibility of property ownership.

One reason to buy your site is that you can build up equity. Rather than pay rent to a landlord, you can pay off a mortgage and eventually own the property.

Separating the Ownership

One risk in buying a business site is that if the business gets into financial trouble, the creditors may go after the building as well. For this reason, most people who buy a site for their business keep the ownership out of the business. For example, the business will be a corporation, and the real estate will be owned personally by the owner or by a trust unrelated to the business.

Expansion

Before buying a site, you should consider the growth potential of your business. If it grows quickly, will you be able to expand at that site or will you have to move? Might the property next door be available for sale in the future if you need it? Can you get an option on it?

If the site is a good investment whether or not you have your business, then by all means, buy it. However, if its main use is for your business, think twice.

Zoning

Some of the concerns when buying a site are the same as when renting. You will want to make sure that the zoning permits the type of business you wish to start, or that you can get a variance without a large expense or delay. Be aware that just because a business is now using the site does not mean that you can expand or remodel the business at that site. Check with the zoning department of your local government and find out exactly what is allowed.

Signs   Signs are another concern. Some cities have regulated signs and do not allow new or larger ones. Some businesses have used these laws to get publicity. A car dealer who was told to take down a large number of American flags on his lot filed a federal lawsuit and rallied the community behind him.

ADA Compliance   ADA compliance is another concern when buying a commercial building. Find out from the building department if the building is in compliance, and if not, what needs to be done to put it in compliance. If you remodel, the requirements may be more strict.

> **NOTE:** *When dealing with public officials, keep in mind that they do not always know what the law is, or do not accurately explain it. They often try to intimidate people into doing things that are not required by law. Read the requirements yourself and question the officials if they seem to be interpreting it incorrectly. Seek legal advice if officials refuse to reexamine the law or move away from an erroneous position.*
>
> *Also, consider that keeping them happy may be worth the price. If you are already doing something they have overlooked, do not make a big deal over a little thing they want changed, or they may subject you to a full inspection or audit.*

CHECKING GOVERNMENTAL REGULATIONS

When looking for a site for your business, you should investigate the different governmental regulations in your area. For example, a location just outside the city or county limits might have a lower licensing fee, a lower sales tax rate, and less strict sign requirements.

Licensing Your Business

The federal and state legislatures, as well as local governments, have an interest in protecting consumers from bad business practices. In order to ensure that consumers are protected from unscrupulous business people and to require a minimum level of service to the public, the federal, state, and local governments have developed hundreds of licensing requirements that cover occupations and services ranging from attorneys to barbers to day care providers.

OCCUPATIONAL LICENSES AND ZONING

Before opening your business, you are supposed to obtain a county occupational license. If you will be working within a city, you also need a city occupational license. Businesses that work in several cities, such as builders, must obtain a license from each city in which they do work. This does not have to be done until you actually begin a job in a particular city.

County occupational licenses can be obtained from the tax collector in the county courthouse. City licenses are usually available at city hall. Be sure to find out if zoning allows your type of business before buying or leasing property, because the licensing departments will check the zoning before issuing your license.

If you will be preparing or serving food, you need to check with the local health department, the Pennsylvania Department of Environment Protection, and in some limited circumstances, the Pennsylvania Department of Agriculture, to be sure that the premises are in compliance.

Home Business

Problems occasionally arise when people attempt to start businesses in their homes. Small, newer businesses cannot afford to pay rent for commercial space, and cities often try to forbid business in residential areas. Getting a county occupational license or advertising a fictitious name may give notice to the city that a business is being conducted in a residential area.

Some people avoid the problem by starting their businesses without occupational licenses, figuring that the penalties for not having a license (if they are caught) are less expensive than the cost of office space. Others get the county license and ignore the city rules. If a person regularly parks commercial trucks and equipment on his or her property, there will probably be complaints from neighbors and the city will probably take legal action. However, if a person's business consists merely of making phone calls out of the home and keeping supplies there, a problem may never arise.

If a problem does arise regarding a home business that does not disturb the neighbors, a good argument can be made that the zoning law that prohibits the business is unconstitutional. When zoning laws were first instituted, they were not meant to stop people from doing things in a residence that had historically been part of the life in a residence. Consider an artist. Should a zoning law prohibit a person from painting pictures at home? If the artist sells them there for a living, is there a difference? Can the government force the artist to rent commercial space just because he or she wants to sell the paintings?

Similar arguments can be made for many home businesses. For hundreds of years, people performed income-producing activities in their homes. However, court battles with a city are expensive and probably not worth the effort for a small business. The best course of action is to keep a low profile. Using a post office box is sometimes helpful in diverting attention away from the residence.

STATE-REGULATED PROFESSIONS

Many professionals require special state licenses. You will probably be called upon to produce such a license when applying for an occupational license.

If you are in a regulated profession, you should be aware of the laws that apply to your profession. Pages 52–58 contain a list of professions and the departments or bureaus covering them. Contact the department or bureau directly and ask for an informational packet containing the laws and regulations covering the profession. The information is almost always free, up-to-date, and easier to get than looking for information in the library. Even if you do not think your profession is regulated, you should read through the list anyway. Some of those included may surprise you.

THE BUREAU OF PROFESSIONAL AND OCCUPATIONAL AFFAIRS

The Department of State has jurisdiction over many professions through its Bureau of Professional and Occupational Affairs. These professions usually require the successful completion of a licensing exam, and usually require you to practice your profession in a certain manner (ethically). If you do not, you may be taken before an administrative law judge and have your license (and livelihood) taken away.

There are laws and regulations that govern the practice of these professions. *Laws* are statutes implemented by the legislature and signed into law by the governor. *Regulations* are procedures and requirements contained in the Pennsylvania Code, and are created by the body in charge of enforcing the requirements of the law. For example, the law may say that you have to take a test administered by the state to become a chiropractor, but the regulations will specify the procedure that you must follow to apply for the test.

The following departments and bureaus regulate certain professions. Information regarding these professions can be obtained through **www.state.pa.us**, by following the hyperlink to "Government in PA."

Bureau of Professional and Occupational Affairs

Accountants
Architects
Auctioneers
Barbers
Chiropractors
Cosmetologists
Dentists
Funeral Directors
Health Professionals
Landscape Architects
Medicine
Nurses
Nursing Home Administrators
Occupational Therapists
Optometrists
Osteopaths
Pharmacists
Physical Therapists
Podiatrists
Professional Engineers
Psychologists
Real Estate Agents
Real Estate Appraisers
Social Workers
Speech-language and Hearing Therapists
Vehicle Manufacturers
Veterinarians

Department of Agriculture

Amusement Ride Inspectors
Approved Food Safety and Laboratory Services Inspectors
Egg Inspectors
Fur Dealers
Horse Racing Owners and Drivers/Jockeys
Livestock Brokers

Livestock Dealers
Nursery (plants) Dealers and Agents
Pesticide Dealers
Poultry Technicians
Solid Fuel Weighmasters

Department of Insurance
Auto Appraisers
Bail Bondspersons
Insurance Adjusters
Insurance Agencies
Insurance Agents

Department of Health
Emergency Medical Services Instructors
Emergency Medical Technicians

Department of Labor and Industry
Entertainers
Entertainment Agents
Motion Picture Projectionists
Pilots

Department of Transportation
Truck Drivers (Commercial Driver's License—CDL)

This list is by no means exhaustive. You are encouraged to contact either your elected state official, whose phone number will appear in the government pages of your telephone directory, or the department that you think best describes what you plan to do.

In addition to the above required licenses, some activities need to be registered, certified, or licensed, although the specific individual may not need to be licensed to perform the activity. Again, the following list is not at all exhaustive, and you are cautioned to seek help for any questions through your elected official's office or through the appropriate department. Remember, if you do not know, ask. Knowing for sure what you need before you start your business or occupation will save time, money, and heartache later. Besides, your taxes support your elected officials and the departments—so get your money's worth. Also, you can access the appropriate department website for further information at **www.state.pa.us**.

Department of Agriculture

Animal Feed

Areas where food is prepared for commercial consumption—especially frozen desserts and nonalcoholic drinks

Bakeries

Cattle Branding

Cold Storage Warehouses

Commercial Fertilization

"Garbage Licenses" (feeding garbage to pigs)

Greenhouses

Horse Slaughtering

Kennels

Liming (for treating soil)

Meat Packing

Nurseries (plants)

Poultry Hauling

Rendering Plants

Selling Milk and Dairy

Soil Conditioners and Plant Growth Substances

Stallion-jack

Department of Banking

Consumer Discount Companies

Sales Finance Companies

Secondary Mortgage Loan Companies

Department of Conservation and Natural Resources

Firewood Gathering from State Forests

Ginseng Harvesting

Ground Pine Removal

Road Use through State Forests

Snowmobile Registration

State Forest Camping

State Park Camping

State Park Picnicking

Wild Plant Management

Department of Education
    Private Academic Schools
    Private Driver Training Schools
    Private Licensed Business, Correspondence, and Trade Schools

Department of Environmental Protection
    Agricultural Utilization of Sewerage Sludge
    Air Quality Plans and Operation
    Asbestos Removal
    Beneficial Use of Municipal Waste
    Beneficial Use of Residual Waste
    Blasting
    Boat Launching
    Boat Mooring
    Bottled or Vended Drinking Water
    Coal Mining
    Coal Preparation
    Coal Refuse Disposal
    Coal Surface Mining
    Composting
    Constructing and Demolishing Waste Landfills
    Dam Safety
    Deep Mine Blasting and Storage of Explosives
    Demonstration of Municipal and Residual Waste Facilities
    Earth Disturbance
    Eating and Drinking Places
    Facilities for the Transfer of Municipal and Residual Waste
    Incineration Resource Recovery
    Land Disposal of Sewerage Sludge
    Land Reclamation of Sewerage Sludge
    Marina Slips
    Mineral Prospecting
    Mining Authorization Letters
    Mining Equipment Approval
    Municipal Waste for Landfills
    Municipal Waste Processing and Disposal
    Non-Coal Surface Mining
    Noncommunity Water Systems
    Oil and Gas
    Public Water Supply Systems

Radiation-related activities require registration and licensure through the U.S. Nuclear Regulatory Commission, as well as licensing and permits through the state (these activities include, but are not limited to, radiation-producing machines and radioactive material handling and storage)

Radon Testing and Mitigation

Sanitation Licenses, which include campgrounds, organized camps, organized camp certificate of registration, private academic school license inspection, and seasonal farm camps

Seismic Surveying

Storage of Explosives

Submerged Lands Licenses

Transporting Chemotherapeutic Waste

Vulnerable Plants

Water Obstructions and Encroachment

Department of Health

Abortion Clinics

Accreditation Medical Command Facilities

Accreditation Training Institutes

Ambulance Services

Birthing Centers

Clinical Laboratories

Clinical Labs performing blood analysis, blood lead analysis, Erythrocyte Protoporphyrin analysis, urine drug tests, and breath alcohol testing devices

Drug and Alcohol Facilities

Drug, Devices, and Cosmetic Sales

Home Health Agencies

Hospitals

Mammography Screening

Nursing Homes

Occupancy Permits for Health Care Facilities

Portable X-Ray Machines

Department of Insurance

Health Maintenance Organizations

Preferred Provider Organizations

Prepaid Capitated Dental Plans

Department of Labor and Industry
Boiler Operators
Elevator Inspection and Installation
Manufacturing of Bedding, Upholstery, and Stuffed Toys
Private Employment Agencies
Vocational Rehabilitation Facilities
Workers' Compensation

Pennsylvania Fish and Boat Commission
Commercial Fishing
Commercial Hatchery
Fishing Agencies
Live Bait Dealers
Passenger Boat Operators
Regulated Fishing Lake Fishing

Pennsylvania Game Commission
Regulated Hunting Grounds
Taxidermy
Wildlife Menageries
Wildlife Pest Control
Wildlife Propagation

Pennsylvania Securities Commission
Registration of Securities
Securities Exemption

Public Utility Commission
Courier Services
Limousines
Taxi Services
Transportation Companies
Trucking Companies

Department of Public Welfare
Adoption
Adult Day Care Facilities
Child Day Care
Community Residential Facilities
Day Treatment Services

Foster Families
Intermediate Care Facilities for the Mentally Retarded
Intermediate Care Facilities
Personal Care Homes
Residential and Maternity Homes

Department of Revenue

Gasoline Regulated Distribution
Small Games of Chance (you must also get a permit from your
county's Office of Treasurer—some counties permit small
games of chance and others do not)
State and Local Sales, Use, and Occupancy

Department of State

Charitable Organizations
Corporations
Fictitious Names
Out-of-State Corporations

Department of Transportation

Airport Landing Fields
All-Terrain Vehicles
Inspection Stations
Junkyards

FEDERAL LICENSES

So far, there are few businesses that require federal registration. If
you are in any of the types of businesses listed in this section, you
should check with the federal agency responsible.

Radio or television stations, or manufacturers of equipment emitting
radio waves:

Federal Communications Commission
445 12th Street, SW
Washington, DC 20554
www.fcc.gov

Manufacturers of alcohol, tobacco, or firearms:

Bureau of Alcohol, Tobacco, Firearms, and Explosives
Office of Public and Governmental Affairs
650 Massachusetts Avenue, NW
Room 8290
Washington, DC 20226
www.atf.treas.gov

Securities brokers and providers of investment advice:

Securities and Exchange Commission
100 F Street, NW
Washington, DC 20546
www.sec.gov

Manufacturers of drugs and processors of meat:

Food and Drug Administration
5600 Fishers Lane
Rockville, MD 20857
www.fda.gov

Interstate carriers:

Surface Transportation Board
1925 K Street, NW
Washington, DC 20423
www.stb.dot.gov

Exporting:

Bureau of Industry and Security
Department of Commerce
14th Street & Constitution Avenue, NW
Washington, DC 20230
www.bis.doc.gov

chapter 8

Contract Laws

As a business owner, you will need to know the basics of forming a simple contract for your transactions with both customers and vendors. There is a lot of misunderstanding about what the law is, and people may give you erroneous information. Relying on it can cost you money. This chapter gives you a quick overview of the principles that apply to your transactions and the pitfalls to avoid. If you face more complicated contract questions, you should consult a law library or an attorney familiar with small business law.

TRADITIONAL CONTRACT LAW

One of the first things taught in law school is that a contract is not legal unless three elements are present—offer, acceptance, and consideration. The rest of the semester dissects exactly what may be a valid offer, acceptance, and consideration. For your purposes, the important things to remember are as follows.

✪	If you make an offer to someone, it may result in a binding contract, even if you change your mind or find out it was a bad deal for you.

✪ Unless an offer is accepted and both parties agree to the same terms, there is no contract.

✪ A contract does not always have to be in writing. Some laws require certain contracts to be in writing, but as a general rule, an oral contract is legal. The problem is in proving that the contract existed.

✪ Without *consideration* (the exchange of something of value or mutual promises), there is not a valid contract.

Basic Contract Rules

Some of the most important contract rules for a business owner are as follows.

✪ *An advertisement is not an offer.* Suppose you put an ad in the newspaper offering "New IBM computers only $995," but there is a typo in the ad and it says $9.95. Can people come in and say "I accept, here's my $9.95," creating a legal contract? Fortunately, no. Courts have ruled that an ad is not an offer that a person can accept. It is an invitation to come in and make offers, which the business can accept or reject.

✪ *The same rule applies to the price tag on an item.* If someone switches price tags on your merchandise, or if you accidentally put the wrong price on it, you are not required by law to sell it at that price. However, many merchants honor a mistaken price, because refusing to do so would constitute bad will and probably lose a customer. If you intentionally put a lower price on an item, intending to require a buyer to pay a higher price, you may be in violation of *bait and switch* laws.

✪ *When a person makes an offer, several things may happen.* It may be accepted, creating a legal contract; it may be rejected; it may expire before it has been accepted; or, it may be withdrawn before acceptance. A contract may expire either by a date made in the offer ("This offer remains open until noon on January 29, 2007") or after a reasonable amount of time. What is reasonable is a legal question that a court must decide. If someone makes you an offer to sell goods, clearly you cannot come back five years later and accept. Whether you can accept a week later or a month later and create a legal contract depends on the type of goods and the circumstances.

✪   *A person accepting an offer cannot add any terms to it.* If you offer to sell a car for $1,000, and the other party says he or she accepts as long as you put new tires on it, there is no contract. An acceptance with changed terms is considered a rejection and a counteroffer.

✪   *When someone rejects your offer and makes a counteroffer, a contract can be created by your acceptance of the counteroffer.*

These rules can affect your business on a daily basis. Suppose you offer to sell something to one customer over the phone, and five minutes later another customer walks in and offers you more for it. To protect yourself, you should call the first customer and withdraw your offer before accepting the offer of the second customer. If the first customer accepts before you have withdrawn your offer, you may be sued if you have sold the item to the second customer.

Exceptions   There are a few exceptions to the basic rules of contracts. Some of the important exceptions you need to know are as follows.

✪   *Consent to a contract must be voluntary.* If it is made under a threat, the contract is not valid. If a business refuses to give a person's car back unless they pay $500 for changing the oil, the customer could probably sue and get the $500 back.

✪   *Contracts to do illegal acts or acts against public policy are not enforceable.* If an electrician signs a contract to put some wiring in a house that is not legal, the customer could probably not force him or her to do it, because the court would refuse to require an illegal act.

✪   *If either party to an offer dies, then the offer expires and cannot be accepted by the heirs.* If a painter is hired to paint a portrait, and dies before completing it, his wife, for example, cannot finish it and require payment. However, a corporation does not die, even if its owners die. If a corporation is hired to build a house and the owner of the corporation dies, the heirs may take over the corporation, finish the job, and require payment.

✪ *Contracts made under misrepresentation are not enforceable.* For example, if someone tells you a car has 35,000 miles on it and you later discover it has 135,000 miles, you may be able to rescind the contract for fraud and misrepresentation.

✪ *If there was a mutual mistake, a contract may be rescinded.* For example, if both you and the seller thought the car had 35,000 miles on it and both relied on that assumption, the contract could be rescinded. However, if the seller knew the car has 135,000 miles on it, but you assumed it had 35,000 and did not ask, you probably could not rescind the contract.

STATUTORY CONTRACT LAW

The previous section discussed the basics of contract law and some of the additional rules for when a contract can be made unenforceable. These are not usually stated in the statutes, but are the legal principles decided by judges over the past hundreds of years. In recent times, the legislatures have made numerous exceptions to these principles. In most cases, these laws have been passed when the legislature felt that traditional law was not fair.

Statutes of Fraud

Statutes of fraud state when a contract must be in writing to be valid. Some people believe a contract is not valid unless it is in writing, but that is not so. Only those types of contracts mentioned in the statutes of fraud must be in writing. Of course, an oral contract is much harder to prove in court than one that is in writing.

In Pennsylvania, some of the contracts that must be in writing are as follows:

✪ sales of any interest in real estate;

✪ leases of real estate over three years;

- ✪ guarantees of debts of another person (*Tudor Development Group, Inc v. U.S. Fidelity and Guarantee Co.*, 692 F. Supp. 461 (1988));

- ✪ sales of goods of over $500 (13 Pa.C.S. Sec. 2201); and,

- ✪ sales of personal property of over $5,000 (13 Pa.C.S. Sec. 1206).

Consumer Protection Laws

Due to the alleged unfair practices by some types of businesses, laws have been passed controlling the types of contracts they may use. Most notable among these are health clubs and door-to-door solicitations. The laws covering these businesses usually give the consumer a certain time to cancel the contract. These advertising and promotion laws are described in Chapter 13.

The *Pennsylvania Plain Language Consumer Contract Act* (73 P.S. Secs. 2201–2212) requires that consumer contracts be easily readable. Under the regulations (37 Pa. Code Secs. 307.1–307.10), both the wording and the look of the contract must be user-friendly. For example:

- ✪ words, sentences, and paragraphs should be short;

- ✪ active verbs should be used;

- ✪ double negatives should not be used;

- ✪ sentences should have no more than one condition;

- ✪ cross-references should not be used;

- ✪ the ink should contrast with the paper; and,

- ✪ headings should be in boldface type.

The Office of the Attorney General provides a packet of materials about compliance with the Act and will preapprove contracts submitted to it. For more information, call or write:

Office of Attorney General
Bureau of Consumer Protection
14th Floor
Strawberry Square
Attn: PLA
Harrisburg, PA 17120
717-787-9707
800-441-2555

PREPARING YOUR CONTRACTS

Before you open your business, you should obtain or prepare the contracts or policies you will use in your business. In some businesses, such as a restaurant, you will not need much. Perhaps you will want a sign near the entrance stating "shirt and shoes required" or "diners must be seated by 10:30 p.m."

However, if you are a building contractor or a similar business, you will need detailed contracts to use with your customers. If you do not clearly spell out your rights and obligations, you may end up in court and lose thousands of dollars in profits.

Of course, the best way to have an effective contract is to have an attorney experienced in the subject prepare one to meet the needs of your business. However, since this may be too expensive for your new operation, you may want to go elsewhere. Three sources for the contracts you will need are other businesses like yours, trade associations, and legal form books. You should obtain as many different contracts as possible, compare them, and decide which terms are most comfortable for you.

Attorney General's Review

Also, under certain circumstances, the Pennsylvania Attorney General's office will review a contract that you have drafted, and issue a letter stating whether or not such a contract is acceptable. This service is free, but time-consuming. However, if you have a letter of satisfaction from the Attorney General, any questions that may arise from your contract that pertain to its propriety can be answered or defended. Call 717-787-9707 for information regarding this service.

Insurance

There are few laws requiring you to have insurance. However, if you do not have insurance, you may face liability that could ruin your business. You should be aware of the types of insurance available and weigh the risks of a loss against the cost of a policy.

Be aware that there can be a wide range of prices and coverage in insurance policies. You should get at least three quotes from different insurance agents, and ask each one to explain the benefits of his or her policy.

WORKERS' COMPENSATION

If you have *any* full- or part-time employees, you are required by Pennsylvania law to carry workers' compensation insurance. Workers' compensation may be obtained from most insurance companies or from the *State Workmen's Insurance Fund*. Although this insurance is expensive, such coverage will protect you against suits by employees or their heirs in case of accidents, and against claims that could potentially put you out of business. To obtain insurance through the State Workmen's Insurance Fund, call their offices at 570-963-4635. In some instances, you may be approved for self-insurance, although it is usually large and wealthy corporations that get approved. Call the Department of Labor and Industry at 717-783-4476 to request information about self-insurance.

However, do not think you can get away with failing to provide workers' compensation insurance in order to save money. Failure to provide workers' compensation insurance when required is serious. An employer is guilty of a third degree misdemeanor for each failure to provide workers' compensation insurance. If the failure is deemed by the court to be intentional, the employer is guilty of a felony of the third degree for each violation. Each day that there is a failure to carry workers' compensation is considered a separate offense.

There are other requirements of the workers' compensation law, such as reporting any on-the-job deaths of workers within twenty-four hours. Also, it is a misdemeanor to deduct the amount of the premiums from the employee's wages.

Those who are exempt from the law are supposed to file an affidavit each year with the state stating that they are exempt. Also, a notice must be posted in the workplace stating that employees are not entitled to workers' compensation benefits.

This law has been subject to frequent change lately, so you should check with the Bureau of Workers' Compensation for the latest requirements. Ask for the their latest publication. Call 800-482-2383 or write:

Bureau of Workers' Compensation
Room 102
1171 South Cameron Street
Harrisburg, PA 17104-2501

LIABILITY INSURANCE

In most cases, you are not required to carry liability insurance. Liability insurance can be divided into two main areas—coverage for injuries on your premises and by your employees, and coverage for injuries caused by your products or services.

Coverage for the first type of injury is usually very reasonably priced. Injuries in your business or by your employees (such as in an auto accident) are covered by standard premises or auto policies. However, coverage for injuries by products may be harder to find and more expensive. Juries have been known to award high judgments for accidents involving products that had little impact on an accident. This has caused the price for insurance to increase dramatically.

Asset Protection

If insurance is unavailable or unaffordable, you can go without and use a corporation or other asset protection device to protect yourself from liability. The best way to find out if insurance is available for your type of business is to check with other businesses. If there is a trade group for your industry, their newsletter or magazine may contain ads for insurers.

Umbrella Policy

As a business owner, you will be a more visible target for lawsuits, even if there is little merit to them. Lawyers know that a nuisance suit is often settled for thousands of dollars. Because of your greater exposure, you should consider getting a personal *umbrella policy*. This is a policy that covers you for claims of up to a million (or even two or five million dollars) and is very reasonably priced.

HAZARD INSURANCE

One of the worst things that can happen to your business is a fire, flood, or other disaster. With lost customer lists, inventory, and equipment, many businesses have been forced to close after such a disaster.

The premium for such insurance is usually reasonable and could protect you from loss of your business. As an additional protection, you should keep backup copies of your important records at your home or another location. For information on the Federal Flood Insurance Program, contact the Pennsylvania Emergency Management Agency at:

Pennsylvania Emergency Management Agency (PEMA)
Executive Office
P.O. Box 3221
Harrisburg, PA 17105
717-651-2007

HOME BUSINESS INSURANCE

There is a special insurance problem for home businesses. Most homeowner and tenant insurance policies do not cover business activities. In fact, under some policies, you may be denied coverage if you use your home for a business.

If you merely use your home to make business phone calls and send letters, you will probably not have a problem and not need extra coverage. However, if you own equipment or have dedicated a portion of your home exclusively to the business, you could have a problem. Check with your insurance agent for the options that are available to you.

If your business is a sole proprietorship, and you have, say, a computer that you use both personally and for your business, it would probably be covered under your homeowners policy. If you incorporated your business and bought the computer in the name of the corporation, coverage might be denied. If a computer is your main business asset, you could get a special insurance policy in the company name covering just the computer. One company that offers such a policy is Safeware, and you can call them at 800-723-9273 or 800-800-1492.

AUTOMOBILE INSURANCE

If you or any of your employees will be using an automobile for business purposes, be sure that such use is covered. Sometimes a policy may include an exclusion for business use. Check to be sure your liability policy covers you if one of your employees causes an accident while running a business errand.

HEALTH INSURANCE

While new businesses can rarely afford health insurance for their employees, the sooner they can obtain it, the better chance they will have to find and keep good employees. As a business owner, you will certainly need health insurance for yourself (unless you have a working spouse who can cover the family), and you can sometimes get a better rate if you purchase a small business package.

EMPLOYEE THEFT

If you fear employees may be able to steal from your business, you may want to have them *bonded*. This can cover all existing and new employees. You may also require a background check of your new employees. For a reasonable cost, background checks are conducted through the Pennsylvania State Police. A check takes about eight weeks.

Some employee positions are required by the state to have background checks. Most notable are day care workers and those who come into contact with children, such as coaches and school personnel.

Your Business and the Internet

The Internet has opened up a world of opportunities for businesses. It was not long ago that getting national visibility cost a fortune. Today, a business can set up a Web page for a few hundred dollars, and with some clever publicity and a little luck, millions of people around the world will see it.

This new world has new legal issues and new liabilities. Not all of them have been addressed by laws or by the courts. Before you begin doing business on the Internet, you should know the existing rules and the areas where legal issues exist.

DOMAIN NAMES

A *domain name* is the address of your website. For example, www.apple.com is the domain name of Apple Computer Company. The last part of the domain name, the ".com" (or "dot com") is the *top-level domain*, or TLD. Dot com is the most popular, but others are currently available in the United States, including .net and .org. (Originally, .net was only available to network service providers and .org only to nonprofit organizations, but regulations have eliminated those requirements.)

It may seem like most words have been taken as a dot com name, but if you combine two or three short words or abbreviations, a nearly unlimited number of possibilities are available. For example, if you have a business dealing with automobiles, most likely someone has already registered automobile.com and auto.com. You can come up with all kinds of variations, using adjectives or your name, depending on your type of business:

autos4u.com	joesauto.com	autobob.com
myauto.com	yourauto.com	onlyautos.com
greatauto.com	autosfirst.com	usautos.com
greatautos.com	firstautoworld.com	4autos.com

One site that provides both low-cost registrations and suggestions for name variations is **www.registerfly.com**.

When the Internet first began, some individuals realized that major corporations would soon want to register their names. Since the registration was easy and cheap, people registered names they thought would ultimately be used by someone else.

At first, some companies paid high fees to buy their names from the registrants. One company, Intermatic, filed a lawsuit instead of paying. The owner of the domain name they wanted had registered numerous domain names, such as britishairways.com and ussteel.com. The court ruled that since Intermatic owned a trademark on the name, the registration of their name by someone else violated that trademark, and that Intermatic was entitled to it.

Since then, people have registered names that are not trademarks, such as CalRipkin.com, and have attempted to charge the individuals with those names to buy their domain. In 1998, Congress passed the *Anti-Cybersquatting Consumer Protection Act*, making it illegal to register a domain with no legitimate need to use it.

This law helped a lot of companies protect their names, but then some companies started abusing it and tried to stop legitimate users of names similar to theirs. This is especially likely against small companies. An organization that has been set up to help small companies protect their domains is the *Domain Name Rights Coalition*. Its website is

www.netpolicy.com. Other good information on domain names can be found at **www.bitlaw.com/internet/domain.html**.

Registering a domain name for your own business is a simple process. There are many companies that offer registration services. For a list of those companies, visit the site of the *Internet Corporation for Assigned Names and Numbers* (ICANN) at **www.icann.org**. You can link directly to any member's site and compare the costs and registration procedures required for the different top-level domains.

WEB PAGES

There are many new companies eager to help you set up a website. Some offer turnkey sites for a low, flat rate, while custom sites can cost tens of thousands of dollars. If you have plenty of capital, you may want to have your site handled by one of these professionals. However, setting up a website is a fairly simple process, and once you learn the basics, you can handle most of it in-house.

If you are new to the Web, you may want to look at **www.learn thenet.com** and **www.webopedia.com**, which will help you become familiar with the Internet jargon and give you a basic introduction to the Web.

Site Setup There are seven steps to setting up a website: site purpose, design, content, structure, programming, testing, and publicity. Whether you do it yourself, hire a professional site designer, or employ a college student, the steps toward creating an effective site are the same.

Before beginning your own site, you should look at other sites, including those of major corporations and of small businesses. Look at the sites of all the companies that compete with you. Look at hundreds of sites and click through them to see how they work (or do not work).

Site purpose. To know what to include on your site, you must decide what its purpose will be. Do you want to take orders for your products or services, attract new employees, give away samples, or show off your company headquarters? You might want to do several of these things.

Site design. After looking at other sites, you can see that there are numerous ways to design a site. It can be crowded, or open and airy; it can have several windows (frames) open at once or just one; and, it can allow long scrolling or just click-throughs.

You will have to decide whether the site will have text only; text plus photographs and graphics; or, text plus photos, graphics, and other design elements, such as animation or Java script. Additionally, you will begin to make decisions about colors, fonts, and the basic graphic appearance of the site.

Site content. You must create the content for your site. For this, you can use your existing promotional materials, new material just for the website, or a combination of the two. Whatever you choose, remember that the written material should be concise, free of errors, and easy for your target audience to read. Any graphics (including photographs) and written materials not created by you require permission. You should obtain such permission from the lawful copyright holder in order to use any copyrighted material. Once you know your site's purpose, look, and content, you can begin to piece the site together.

Site structure. You must decide how the content (text plus photographs, graphics, animation, etc.) will be structured—what content will be on which page, and how a user will link from one part of the site to another. For example, your first page may have the business name and then choices to click on, such as "about us," "opportunities," or "product catalog." Have those choices connect to other pages containing the detailed information, so that a user will see the catalog when he or she clicks on "product catalog." Your site could also have an option to click on a link to another website related to yours.

Site programming and setup. When you know nothing about setting up a website, it can seem like a daunting task that will require an expert. However, *programming* here means merely putting a site together. There are inexpensive computer programs available that make it very simple.

Commercial programs such as Microsoft FrontPage, Dreamweaver, Pagemaker, Photoshop, MS Publisher, and PageMill allow you to set up Web pages as easily as laying out a print publication. These programs will convert the text and graphics you create into HTML, the programming language of the Web. Before you choose Web design software and design your site, you should determine which Web hosting service you will use. Make sure that the design software you use is compatible with the host server's system. The Web host is the provider that will give you space on its server and that may provide other services to you, such as secure order processing and analysis of your site to see who is visiting and linking to it.

If you have an America Online (AOL) account, you can download design software and a tutorial for free. You do not have to use AOL's design software in order to use this service. You are eligible to use this site whether you design your own pages, have someone else do the design work for you, or use AOL's templates. This service allows you to use your own domain name and choose the package that is appropriate for your business.

If you have used a page layout program, you can usually get a simple Web page up and running within a day or two. If you do not have much experience with a computer, you might consider hiring a college student to set up a Web page for you.

Site testing. Some of the website setup programs allow you to thoroughly check your new site to see if all the pictures are included and all the links are proper. There are also websites you can go to that will check out your site. Some even allow you to improve your site, such as by reducing the size of your graphics so they download faster. Use a major search engine listed on page 78 to look for companies that can test your site before you launch it on the Web.

Site publicity. Once you set up your website, you will want to get people to look at it. *Publicity* means getting your site noticed as much as possible by drawing people to it.

The first thing to do to get noticed is to be sure your site is registered with as many *search engines* as possible. These are pages that people use to find things on the Internet, such as Yahoo and Google. They do not automatically know about you just because you created a website. You must tell them about your site, and they must examine and catalog it.

For a fee, there are services that will register your site with numerous search engines. If you are starting out on a shoestring, you can easily do it yourself. While there are hundreds of search engines, most people use a dozen or so of the bigger ones. If your site is in a niche area, such as genealogy services, then you would want to be listed on any specific genealogy search engines. Most businesses should be mainly concerned with getting on the biggest ones.

By far the biggest and most successful search engine today is Google (**www.google.com**). Some of the other big ones are:

www.altavista.com	www.hotbot.com
www.excite.com	www.lycos.com
www.fastsearch.com	www.metacrawler.com
www.go.com	www.northernlight.com
www.goto.com	www.webcrawler.com

Most of these sites have a place to click to "add your site" to their system. Some sites charge hundreds of dollars to be listed. If your site contains valuable information that people are looking for, you should be able to do well without paying these fees.

Getting Your Site Known

A *meta tag* is an invisible subject word added to your site that can be found by a search engine. For example, if you are a pest control company, you may want to list all of the scientific names of the pests you control and all of the treatments you have available, but you may not need them to be part of the visual design of your site. List these words as meta tags when you set up your page so people searching for those words will find your site.

Some companies thought that a clever way to get viewers would be to use commonly searched names or names of major competitors as meta tags to attract people looking for those big companies. For example, a small delivery service that has nothing to do with UPS or FedEx might use those company names as meta tags so people looking for them would find the smaller company. While it may sound like a good idea, it has been declared illegal trademark infringement. Today, many companies have computer programs scanning the Internet for improper use of their trademarks.

Once you have made sure that your site is passively listed in all the search engines, you may want to actively promote your site. However, self-promotion is seen as a bad thing on the Internet, especially if its purpose is to make money.

Newsgroups are places on the Internet where people interested in a specific topic can exchange information. For example, expectant mothers have a group where they can trade advice and experiences. If you have a product that would be great for expectant mothers, that would be a good place for it to be discussed. However, if you log into the group and merely announce your product, suggesting people order it from your website, you will probably be *flamed* (sent a lot of hate mail).

If you join the group, however, and become a regular, and in answer to someone's problem, mention that you "saw this product that might help," your information will be better received. It may seem unethical to plug your product without disclosing your interest, but this is a procedure used by many large companies. They hire *buzz agents* to plug their product all over the Internet and create positive *buzz* for the product. So, perhaps it has become an acceptable marketing method and consumers know to take plugs with a grain of salt. Let your conscience be your guide.

Keep in mind that Internet publicity works both ways. If you have a great product and people love it, you will get a lot of business. If you sell a shoddy product, give poor service, and do not keep your customers happy, bad publicity on the Internet can kill your business. Besides being an equalizer between large and small companies, the Internet can be a filtering mechanism between good and bad products.

Spamming   Sending unsolicited email advertising (called *spam*) started out as a mere breach of Internet etiquette (netiquette), but has now become a state and federal crime. The ability to reach millions of people with advertising at virtually no cost was too good for too many businesses to pass up, and this resulted in the clogging of most users' email boxes and near shut down of some computer systems. Some people ended up with thousand of offers every day.

To prevent this, many states passed anti-spamming laws and Congress passed the Controlling the Assault of Non-Solicited Pornography and Marketing (CAN-SPAM) Act. This law:

- ✪ bans misleading or false headers on email;

- ✪ bans misleading subject lines;

- ✪ requires allowing recipients to opt out of future mailings;

- ✪ requires the email be identified as advertising; and,

- ✪ requires the email include a valid physical address.

Each violation can result in up to an $11,000 fine and the fines can be raised if advertisers violate other rules, such as not harvesting names and not using permutations of existing names. More information can be found on the Federal Trade Commission's website at **www.ftc.gov**.

Advertising   Advertising on the Internet has grown in recent years. At first, small, thin rectangular ads appeared at the top of websites; these are called *banner ads*. Lately they have grown bigger, can appear anywhere on the site, and usually blink or show a moving visual.

The fees can be based on how many people view an ad, how many click on it, or both. Some larger companies, such as Amazon.com, have affiliate programs in which they will pay a percentage of a purchase if a customer comes from your site to theirs and makes a purchase. For sites that have thousands of visitors the ads have been profitable— some sites reportedly make over $100,000 a year.

Example:
One financially successful site is Manolo's Shoe Blog (http://shoeblogs.com). It is written by a man who loves shoes, has a great sense of humor, and writes in endearing broken English. Because he is an expert in his field, his suggestions are taken by many readers who click through to the products and purchase them.

LEGAL ISSUES

Before you set up a Web page, you should consider the many legal issues associated with it.

Jurisdiction

Jurisdiction is the power of a court in a particular location to decide a particular case. Usually, you have to have been physically present in a jurisdiction or have done business there before you can be sued there. Since the Internet extends your business's ability to reach people in faraway places, there may be instances when you could be subject to legal jurisdiction far from your own state (or country). There are a number of cases that have been decided in this country regarding the Internet and jurisdiction, but very few cases have been decided on this issue outside of the United States.

In most instances, U.S. courts use the pre-Internet test—whether you have been present in another jurisdiction or have had enough contact with someone in the other jurisdiction. The fact that the Internet itself is not a place will not shield you from being sued in another state when you have shipped you company's product there, have entered into a contract with a resident of that state, or have defamed a foreign resident with content on your website.

According to the court, there is a spectrum of contact required between you, your website, and consumers or audiences. (*Zippo Manufacturing Co. v. Zippo Dot Com, Inc.,* 952 F. Supp. 1119 (W.D. Pa 1997).) The more interactive your site is with consumers, the more you target an audience for your goods in a particular location, and the farther you reach to send your goods out into the world, the more it becomes possible for someone to sue you outside of your own jurisdiction. You must weigh these risks against the benefits when constructing and promoting your website.

The law is not even remotely final on these issues. The American Bar Association, among other groups, is studying this topic in detail. At present, no final, global solution or agreement about jurisdictional issues with websites exists.

One way to protect yourself from the possibility of being sued in a faraway jurisdiction would be to state on your website that those using the site or doing business with you agree that "jurisdiction for any actions regarding this site" or your company will be in your home county.

For extra protection, you can have a preliminary page that must be clicked before entering your website. However, this may be overkill for a small business with little risk of lawsuits. If you are in any business for which you could have serious liability, you should review some competitors' sites and see how they handle the liability issue. They often have a place to click for "legal notice" or "disclaimer" on their first page.

You may want to consult with an attorney to discuss the specific disclaimer you will use on your website, where it should appear, and whether you will have users of your site actively agree to this disclaimer or just passively read it. However, these disclaimers are not enforceable everywhere in the world. Until there is global agreement on jurisdictional issues, this may remain an area of uncertainty for some time to come.

Libel

Libel is any publication that injures the reputation of another. This can occur in print, writing, pictures, or signs. All that is required for publication is that you transmit the material to at least one other person. When putting together your website, you must keep in mind that it is visible to millions of people all over the planet, and that if you libel a person or company, you may have to pay damages. Many countries do not have the freedom of speech that we do, and a statement that is not libel in the United States may be libelous elsewhere. If you are concerned about this, alter the content of your site or check with an attorney about libel laws in the country you think might take action against you.

Copyright Infringement

It is so easy to copy and borrow information on the Internet that it is easy to infringe copyrights without even knowing it. A *copyright* exists for a work as soon as the creator creates it. There is no need to register the copyright or to put a copyright notice on it. Therefore, practically everything on the Internet belongs to someone.

Linking and Framing

Some people freely give their works away. For example, many people have created Web artwork (*gifs* and *animated gifs*) that they freely allow people to copy. There are numerous sites that provide hundreds or thousands of free gifs that you can add to your Web pages. Some require you to acknowledge the source and some do not. You should always be sure that the works are free for the taking before using them.

Linking and Framing

One way to violate copyright laws is to improperly link other sites to yours, either directly or with framing. *Linking* is when you provide a link that takes the user to the linked site. *Framing* occurs when you set up your site so that when you link to another site, your site is still viewable as a frame around the linked-to site.

While many sites are glad to be linked to others, some, especially providers of valuable information, object. Courts have ruled that linking and framing can be a copyright violation. One rule that has developed is that it is usually okay to link to the first page of a site, but not to link to some valuable information deeper within the site. The rationale for this is that the owner of the site wants visitors to go through the various levels of their site (viewing all the ads) before getting the information. By linking directly to the information, you are giving away their product without the ads.

The problem with linking to the first page of a site is that it may be a tedious or difficult task to find the needed page from there. Many sites are poorly designed and make it nearly impossible to find anything.

If you wish to link to another page, the best solution is to ask permission. Email the webmaster or other person in charge of the site, if an email address is given, and explain what you want to do. If they grant permission, be sure to print out a copy of their email for your records.

Privacy

Since the Internet is such an easy way to share information, there are many concerns that it will cause a loss of individual privacy. The two main concerns arise when you post information that others consider private, and when you gather information from customers and use it in a way that violates their privacy.

While public actions of politicians and celebrities are fair game, details about their private lives are sometimes protected by law, and details about persons who are not public figures are often protected. The laws in each state are different, and what might be allowable in one state could be illegal in another. If your site will provide any personal information about individuals, you should discuss the possibility of liability with an attorney.

Several well-known companies have been in the news lately for violations of their customers' privacy. They either shared what the customer was buying or downloading, or looked for additional information on the customer's computer. To let customers know that you do not violate certain standards of privacy, you can subscribe to one of the privacy codes that have been created for the Internet. These allow you to put a symbol on your site guaranteeing to your customers that you follow the code.

The following are the websites of two organizations that offer this service and their fees at the time of this publication.

www.privacybot.com	$100
www.bbbonline.com	$200 to $7,000

Protecting Yourself

The easiest way to protect yourself personally from the various possible types of liability is to set up a corporation or limited liability company to own the website. This is not foolproof protection since, in some cases, you could be sued personally as well—but it is one level of protection.

COPPA

If your website is aimed at children under the age of thirteen, or if it attracts children of that age, then you are subject to the federal *Children Online Privacy Protection Act of 1998* (COPPA). This law requires such websites to:

- ✪ give notice on the site of what information is being collected;

- ✪ obtain verifiable parental consent to collect the information;

- ✪ allow the parent to review the information collected;

- ✪ allow the parent to delete the child's information or to refuse to allow the use of the information;

- ✪ limit the information collected to only that necessary to participate on the site; and,

- ✪ protect the security and confidentiality of the information.

HIRING A WEBSITE DESIGNER

If you hire someone to design your website, you should make sure of what rights you are buying. Under copyright law, when you hire someone to create a work, you do not get all rights to that work unless you clearly spell that out in a written agreement.

For example, if your designer creates an artistic design to go on your website, you may have to pay extra if you want to use the same design on your business cards or letterhead. Depending on how the agreement is worded, you may even have to pay a yearly fee for the rights.

If you spend a lot of money promoting your business and a logo or design becomes important to your image, you would not want to have to pay royalties for the life of your business to someone who spent an hour or two putting together a design. Whenever you purchase a creative work from someone, be sure to get a written statement of what rights you are buying. If you are not receiving all rights for all uses for all time, you should think twice about the purchase.

If the designer also is involved with hosting your site, you should be sure you have the right to take the design with you if you move to another host. You should get a backup of your site on a CD in case it is ever lost or you need to move it to another site.

FINANCIAL TRANSACTIONS

The existing services for sending money over the Internet, such as PayPal, usually offer more risk and higher fees than traditional credit card processing. Under their service agreements, you usually must agree that they can freeze your account at any time and can take money out of your bank account at any time. Some do not offer an appeal process. Before signing up for any of these services, you should read their service agreement carefully and check the Internet for other peoples' experiences with them. For example, for information on PayPal you can check **www.nopaypal.com**.

For now, the easiest way to exchange money on the Internet is through traditional credit cards. Because of concerns that email can be abducted in transit and read by others, most companies use a secure site in which customers are guaranteed that their card data is encrypted before being sent.

When setting up your website, you should ask the provider if you can be set up with a secure site for transmitting credit card data. If they cannot provide it, you will need to contract with another software provider. Use one of the major search engines listed on page 78 to look for companies that provide credit card services to businesses on the Internet.

As a practical matter, there is very little to worry about when sending credit card data by email. If you do not have a secure site, another option is to allow purchasers to fax or phone in their credit card data. However, keep in mind that this extra step will lose some business unless your products are unique and your buyers are very motivated.

The least effective option is to provide an order form on the site that can be printed out and mailed in with a check. Again, your customers must be really motivated or they will lose interest after finding out this extra work is involved.

FTC RULES

Because the Internet is an instrument of interstate commerce, it is a legitimate subject for federal regulation. The *Federal Trade Commission* (FTC) first said that all of its consumer protection rules applied to the Internet, but lately it has been adding specific rules and issuing publications. The following publications are available from the FTC website at **www.ftc.gov/bcp/menu-internet.htm** or by mail from:

Consumer Response Center
Federal Trade Commission
600 Pennsylvania, NW
Room H-130
Washington, DC 20580

✪ *Advertising and Marketing on the Internet: The Rules of the Road*

✪ *Appliance Labeling Rule Homepage*

✪ *BBB-Online: Code of Online Business Practices*

✪ *Big Print. Little Print. What's the Deal? How to Disclose the Details*

✪ *Businessperson's Guide to the Mail and Telephone Order Merchandise Rule*

✪ *CAN-SPAM Act: Requirements for Commercial Emailers*

✪ *Complying with the Telemarketing Sales Rule*

✪ *Disclosing Energy Efficiency Information: A Guide for Online Sellers of Appliances*

✪ *Dot Com Disclosures: Information About Online Advertising*

✪ *Electronic Commerce: Selling Internationally. A Guide for Business*

✪ *How to Comply With the Children's Online Privacy Protection Rule*

✪ *Frequently Asked Questions About the Children's Online Privacy Protection Rule*

✪ *Internet Auctions: A Guide for Buyer and Sellers*

✪ *"Remove Me" Responses and Responsibilities: Email Marketers Must Honor "Unsubscribe" Claims*

✪ *Securing Your Server—Shut the Door on Spam*

✪ *Security Check: Reducing Risks to Your Computer Systems*

✪ *Selling on the Internet: Prompt Delivery Rules*

✪ *TooLate.Com: The Lowdown on Late Internet Shipments*

✪ *Website Woes: Avoiding Web Service Scams*

✪ *What's Dot and What's Not: Domain Name Registration Scams*

✪ *You, Your Privacy Policy & COPPA*

FRAUD

Because the Internet is somewhat anonymous, it is a tempting place for those with fraudulent schemes to look for victims. As a business consumer, you should exercise caution when dealing with unknown or anonymous parties on the Internet.

The U.S. Department of Justice, the FBI, and the National White Collar Crime Center jointly launched the Internet Crime Complaint Center (ICCC). If you suspect that you are the victim of fraud online, whether as a consumer or a business, you can report incidents to the ICCC on their website, **www.ic3.gov**. The ICCC is currently staffed by FBI agents and representatives of the National White Collar Crime Center, and will work with state and local law enforcement officials to prevent, investigate, and prosecute high-tech and economic crime online.

Health and Safety Laws

As a reaction to the terrible work conditions prevalent in the factories and mills of the nineteenth century industrial age, Congress and the states developed many laws intended to protect the health and safety of the nation's workers. These laws are difficult to understand and often seem to be very unfair to employers. Therefore, this is an area that you need to pay particular attention to as a new business. Failure to do so can result in terrible consequences for you.

FEDERAL LAWS

The federal government's laws regarding health and safety of workers are far-reaching and very important to consider in running your business, especially if you are a manufacturer or in the oil and gas, food production, or agriculture industries.

OSHA   The point of the *Occupational Safety and Health Administration* (OSHA) is to place the duty on the employer to keep the workplace free from recognized hazards that are likely to cause death or serious bodily injury to workers. The regulations are not as cumbersome for small businesses as for larger enterprises. If you have ten or fewer employees, or if you are in a certain type of business, you do not have to keep a record of illnesses, injuries, and exposure to hazardous substances for your employees. If you have eleven or more employees, OSHA's rules will apply. One important rule to know is that within forty-eight hours of an on-the-job death of an employee, or injury of five or more employees on the job, the area director of OSHA must be contacted.

For more information, you should write or call an OSHA office:

U.S. Department of Labor
200 Constitution Avenue, NW
Room N-3101
Washington, DC 20210
202-219-4667

You can also visit their website at **www.osha-slc.gov** to obtain copies of their publications, *OSHA Handbook for Small Business* (OSHA 2209), and *OSHA Publications and Audiovisual Programs Catalog* (OSHA 2019). They also have a poster that is required to be posted in the workplace. Find it at **www.osha.gov/publications/poster.html**.

The *Hazard Communication Standard* requires that employees be made aware of the hazards in the workplace. (29 C.F.R. 1910.1200.) It is especially applicable to those working with chemicals, but this can include even offices that use copy machines. Businesses using hazardous chemicals must have a comprehensive program for informing employees of the hazards and for protecting them from contamination.

For more information, you can contact OSHA at the previously mentioned address, phone number, or website. They can supply a copy of the regulation and a booklet called *OSHA 3084*, which explains the law.

EPA   The *Worker Protection Standard for Agricultural Pesticides* requires safety training, decontamination sites, and of course, posters. The *Environmental Protection Agency* (EPA) will provide information in compliance with this law. They can be reached at 800-490-9198, or on their website at **www.epa.gov**.

They can be reached by mail at:

Environmental Protection Agency
401 M Street, SW
Washington, DC 20460

FDA   The *Pure Food and Drug Act* of 1906 prohibits the misbranding or adulteration of food and drugs. It also created the *Food and Drug Administration* (FDA), which has promulgated many regulations and must give permission before a new drug can be introduced into the market. If you will be dealing with any food or drugs, you should keep abreast of their policies. Their website is **www.fda.gov**, their small business site is **www.fda.gov/ora/ fed_state/small_business**, and their local small business representative can be reached at:

FDA, Mid-Atlantic Region
Small Business Representative
900 U.S. Customhouse
2nd and Chestnut Street
Philadelphia, PA 19106
215-597-4394 ext. 4003

Hazardous   There are regulations that control the shipping and packing of haz-
Materials   ardous materials. For more information, contact the Office of
Transportation   Hazardous Materials Transportation at:

Office of Hazardous Materials Transportation
400 Seventh Street, SW
Washington, DC 20590
202-426-0656

PENNSYLVANIA LAWS

Pennsylvania has additional occupations it regulates as hazardous. It also has specific occupational safety laws concerning buildings and certain products.

Hazardous Occupations

Under Act 177 of 1913, railroading, operating street railways, generating and selling electricity, telegraph and telephone business, express business, blasting and dynamiting, operating automobiles for public use, and boating when the boat is powered by steam, gas, or electricity are considered hazardous occupations. The owners of such enterprises are liable for injuries or deaths of their employees, unless they can rebut a presumption against them that they have not used reasonable care. In cases where the employee is at fault, the damages are apportioned. Employers may not contract with employees to avoid the liability of this law.

Occupational and Industrial Safety

In addition to the federal safety requirements under OSHA, Pennsylvania has four specific laws that relate to occupational and industrial safety. These laws are:

❂ the *Required Buildings Be Constructed to Be Usable by the Physically Handicapped Act* (this is in addition to the federal Americans with Disabilities Act—see Chapter 12);

❂ the *Fire and Panic Act*;

❂ the *Bedding and Upholstery Act*; and,

❂ the *Stuffed Toy Manufacturers Act*.

Fire and Panic Act. The *Fire and Panic Act* regulates the safety of buildings, and assesses fees and penalties for violations. It is very important and very complicated, and compliance can be costly, especially if you are locating your business in an older building. You are urged to begin the process for submitting your plans for examination and approval as soon as you know where you will be locating your business, especially if you will be leasing or renting property, because occupancy will not be permitted until plans are approved.

Because the Fire and Panic Act is complicated, rather than breaking down the Act here, you are urged to contact the Department of Labor and Industry's Bureau of Occupational and Industrial Safety Building Plans Examination Section in Harrisburg at 717-787-3806. Trained building examiners will look at drawings of your building, compare it to the Building Code, and either make notation of areas of noncompliance that must be corrected or approve the drawings. This is not an arbitrary process—it is one of mathematics and measurements.

The good news is, your plans will eventually be approved if the required changes are made. The bad news is that the changes may be costly, and you have to comply with local ordinances that may (and often do) differ from the state code. If the local ordinance differs, you may need to seek a variance before the local zoning board. Contact the city or municipal government building where you intend to locate your office to determine if there are any local ordinances that may apply.

Bedding and Upholstery Act. Those tags on your cushions and furniture that say "do not remove under penalty of law" are required by the *Bedding and Upholstery Act.* This Act governs the manufacturing, repairing, renovating, cleansing, sterilizing, and disinfecting of mattresses, pillows, bolsters, feather beds, and other filled bedding, cushions, upholstered furniture, and bulk materials intended for use in such products and for sale or lease. Basically, the Act requires that the above named items be made with new, clean, or disinfected and sterilized materials. Enforcement of this Act lies with the Department of General Services. Their phone number is 717-787-4705.

Stuffed Toy Manufacturing Act. The *Stuffed Toy Manufacturing Act* regulates the manufacturing of stuffed toys for sale, gift, or use. Manufacturers must pay to register their business with the Department of General Services and obtain a certificate of registration. The Stuffed Toy Act requires that stuffed toys be made with new materials that are free from dangerous or harmful substances, and requires a certificate of disinfection of materials of animal origin before their use. Do note that if you have a business making stuffed toys as a *leisure pursuit* and your gross income from the sale of these toys is less than $1,000 a year, you are exempted from the registration fee, but this does not relieve you of the requirement to comply with the Act's other provisions.

Employment and Labor Laws

As they have with health and safety laws, Congress and the states have heavily regulated the actions that employers can take with regard to hiring and firing, improper employment practices, and discrimination. Because the penalties can be severe, educate yourself on the proper actions to take and, if necessary, consult a labor and employment lawyer prior to making important employee decisions.

HIRING AND FIRING LAWS

For small businesses, there are not many rules regarding who you may hire or fire. The ancient law that an employee can be fired at any time (or may quit at any time) still prevails for small businesses. In certain situations and as you grow, however, you will come under a number of laws that affect your hiring and firing practices.

One of the most important things to consider when hiring someone is that if you fire him or her, that fired employee may be entitled to unemployment compensation. If so, your unemployment compensation tax rate will go up and it can cost you a lot of money. Therefore, you should only hire people you are sure you will keep, and you should avoid situations where your former employees can make claims against your company.

One way this can be done is by hiring only part-time employees. The drawback to this is that you may not be able to attract the best employees. When hiring dishwashers or busboys, this may not be an issue, but when hiring someone to develop a software product, you do not want him or her to leave halfway through the development.

A better solution is to screen applicants to begin with and only hire those who you feel certain will work out. Of course, this is easier said than done. Some people interview well but then turn out to be incompetent at the job.

The best record to look for is someone who has stayed a long time at each of his or her previous jobs. Next best is someone who has not stayed as long (for good reasons), but has always been employed. The worst type of hire would be someone who is or has been collecting unemployment compensation.

The reason those who have collected compensation are a bad risk is that if they collect in the future, even if it is not your fault, your employment of them could make you chargeable for their claim. For example, say you hire someone who has been on unemployment compensation and he or she works out well for a year, but then quits to take another job, and is fired after a few weeks. In this situation, you would be chargeable for most of his or her claim, because the last five quarters of work are analyzed. Look for a steady job history.

Often, the intelligence of an employee is more important than his or her experience. An employee with years of typing experience may be fast, but unable to figure out how to use your new computer, whereas an intelligent employee can learn the equipment quickly and eventually gain speed. Of course, common sense is important in all situations.

The bottom line is that you cannot know if an employee will be able to fill your needs from a résumé and interview. Once you have found someone who you think will work out, offer that person a job with a ninety-day probationary period. If you are not completely satisfied with the employee after the ninety days, offer to extend the probationary period for ninety additional days rather than end the relationship immediately. Of course, all of this should be in writing.

Background Checks

Beware that a former boss may be a good friend or even a relative. It has always been considered acceptable to exaggerate on résumés, but in recent years, some applicants have been found to be completely fabricating sections of their education and experience. Checking references is important.

Polygraph Tests

Under the federal *Employee Polygraph Protection Act,* you cannot require an employee or prospective employee to take a polygraph test unless you are in the armored car, guard, or pharmaceutical business.

Drug Tests

Under the Americans with Disabilities Act (ADA), drug testing can only be required of applicants who have been offered jobs conditioned upon passing the drug test.

FIRING

In most cases, unless you have a contract with an employee for a set time period, you can fire him or her at any time. This is only fair, since the employee can quit at any time. This type of employment is called *at will*. You should make it clear when offering a job to someone that, upon acceptance, he or she will be an at-will employee. The exceptions to this are if you fired someone based on illegal discrimination, for filing some sort of health or safety complaint, or for refusing your sexual advances.

NEW HIRE REPORTING

In order to track down parents who do not pay child support, a federal law was passed in 1996 that requires the reporting of new hires. The *Personal Responsibility and Work Opportunity Reconciliation Act of 1996* (PRWORA) provides that such information must be reported by employers to their state government.

Within twenty days of hiring a new employee, an employer must provide the state with information about the employee, including his or her name, Social Security number, and address. This information can be submitted in several ways, including by mail, fax, magnetic tape, or over the Internet. There is a special form that can be used for this reporting; however, an employer can simply use the W-4 form for this purpose. Since this form must be filled out for all employees anyway, it would be pointless to use a separate form for the new hire reporting. A copy of the **W-4 FORM** is included in Appendix C. It may be faxed to 717-657-4473 or mailed to:

Pennsylvania New Hire Reporting Program
P.O. Box 69400
Harrisburg, PA 17106

For more information about the program, call 888-724-9400, visit **www.panewhires.com**, or email **info@panewhires.com**.

EMPLOYMENT AGREEMENTS

To avoid misunderstanding with employees, you should use an employment agreement or an employee handbook. These can spell out in detail the policies of your company and the rights of your employees. These agreements can protect your trade secrets and spell out clearly that employment can be terminated at any time by either party.

Make sure that your agreement is fair and clear, because you have the upper hand in this situation and you would not want a court to find that you abused that bargaining power with an unreasonable employee agreement.

If having an employee sign an agreement is awkward, you can usually obtain the same rights by putting the company policies in an employee manual. Each existing and new employee should be given a copy along with a letter stating that the rules apply to all employees, and that by accepting or continuing employment at your company, they agree to abide by the rules. Having an employee sign a receipt for the letter and manual is proof that he or she received it.

One danger of an employment agreement or handbook is that it may be interpreted to create a long-term employment contract. To avoid this, be sure that you clearly state in the agreement or handbook that the employment is at will and can be terminated at any time by either party.

Some other things to consider in an employment agreement or handbook are:

✪   what the salary and other compensation will be;

✪   what the hours of employment will be;

✪   what the probationary period will be;

✪   that the employee cannot sign any contracts binding the employer; and,

✪   that the employee agrees to arbitration rather than filing a lawsuit if serious disagreements arise.

INDEPENDENT CONTRACTORS

One way to avoid problems with employees and taxes at the same time is to have all of your work done through independent contractors. This can relieve you of most of the burdens of employment laws, as well as the obligation to pay Social Security and Medicare taxes for the workers.

An independent contractor is, in effect, a separate business that you pay to do a job. You pay them just as you pay any company from which you buy products or services. At the end of the year, if the amount paid exceeds $600, you must issue a 1099 form, which is similar to the W-2 that you would issue to employees.

This may seem too good to be true, and in some situations it is. The IRS does not like independent contractor arrangements, because it is too easy for the independent contractors to cheat on their taxes. To limit the use of independent contractors, the IRS has strict regulations on who may and may not be classified as an independent contractor. Also, companies who do not appear to pay enough in wages for their field of business are audited.

Using independent contractors for jobs not traditionally done by independent contractors puts you at high risk for an IRS audit. For example, you could not get away with hiring a secretary as an independent contractor. One of the most important factors considered in determining if a worker can be an independent contractor is the amount of control the company has over his or her work. If you need someone to paint your building and you agree to pay a certain price to have it done according to the painter's own methods and schedule, you can pay the painter as an independent contractor. However, if you tell the painter when and how to do the work, and provide the tools and materials, the painter will be classified as an employee.

If you just need some typing done and you take it to a typing service and pick it up when it is ready, you will be safe in treating those workers as independent contractors. However, if you need someone to come into your office to type on your machine at your schedule, you will probably be required to treat that person as an employee for tax purposes.

The IRS has a form you can use in determining if a person is an employee or an independent contractor, called **DETERMINATION OF WORKER STATUS (IRS FORM SS-8)**. It is included in Appendix C of this book along with instructions. (see form 6, p.233.)

Independent Contractors vs. Employees

In deciding whether to make use of independent contractors or employees, you should weigh the following advantages and disadvantages.

Advantages.

- ✪ *Lower taxes.* You do not have to pay Social Security, Medicare, unemployment, or other employee taxes.

- ✪ *Less paperwork.* You do not have to handle federal withholding deposits or the monthly employer returns to the state or federal government.

✪ *Less insurance.* You do not have to pay workers' compensation insurance or insurance against their possible liabilities.

✪ *More flexibility.* You can use independent contractors only when you need them.

Disadvantages.

✪ The IRS and state tax offices are strict about which workers can be qualified as independent contractors. They will audit companies whose use of independent contractors does not appear to be legitimate.

✪ If your use of independent contractors is found to be improper, you may have to pay back taxes and penalties, and may have problems with your pension plan.

✪ While employees usually cannot sue you for their injuries (if you have covered them with workers' compensation), independent contractors can sue you if their injuries were your fault.

✪ If you are paying someone to produce a creative work (writing, photography, artwork), you receive fewer rights to the work of an independent contractor.

✪ You have less control over the work of an independent contractor and less flexibility in terminating him or her if you are not satisfied that the job is being done the way you require.

✪ You have less loyalty from an independent contractor who works sporadically for you and possibly others than you have from your own full-time employees.

For some businesses, the advantages outweigh the disadvantages. For others, they do not. Consider your business plans and the consequences from each type of arrangement. Keep in mind that it will be easier to start with independent contractors and switch to employees than to hire employees and have to fire them to hire independent contractors.

TEMPORARY WORKERS

Another way to avoid the hassles of hiring employees is to get workers from a temporary agency. In this arrangement, you may pay a higher amount per hour for the work, but the agency will take care of all of the tax and insurance requirements. Since these can be expensive and time-consuming, the extra cost may be well worth it.

Whether or not temporary workers will work for you depends upon the type of business you are in and tasks you need performed. For such jobs as sales management, you would probably want someone who will stay with you long-term and develop relationships with the buyers, but for order fulfillment, temporary workers might work out well.

Another advantage of temporary workers is that you can easily stop using those who do not work out well for you. Conversely, if you find one who is ideal, you may be able to hire him or her on a full-time basis.

In recent years, a new wrinkle has developed in the temporary worker area. Many large companies are beginning to use them because they are so much cheaper than paying the benefits demanded by full-time employees. For example, Microsoft Corp. had as many as 6,000 temporary workers, some of whom worked for them for years. Some of the temporary workers won a lawsuit that declared they are really employees and are entitled to the same benefits of other employees (such as pension plans).

The law is not yet settled in this area, regarding what arrangements will result in a temporary worker being declared an employee. That will take several more court cases, some of which have already been filed. A few things you can do to protect yourself include the following.

- Be sure that any of your benefit plans make it clear that they do not apply to workers obtained through temporary agencies.

- Do not keep the same temporary workers for longer than a year.

✪ Do not list temporary workers in any employee directories or hold them out to the public as your employees.

✪ Do not allow them to use your business cards or stationery.

DISCRIMINATION LAWS

There are numerous federal laws forbidding discrimination based upon race, sex, pregnancy, color, religion, national origin, age, or disability. The laws apply to both hiring and firing, and to employment practices such as salaries, promotions, and benefits. Most of these laws only apply to an employer who has fifteen or more employees for twenty weeks of a calendar year, or has federal contracts or subcontracts. Therefore, you most likely will not be required to comply with the law immediately upon opening your business. However, there are similar state laws that may apply to your business that have a lower employee threshold.

One exception to the fifteen or more employees rule is the *Equal Pay Act*. This act applies to employers with two or more employees, and requires that women be paid the same as men in the same type of job.

Employers with fifteen or more employees are required to display a poster regarding discrimination. This poster is available from the Equal Employment Opportunity Commission on their website at **www.dol.gov/esa/regs/compliance/posters/eeo.htm**. Employers with one hundred or more employees are required to file an annual report with the EEOC.

Discriminatory Interview Questions

When hiring employees, some questions are illegal or inadvisable to ask. The following data *should not* be collected on your employment application or in your interviews, unless the information is somehow directly tied to the duties of the job.

✪ Do not ask about an applicant's citizenship or place of birth. However, after hiring an employee, you must ask about his or her right to work in this country.

- ✪ Do not ask a female applicant her maiden name. You can ask if she has been known by any other name in order to do a background check.

- ✪ Do not ask if applicants have children, plan to have them, or have child care. You can ask if an applicant will be able to work the required hours.

- ✪ Do not ask if the applicant has religious objections for working Saturday or Sunday. You can mention if the job requires such hours and ask whether the applicant can meet this job requirement.

- ✪ Do not ask an applicant's age. You can ask if an applicant is age 18 or over, or if it is a liquor-related job, you can ask if the applicant is age 21 or over.

- ✪ Do not ask an applicant's weight.

- ✪ Do not ask if an applicant has AIDS or is HIV-positive.

- ✪ Do not ask if the applicant has filed a workers' compensation claim.

- ✪ Do not ask about the applicant's previous health problems.

- ✪ Do not ask if the applicant is married or whether the spouse would object to the job, hours, or duties.

- ✪ Do not ask if the applicant owns a home, furniture, or car, as it is considered racially discriminatory.

- ✪ Do not ask if the applicant was ever arrested. You can ask if the applicant was ever convicted of a crime.

ADA   Under the *Americans with Disabilities Act of 1990* (ADA), employers who do not make *reasonable accommodations* for disabled employees will face fines of up to $100,000, as well as other civil penalties and civil damage awards.

While the goal of creating more opportunities for the disabled is a good one, the result has put all of the costs of achieving this goal on businesses that are faced with disabled applicants. In fact, studies done since the law was passed have shown that employers have hired fewer disabled applicants than before the law was passed, possibly due to the costs of reasonable accommodations and the fear of being taken to court.

The ADA is very vague. When it passed, some feared it could be taken to ridiculous lengths—such as forcing companies to hire blind applicants for jobs that require reading, and then forcing them to hire people to read for the blind employees. In the years since its enactment, some of the critics' fears have been met. In some famous rulings, the EEOC said:

- rude, disruptive, and chronically late employees could be protected by the ADA if they had some type of mental disability;

- recovering drug addicts and alcoholics are protected by the ADA;

- obesity can be a disability covered by the ADA;

- workers who are disturbed by the sight of other workers because of emotional imbalance must be given private work areas; and,

- airlines cannot discriminate against persons blind in one eye when hiring pilots.

When the ADA was passed, it was estimated that three million Americans were blind, deaf, or in wheelchairs, but it has been estimated that the ADA now applies to forty-nine million Americans with every type of physical or mental impairment. Of the ADA cases that go to court, 92% are won by businesses. While this may sound good, considering the cost of going to court, the expense of this litigation is devastating for the businesses. Many of these lawsuits occur because the law is worded so vaguely.

Some lawyers in the Miami area have been sending disabled people around the state to see if businesses comply with the ADA. When they find a violation, they immediately file a lawsuit. Because defending such a suit is expensive, the businesses routinely settle with the law firm for several thousand dollars. One newspaper discovered that once the settlement is paid, the law firms rarely care if the business complies with the law—they just move to the next town and file more suits.

If your business is the victim of such a scheme, you should consider getting together with other businesses and fighting the cases. This type of activity was not what the ADA was meant for, and perhaps it could be ruled to be extortion or even a violation of racketeering laws.

The ADA currently applies to employers with fifteen or more employees. Employers who need more than fifteen employees might want to consider contracting with independent contractors to avoid problems with this law, particularly if the number of employees is only slightly larger than fifteen.

For more information on how this law affects your business, see the U.S. Department of Justice website at **www.usdoj.gov/crt/ada/ business.htm**.

Tax Benefits

There are three types of tax credits to help small businesses with the burden of these laws.

1. Businesses can deduct up to $15,000 a year for making their premises accessible to the disabled and can depreciate the rest. (Internal Revenue Code (I.R.C.) Section 190.)

2. Small businesses (under $1,000,000 in revenue and under thirty employees) can get a tax credit each year for 50% of the cost of making their premises accessible to the disabled, but this only applies to the amount between $250 and $10,500.

3. Small businesses can get a credit of up to 40% of the first $6,000 of wages paid to certain new employees who qualify through the *Pre-Screening Notice and Certification Request* (IRS form 8850).

Records

To protect against potential claims of discrimination, all employers should keep detailed records showing reasons for hiring or not hiring applicants, and for firing employees.

Pennsylvania Law

In addition to federal laws, you must obey Pennsylvania discrimination laws.

Universal Accessibility Act. The *Universal Accessibility Act* (UAA), which is applicable in addition to the ADA, requires any private building used by the public to be accessible by the handicapped pursuant to this Act *if* the building was built or remodeled after September 1, 1965 (the effective date of this Act).

Equal Pay Act. The Pennsylvania Equal Pay Act is Pennsylvania's counterpart to the federal law providing for equal pay for the same job to both sexes. This state statute is meant to fill the gap of workers not covered by federal law, and therefore, does not apply to workers who are under the Fair Labor Standards Act, Section 6. The Pennsylvania Equal Pay Act requires employers to post an abstract of Act 694. The abstract is prepared by the Department of Labor and Industry, and a copy may be obtained by calling the Bureau of Labor Standards in your region: Altoona, 814-946-7374; Harrisburg, 717-787-4671; Philadelphia, 215-560-1858; Pittsburgh, 412-565-5300; or, Scranton, 570-963-4577.

SEXUAL HARASSMENT

As an employer, you can be liable for the acts of your employees. One of the latest types of acts that employers have been help liable for is sexual harassment of customers, employees, and others. While you cannot control every act of every employee, if you indicate to employees that such behavior is unacceptable and set up a system to resolve complaints, you will do much to protect yourself against lawsuits.

The EEOC has held the following in sexual harassment cases.

✮   The victim as well as the harasser may be a woman or a man.

✮   The victim does not have to be of the opposite sex.

- ✪ The harasser can be the victim's supervisor, an agent of the employer, a supervisor in another area, a coworker, or a nonemployee.

- ✪ The victim does not have to be the person harassed, but could be anyone affected by the offensive conduct.

- ✪ Unlawful sexual harassment may occur without economic injury to or discharge of the victim.

- ✪ The harasser's conduct must be unwelcome.

Some of the actions that have been considered harassment are:

- ✪ displaying sexually explicit posters in the workplace;

- ✪ requiring female employees to wear revealing uniforms;

- ✪ rating the sexual attractiveness of female employees as they pass male employees' desks;

- ✪ continued sexual jokes and innuendos;

- ✪ demands for sexual favors from subordinates;

- ✪ unwelcomed sexual propositions or flirtation;

- ✪ unwelcomed physical contact; and,

- ✪ whistling or leering at members of the opposite sex.

In 1993, the United States Supreme Court ruled that an employee can make a claim for sexual harassment even without proof of a specific injury. However, lower federal courts in more recent cases have dismissed cases where no specific injury was shown. These new cases may indicate that the pendulum has stopped moving toward expanded rights for the employee.

On the other hand, another recent case ruled that an employer can be liable for the harassment of an employee by a supervisor—even if the employer was unaware of the supervisor's conduct—if the employer did not have a system in place to allow complaints against harassment. This area of law is still developing, but to avoid a possible lawsuit, you should be aware of the things that could potentially cause liability and avoid them.

Some things a business can do to protect against claims of sexual harassment include the following.

- ✪ Distribute a written policy against all kinds of sexual harassment to all employees.

- ✪ Encourage employees to report all incidents of sexual harassment.

- ✪ Ensure there is no retaliation against those who complain.

- ✪ Make clear that your policy is zero tolerance.

- ✪ Explain that sexual harassment includes both requests for sexual favors and a work environment that some employees may consider hostile.

- ✪ Allow employees to report harassment to someone other than their immediate supervisor, in case that person is involved in the harassment.

- ✪ Promise as much confidentiality as possible to complainants.

Pennsylvania Law

The *Pennsylvania Human Relations Act* prohibits sexual harassment on the job. There are three kinds of sexual harassment as defined in the Act:

1. physical;

2. verbal; and,

3. visual.

Physical harassment includes touching, fondling, kissing, and so on, and can include assault or rape. *Verbal harassment* includes demands for sexual favors, whistles, jokes of a sexual nature, and so on. *Visual harassment* includes leering and obscene gestures, or crude cartoons, photographs, or posters. Anyone who feels harassment in such a manner, and who feels that he or she must submit or endure this in order to keep his or her job or get a promotion, may file a civil complaint as well as a complaint before the Pennsylvania Human Relations Commission (HRC). Literature published by the Human Relations Commission advises victims to file complaints on several levels: civil court, administrative court (the HRC), their union (if they are unionized employees), and with the police.

If you are the boss and have not done the harassing, you can and will be sued as well if you know or should have known one of your employees was being victimized and did nothing to stop it. Also, an employee who witnesses the harassment of another can also sue the harasser and the boss or supervisor.

In order to protect yourself, your business, and your employees, you are advised to establish and circulate a policy that explains your position on sexual harassment and defines the behavior that constitutes sexual harassment and the consequences for violations of the policy. It is advisable to include this sexual harassment policy in the employee handbook that you have each employee sign upon hiring. Also, as an employer, to protect yourself, you should provide a procedure so employees can report incidents, and you should encourage your employees to do so. Let them know the incidents will be investigated thoroughly and neutrally, and that offenders will be swiftly punished. Contact the Pennsylvania Human Relations office for assistance in setting up a policy and getting more information about the Human Relations Act.

PA HRC Headquarters
101 South 2nd Street
Suite 300
Harrisburg, PA 17105
717-787-4410

Harrisburg Regional HRC
Uptown Shopping Plaza
2971-E 7th Street
Harrisburg, PA 17110
717-787-9784

Pittsburgh Regional HRC
11th Floor State Office Building
300 Library Avenue
Pittsburgh, PA 15222
412-565-5395

Philadelphia Regional HRC
711 State Office Building
1400 Spring Garden Street
Philadelphia, PA 19130
215-560-2496

WAGE AND HOUR LAWS

The *Fair Labor Standards Act* (FLSA) applies to all employers who are engaged in *interstate commerce* or in the production of goods for interstate commerce (anything that will cross the state line), as well as all employees of hospitals, schools, residential facilities for the disabled or aged, or public agencies. It also applies to all employees of enterprises that gross $500,000 or more per year.

While many small businesses might not think they are engaged in interstate commerce, the laws have been interpreted so broadly that nearly any use of the mail, interstate telephone service, or other interstate services—however minor—is enough to bring a business under the law.

Minimum Wage

The federal wage and hour laws are contained in the *federal Fair Labor Standards Act*. In 1996, Congress passed and President Clinton signed legislation raising the minimum wage to $5.15 an hour beginning September 1, 1997.

In certain circumstances, a wage of $4.25 may be paid to employees under 20 years of age for a ninety-day training period.

For employees who regularly receive more than $30 a month in tips, the minimum wage is $2.13 per hour. If the employee's tips do not bring him or her up to the full $5.15 minimum wage, then the employer must make up the difference. For more information, contact the Department of Labor.

Wage and Hour Division
U.S. Department of Labor
200 Constitution Avenue, NW
Room S-3325
Washington, DC 20210

You can also call the Philadelphia office at 215-596-1193.

Pennsylvania Law

Pennsylvania has several laws that relate to the payment of wages. Among these are:

- the *Equal Pay Law*;

- the *Prevailing Wage Act*;

- the *Wage Payment and Collection Law*; and,

- the *Seasonal Farm Labor Act*.

Equal Pay Law. The *Equal Pay Law* prohibits discrimination of the rate of pay on the basis of sex by paying wages at a rate less than the rate at which wages are paid to employees of the opposite sex. The jobs in question must be for equal work, the performance of which requires equal skill, effort, and responsibility. The jobs must be performed under equal working conditions. An exception to this rule exists where payment is made subject to a seniority system, a merit system, a system that makes payment on the basis of quality or quantity of production, or any factor other than gender. An agreement by the employee to accept less money for the same job as a member of the opposite sex is *not* a defense to a violation of this Act. Any employer subject to this Act cannot lower the wages of the higher paid employee in order to comply with the Act. A violation of this Act subjects the employer to liability for the amount of the unpaid wages, *plus* an equal amount of the unpaid wages as liquidated damages.

Employers must keep records on the wages, wage rate, job classifications, and other terms and conditions of employment for all employees. Failure to maintain the records and to make them available to the Department of Labor and Industry upon request will result in the employer being fined $50 to $200 dollars.

An abstract of this Act must be posted in a conspicuous place. A copy of the abstract may be obtained by calling the Labor Standards Office in your region (the numbers are listed in the government pages of your telephone book). The Equal Pay Law does not apply to anyone who is subject to Section 6 of the Federal Fair Labor Standards Act.

Prevailing Wage Act. The *Prevailing Wage Act* requires that contractors and subcontractors performing a public works contract must pay at least the minimum prevailing wage for the job performed. A public works contract is any contract exceeding $25,000 and paid for, in whole or in part, by the funds of the public body. A public works contract includes contracts for construction, reconstruction, demolition, alteration, and repair work other than maintenance work under contract.

A worker subject to this Act is any laborer, mechanic, skilled or semi-skilled laborer, and apprentices, whether or not their work is performed on the job site. It is the duty of the public body making the contract to determine the prevailing wage rate through the Secretary of the Department of Labor and Industry. Contractors and subcontractors are required to post the prevailing wages for each craft and classification involved in the contract performance.

Wage Payment and Collection Law. The *Wage Payment and Collection Law* requires that wages be paid on regular paydays designated in advance by the employer. The employer is required to notify the employee of the time and place of payment, the rate of pay, and any benefits at the time of hiring.

Seasonal Farm Labor Act. The *Seasonal Farm Labor Act* was intended to improve the conditions of seasonal farm workers by creating standards for their wages, hours, work conditions, housing, sanitation, food facilities, fire protection, and safety. It requires farm labor contractors to obtain certificates of registration, and forbids the isolation of workers from services to which they are entitled. It also limits child labor. Seasonal farm labor camps are inspected by the Department of Environmental Protection, and potable drinking water and adequate, sanitary toilet facilities must be provided.

PENSION AND BENEFIT LAWS

There are no laws requiring small businesses to provide any type of special benefits to employees. Such benefits are given to attract and keep good employees. With pension plans, the main concern is that if you do start one, it must comply with federal tax laws.

Holidays   There are no federal or Pennsylvania laws that require that employees bo given holidays off. You can require them to work Thanksgiving and Christmas, and dock their pay or fire them for failing to show—but you will not have much luck keeping employees with such a policy.

Most companies give full-time employees a certain number of paid holidays, such as: New Year's Day (January 1); Memorial Day (last Monday in May); the Fourth of July; Labor Day (first Monday in September); Thanksgiving (fourth Thursday in November); and, Christmas (December 25). Some, but not many, employers include other holidays, such as Martin Luther King, Jr.'s birthday (January 15); President's Day; and, Columbus Day. If one of the holidays falls on a Saturday or Sunday, many employers give the preceding Friday or following Monday off.

Pennsylvania law says that legal holidays include all of those in the previous paragraph (except President's Day), as well as the following:

- Abraham Lincoln's birthday (February 12);

- George Washington's birthday (February 22);

- Good Friday (varies—usually in April);

- Primary Election Day (varies—usually in May);

- Columbus Day (second Monday in October);

- Veterans' Day (November 11); and,

- General Election Day (varies—usually in November).

However, the fact that these are designated state holidays does not mean anything. In fact, not even the state government is closed on all of these days.

Sick Days   There is no federal or Pennsylvania law mandating that an employee be paid for time that he or she is home sick. In fact, the Pennsylvania Labor Law states that all employers must only pay employees for hours worked. The situation seems to be that the larger the company, the more paid sick leave is allowed. Part-time workers rarely get sick leave, and small business sick leave is usually limited for the simple reason that a small business cannot afford to pay for time that employees do not work.

Some small companies have an official policy of no paid sick leave, but when an important employee misses a day because he or she is clearly sick, it is paid.

Breaks

There are no federal or Pennsylvania laws requiring coffee breaks or lunch breaks. However, it is common sense that employees will be more productive if they have reasonable breaks for nourishment or to use the toilet facilities.

Pension Plans and Retirement Accounts

Few small new businesses can afford to provide pension plans for their employees. The first concern of a small business is usually how the owner can shelter income in a pension plan without having to set up a pension plan for an employee. Under most pension plans, this is not allowed.

IRA. Any individual can put up to $4,000 ($5,000 if age 50 or over) in an Individual Retirement Account (IRA). Unless the person, or his or her spouse, is covered by a company pension plan and has income over a certain amount, the amount put into the account is fully tax-deductible.

Roth IRA. Contributions to a Roth IRA are not tax deductible, but when the money is taken out, it is not taxable. People who expect to still have taxable income when they withdraw from their IRA can benefit from these.

SEP IRA, SAR-SEP IRA, SIMPLE IRA. With these types of retirement accounts, a person can put a much greater amount into a retirement plan and deduct it from their taxable income. Employees must also be covered by such plans, but certain employees are exempt, so it is sometimes possible to use these for the owners alone. The best source for more information is a mutual fund company (such as Vanguard, Fidelity, or Dreyfus) or a local bank, which can set up the plan and provide you with all of the rules. These have an advantage over qualified plans (discussed below), since they do not have the high annual fees.

Qualified Retirement Plans. Qualified retirement plans are 401(k) plans, Keogh plans, and corporate retirement plans. These are covered by the *Employee Retirement Income Security Act* (ERISA), which is a complicated law meant to protect employee pension plans. Congress did not want employees who contributed to pension plans all their lives ending up with nothing if the plan went bankrupt. The law is so complicated and the penalties so severe that some companies are cancelling their pension plans, and applications for new plans are a fraction of what they were previously. However, many banks and mutual funds have created *canned plans*, which can be used instead of drafting one from scratch. Still, the fees for administering them are steep. Check with a bank or mutual fund for details.

FAMILY AND MEDICAL LEAVE LAW

To assist business owners in deciding what type of leave to offer their employees, Congress passed the *Family and Medical Leave Act of 1993* (FMLA). This law requires an employee to be given up to twelve weeks of unpaid leave when:

- the employee or employee's spouse has a child;

- the employee adopts a child or takes in a foster child;

- the employee needs to care for an ill spouse, child, or parent; or,

- the employee becomes seriously ill.

The law only applies to employers with fifty or more employees. Also, the top 10% of an employer's salaried employees can be denied this leave because of the disruption in business their loss could cause.

Pennsylvania Law

There is no Pennsylvania law requiring family or medical leave. Therefore, the federal act controls.

CHILD LABOR LAWS

The federal *Fair Labor Standards Act* contains rules regarding the hiring of children. The basic rules are that children under 16 years old may not be hired at all, except in a few jobs such as acting and newspaper delivery. Those under age 18 may not be hired for dangerous jobs. Children may not work more than three hours a day or eighteen hours a week in a school week, or more than eight hours a day or forty hours a week in a nonschool week. If you plan to hire children, you should check the Federal Fair Labor Standards Act, which is in Chapter 29, United States Code (29 U.S.C.), and also the related regulations, which are in Chapter 29 of the Code of Federal Regulations (29 C.F.R.).

Pennsylvania Law

Generally, a minor under age 14 may not be permitted to work in *any* occupation, except those employed on farms or in domestic service in private homes. The farmer is the only person permitted to hire a minor under age 14 to work on a farm. Children ages 12 to 14 may be employed as caddies, as long as they carry no more than one golf bag at a time and do not work for more than eighteen holes in one day. Children age 11 and over may be employed as newscarriers, and seven-year-olds may be performers in the entertainment field. Other minors and infants may also be cast in motion pictures, but a special permit must be obtained from the Department of Labor and Industry, and certain moral and educational requirements must be met (e.g., a minor cannot be present during the filming of a nude scene) and a minimum number of instructional hours must be fulfilled.

Any working minor must have an employment certificate issued by the child's school, and the certificates must be kept on file by the employer. There are three types of work permits that are issued by the child's school: general; vacation; and, transferrable. The special permit, required for minors to perform in a theatrical or other performance, is obtained from the Department of Labor and Industry and is in addition to the school employment permits. The transferrable work permit may be issued to 16- and 17-year-olds. A new permit is not required each time a child changes jobs, but the employer must notify the school within five days of the child beginning or terminating his or her employment.

It is advisable for the employer to always keep a photocopy of the child's work permit in his or her personnel files, just in case any questions about the child's employment ever arises. The photocopy will function as a legally recognizable record of employment, but only if the employer records the occupation that the minor is engaged in on the photocopy.

Minors ages 14 and 15 may work during the school term for a maximum of four hours a school day, and eight hours any other day. The minor may only work for a maximum of eighteen hours from Monday through Friday, and a total of eight hours on Saturday and/or Sunday. During summer vacation, a minor may work a maximum of eight hours a day, forty-four hours per week. Minors age 14 and 15 may not work after 7 p.m. or before 7 a.m., with the exception of summer, when they can work until 10 p.m. A minor hired to work on a farm by someone other than the farmer in the hatching, raising, or harvesting of poultry may work until 10 p.m., providing that the minor is not in an agricultural occupation deemed hazardous by the U.S. Secretary of Labor. A minor age 11 and up may work as a news carrier, or selling or distributing magazines or other publications, between 5 a.m. and 8 p.m.

Minors aged 16 and 17 may work a maximum of twenty-eight hours a school week (Monday through Friday) if enrolled in a regular day school, plus an additional eight hours on Saturday *and* an additional eight hours on Sunday, but they cannot exceed working eight hours a day. Minors aged 16 and 17 cannot work after midnight Sunday through Thursday or before 6 a.m. any day. On nights preceding a school holiday, 16- and 17-year-olds may work until 1 a.m. On Friday and Saturday night, the minor may work until 1 a.m. There is no limit to night work that a 16- or 17-year-old may work during summer vacation, and there is no limit to night work for any minor legally excused from school attendance.

If a child is 17 and has graduated from high school, or has obtained his or her academic potential as determined by the chief school administrator, that child may be treated as an 18-year-old for purposes of the Child Labor Law. Also, there are special rules that apply to 16- and 17-year-olds that work during the summer at summer resident camps, conferences, or retreats operated by religious or scouting organizations.

A general rule for all minors is that they may only work six days a week, and a thirty-minute meal break must be provided either on or before five consecutive hours of work.

Any employer who violates or permits the Child Labor Law to be violated faces a fine of $100 to $300 for the first offense, and $250 to $1000 and/or ten days in prison for any subsequent offense. While this may not seem terribly steep, if that illegally employed minor is injured while on the job, the employer will be required to pay an additional 50% of the workers' compensation that the child is awarded.

There are two special prohibitions that are not part of the Child Labor Law, but that are very important and are applicable to the employment situation. According to the Vehicle Code, minors 16 and over may operate a vehicle, providing it is not in excess of 30,000 pounds registered gross weight and/or a vehicle towing a trailer that is in excess of 10,000 pounds gross weight. According to the Liquor Code, Section 493(13), any minor 16 and over may be employed as a food waiter or waitress (that means he or she may *not* also carry alcoholic beverages) or as a busboy or bus-girl at an establishment where alcoholic liquors are sold, dispensed, or made. At age 18, a minor may then serve alcoholic beverages at a licensed establishment.

A child is prohibited from engaging in many occupations. Some are practical and obvious, and some seem silly in our modern times. Rather than repeating this exhaustive list here, you are encouraged to obtain a copy of the Child Labor Law abstract that must be posted in a conspicuous place from the Bureau of Labor Standards in your region.

IMMIGRATION LAWS

There are strict penalties for any business that hires aliens who are not eligible to work. You must verify both the identity and the employment eligibility of anyone you hire by using the **EMPLOYMENT ELIGIBILITY VERIFICATION (FORM I-9)**. (see form 4, p.227.) Both you and the employee must fill out the form, and you must check an employee's identification cards or papers. Fines for hiring illegal aliens range from $250 to $2,000 for the first offense and up to $10,000 for the third offense. Failure to maintain the proper paperwork may result in a fine of up to

$1,000. The law does not apply to independent contractors with whom you may contract, and it does not penalize you if the employee used fake identification.

There are also penalties that apply to employers of four or more persons for discriminating against eligible applicants because they appear foreign or because of their national origin or citizenship status.

Appendix C has a list of acceptable documentation, a blank form, and instructions. (see form 4, p.227.) The blank form can also be downloaded at **www.uscis.gov/graphics/formsfee/forms/i-9.htm**.

For more information, call 800-357-2099. For the *Handbook for Employers and Instructions for Completing Form I-9,* check the *United States Citizenship and Immigration Services* (USCIS) website at **www.uscis.gov**.

Foreign employees. If you wish to hire employees who are foreign citizens and are not able to provide the proper documentation, they must first obtain a work visa from USCIS.

Work visas for foreigners are not easy to get. Millions of people around the globe would like to come to the U.S. to work, but the laws are designed to keep most of them out to protect the jobs of American citizens.

Whether or not a person can get a work visa depends on whether there is a shortage of U.S. workers available to fill the job. For jobs requiring few or no skills, it is practically impossible to get a visa. For highly skilled jobs, such as nurses and physical therapists, and for those of exceptional ability, such as Nobel Prize winners and Olympic medalists, obtaining a visa is fairly easy.

There are several types of visas, and different rules for different countries. For example, NAFTA has made it easier for some types of workers to enter the U.S. from Canada and Mexico. For some positions, the shortage of workers is assumed by the USCIS. For others, a business must first advertise a position available in the United States. Only after no qualified persons apply can it hire someone from another country.

The visa system is complicated and subject to regular change. If you wish to hire a foreign worker, you should consult with an immigration specialist or a book on the subject.

Pennsylvania Law

There is no Pennsylvania law pertaining to hiring illegal aliens. Therefore, the federal act controls.

HIRING OFF THE BOOKS

Because of the taxes, insurance, and red tape involved with hiring employees, some new businesses hire people *off the books*. They pay them in cash and never admit they are employees. While the wages paid in cash would not be deductible, they consider this a smaller cost than compliance. Some even use off the books receipts to cover it.

Except when your spouse or child is giving you some temporary help, this is a terrible idea. Hiring people off the books can result in civil fines, loss of insurance coverage, and even criminal penalties. When engaged in dangerous work, like roofing or using power tools, you are risking millions of dollars in potential liability if a worker is killed or seriously injured. It may be more costly and time-consuming to comply with the employment laws, but if you are concerned with long-term growth with less risk, it is the wiser way to go.

FEDERAL CONTRACTS

Companies that do work for the federal government are subject to several laws.

The *Davis-Bacon Act* requires contractors engaged in U.S. government construction projects to pay wages and benefits that are equal to or better than the prevailing wages in the area.

The *McNamara-O'Hara Service Contract Act* sets wages and other labor standards for contractors furnishing services to agencies of the U.S. government.

The *Walsh-Healey Public Contracts Act* requires the Department of Labor to settle disputes regarding manufacturers supplying products to the U.S. government.

MISCELLANEOUS LAWS

In addition to the broad categories of laws affecting businesses, there are several other federal and state laws that you should be familiar with.

Federal Law   Federal law regulates affirmative action, layoffs, unions, and informational posters.

Affirmative action. In most cases, the federal government does not tell employers who they must hire. The only situation in which a small business would need to comply with affirmative action requirements would be if it accepted federal contracts or subcontracts. These requirements could include hiring minorities or veterans of the conflict in Vietnam.

Layoffs. Companies with one hundred or more full-time employees at one location are subject to the *Worker Adjustment and Retraining Notification Act*. This law requires a sixty-day notification prior to certain layoffs and has other strict provisions.

Unions. The *National Labor Relations Act of 1935* gives employees the right to organize a union or to join one. (29 U.S.C. Secs. 151 et seq.) There are things employers can do to protect themselves, but you should consult a labor attorney or a book on the subject before taking action that might be illegal and result in fines.

Poster laws. Poster laws require certain posters to be displayed to inform employees of their rights. Not all businesses are required to display all posters, but the following list should be of help.

✪   All employers must display the wage and hour poster available from the U.S. Department of Labor at **www.dol.gov/esa**.

✪ Employers with fifteen or more employees for twenty weeks of the year must display the sex, race, religion, and ethnic discrimination poster, as well as the age discrimination poster, available from the EEOC at **www.eeoc.gov/publications.html**.

✪ Employers with federal contracts or subcontracts of $10,000 or more must display the sex, race, religion, and ethnic discrimination poster, plus a poster regarding Vietnam Era Veterans (available from the local federal contracting office).

✪ Employers with government contracts subject to the *Service Contract Act* or the *Public Contracts Act* must display a notice to employees working on government contracts available from the Employment Standards Division at **www.dol.gov/esa/whd**.

Pennsylvania Law

Pennsylvania has something called the *Veteran's Preference Act* (VPA). The VPA gives preference to any veteran over any other applicant for a position. This does not mean you are compelled to hire a less-qualified applicant over a better qualified applicant merely because of the applicant's status as a veteran. (*Brickhouse v. Springford School District* 656 A.2d. 483 (Pa. 1995)). The general rule for you to follow is that if you have two applicants of equal skill, qualifications, certifications, and so on (whatever your job requirements are), you are compelled to choose the veteran over the nonveteran.

A lot of information regarding labor rules and regulations can be obtained through the Pennsylvanian Department of Labor and Industry's website at **www.LI.state.pa.us**.

Advertising and Promotion Laws

Because of the unscrupulous and deceptive advertising techniques of some companies, as well as the multitude of con artists trying to steal from innocent consumers, numerous federal and state statutes have been enacted that make it unlawful to use improper advertising and promotional techniques in soliciting business.

ADVERTISING LAWS AND RULES

The federal government regulates advertising through the *Federal Trade Commission* (FTC). The rules are contained in the *Code of Federal Regulations* (C.F.R.). You can find these rules in most law libraries and many public libraries. If you plan on doing any advertising that you think may be questionable, you might want to check the rules. As you read the rules, you will probably think of many violations you see every day.

Federal rules do not apply to every business, and small businesses that operate only within the state and do not use the postal service may be exempt. However, many of the federal rules have been adopted into law by the State of Florida. Therefore, a violation could be prosecuted by the state rather than the federal government.

Some of the important rules are summarized in this section. If you wish to learn more details about the rules, you should obtain copies from your library.

Deceptive Pricing

(C.F.R., Title 16, Ch. I, Part 233.) When prices are being compared, it is required that actual and not inflated prices are used. For example, if an object would usually be sold for $7, you should not first offer it for $10 and then start offering it at 30% off. It is considered misleading to suggest that a discount from list price is a bargain if the item is seldom actually sold at list price. If most surrounding stores sell an item for $7, it is considered misleading to say it has a retail value of $10, even if there are some stores elsewhere selling it at that price.

Bait Advertising

(C.F.R., Title 16, Ch. I, Part 238.) Bait advertising is placing an ad when you do not really want the respondents to buy the product offered, but want them to switch to another item.

Use of "Free," "Half-Off," and Similar Words

(C.F.R., Title 16, Ch. I, Part 251.) Use of words such as "free," "1¢ sale," and the like must not be misleading. This means that the regular price must not include a mark-up to cover the free item. The seller must expect to sell the product without the free item at some time in the future.

Substantiation of Claims

(C.F.R., Title 16; Federal Regulations (F.R.), Title 48, Page 10471 (1983).) The FTC requires that advertisers be able to substantiate their claims. Some information on this policy is contained on the Internet at **www.ftc.gov/bcp/guides/ad3subst.htm**.

Endorsements

(C.F.R., Title 16, Ch. I, Part 255.) This rule forbids endorsements that are misleading. An example is a quote from a film review that is used in such a way as to change the substance of the review. It is not necessary to use the exact words of the person endorsing the product, as long as the opinion is not distorted. If a product is changed, an endorsement that does not apply to the new version cannot be used. For some items, such as drugs, claims cannot be used without scientific proof. Endorsements by organizations cannot be used unless one is sure that the membership holds the same opinion.

Unfairness

(15 U.S.C. Section 45.) Any advertising practices that can be deemed to be *unfair* are forbidden by the FTC. An explanation of this policy is located at **www.ftc.gov/bcp/policystmt/ad-unfair.htm**.

Negative Option Plans

(C.F.R., Title 16, Ch. I, Part 425.) When a seller uses a sales system in which the buyer must notify the seller if he or she does not want the goods, the seller must provide the buyer with a form to decline the sale and at least ten days in which to decline. Bonus merchandise must be shipped promptly, and the seller must promptly terminate shipment for any who so request after completion of the contract.

Laser Eye Surgery

(15 U.S.C. Sections 45, 52–57.) Under the laws governing deceptive advertising, the FTC and the FDA are regulating the advertising of laser eye surgery. Anyone involved in this area should obtain a copy of these rules. They are located on the Internet at **www.ftc.gov/bcp/guides/eyecare2.htm**.

Food and Dietary Supplements

(21 U.S.C. Section 343.) Under the *Nutritional Labeling Education Act of 1990*, the FTC and the FDA regulate the packaging and advertising of food and dietary products. Anyone involved in this area should obtain a copy of these rules. They are located on the Internet at **www.ftc.gov/bcp/menu-health.htm**.

Jewelry and Precious Metals

(F.R., Title 61, Page 27212.) The FTC has numerous rules governing the sale and advertising of jewelry and precious metals. Anyone in this business should obtain a copy of these rules. They are located on the Internet at **www.ftc.gov/bcp/guides/jewel-gd.htm**.

Pennsylvania Law

Most of Pennsylvania's advertising laws are included with the *Unfair Trade Practices and Consumer Protection Act* of 1968.

Misleading advertising. It is illegal to use advertising that is *misleading*, or to use words like "wholesale" or "below cost" unless the goods are actually at or below the retailer's net cost. If demanded by a consumer, a retailer must provide to the Better Business Bureau, the Chamber of Commerce, or the State Attorney's office proof of his or her cost, and must help that person figure out the net cost. Retailers may not advertise items at a special price unless they have reasonable quantities or state in the ad the quantity available (unless they give rain checks). A customer may sue a business under this law and receive his or her attorney's fees, court costs, and actual and punitive damages.

Under the Unfair Trade Practices and Consumer Protection Act of 1968, it is forbidden to make any misrepresentations of goods or services to the public, including any of the following:

- ✪ misrepresenting the owner, manufacturer, distributor, source, or geographical origin of goods;

- ✪ misrepresenting the age, model, grade, style, or standard of goods;

- ✪ misrepresenting the sponsorship, endorsement, approval, or certification of goods or services;

- ✪ misrepresenting the affiliation, connection, or association of any goods or services;

- ✪ misrepresenting the nature, characteristics, standard ingredients, uses, benefits, warranties, guarantees, quantities, or qualities of goods or services;

- ✪ misrepresenting used, altered, deteriorated, or repossessed goods as new (however, goods returned to a seller undamaged may be sold as new);

- ✪ disparaging the goods, services, or business of another by false or misleading representation;

- ✪ advertising goods or services with the intent not to sell them as advertised;

- ✪ advertising goods or services with the intent not to supply reasonably expectable public demand, unless the advertisement discloses a limitation of quantity;

- ✪ making false or misleading statements of fact concerning the reasons for, existence of, or amounts of price reductions;

- promising or offering to give the buyer any compensation or reward for the procurement of a contract for the purchase of goods or services with another, when such payment or reward is contingent upon the occurrence of an event subsequent to the time of the signing of the contract to purchase;

- promising or offering to give the buyer any compensation or reward for the referral of the name of another for the purpose of procuring a contract of purchase with such other person when such payment or reward is contingent upon the occurrence of an event subsequent to the time of the signing of the contract to purchase;

- failing to comply with the terms of any written guarantee or warranty given to the buyer at, prior to, or after a contract for the purchase of goods or services is made;

- knowingly misrepresenting that services, replacements, or repairs are needed if they are not needed;

- making repairs, improvements, or replacements on tangible, real, or personal property, of a nature or quality inferior to or below the standard of that agreed to in writing;

- engaging in any other fraudulent conduct that creates a likelihood of confusion or misunderstanding; and,

- pyramid schemes, which are expressly forbidden by the Act. A *pyramid scheme* is any plan by which goods or services are sold to a person for consideration, and upon the further consideration that the purchaser secure or attempt to secure one or more persons, likewise, to join said plan, each purchaser is to be given the right to secure money, goods, or services, depending upon the number of persons joining the plan. In addition, promoting or engaging in any plan, commonly known as or similar to the so-called *Chain Letter Plan* or *Pyramid Club*, is not permitted.

The terms Chain Letter Plan and Pyramid Club mean any scheme for the disposal or distribution of property, services, or anything of value whereby a participant pays valuable consid-eration, in whole or in part, for an opportunity to receive compensation for introducing or attempting to introduce one or more additional persons to participate in the scheme, or for the opportunity to receive compensation when a person intro-duced by the participant introduces a new participant. As used in this subclause, the term *consideration* means an investment of cash or the purchase of goods, other property, training, or services. It does not include payments made for sales demonstration equipment and materials for use in making sales and not for resale furnished at no profit to any person in the program or to the company or corporation, and the term does not apply to a minimal initial payment of $25 or less.

Note especially that under the Act, if you publish an advertisement or broadcast an advertisement over the radio or on a television station, you are not liable if the ad copy that you are given does *not* comply with the Unfair Trade Practices and Consumer Protection Law and you are unaware that the copy does not comply.

Assignment of indebtedness. Another rule to remember in a sales contract situation is that you may not transfer or assign the indebt-edness to any third party prior to midnight of the fifth day the sales contract was signed. If the seller plans to repossess the goods deliv-ered, he or she must do so within twenty days of the date of notice of cancellation or forfeit all rights to the delivered goods.

A consumer may not waive his or her rights under this Act unless the goods or services are needed to meet a bona fide personal emergency of the buyer, and the buyer furnishes the seller with a separate dated and signed personal statement in the buyer's handwriting, describing the emergency and expressly acknowledging and waiving the right to can-cel the sale within three business days. The Unfair Trade Practices and Consumer Protection Act does not apply to real estate and is applicable to the sale of any other goods in excess of $25.

Penalties for violation of this Act are fairly steep and the Office of the Attorney General is extremely aggressive in enforcing the Act's provisions. An injunction may be issued against you, stopping you from continuing your business practices, and in some instances, preventing you from continuing your business at all until a hearing is held. You may also be required to forfeit your franchise or right to do business. Fines for violation of this Act range from $1,000 to $5,000. In addition, the court may assess punitive damages in the amount of up to three times the amount of damages sustained, but not less than $100.

INTERNET SALES LAWS

There are not yet specific laws governing Internet transactions that are different from laws governing other transactions. The FTC feels that its current rules regarding deceptive advertising, substantiation, disclaimers, refunds, and related matters must be followed by Internet businesses, and that consumers are adequately protected by them. See the first three pages of this chapter and Chapter 10 for that information.

For some specific guidelines on Internet advertising, see the FTC's site at **www.ftc.gov/bcp/conline/pubs/buspubs/ruleroad.htm**.

EMAIL ADVERTISING

The *Controlling the Assault of Non-Solicited Pornography And Marketing Act of 2003* (CAN-SPAM) has put numerous controls on how you can use email to solicit business for your company. It requires unsolicited commercial email messages to be labeled, and the message must include opt-out instructions and the sender's physical address. Some of the prohibited activities under the Act are:

- false or misleading information in an email;

- deceptive subject heading;

- failure to include a functioning return address;

- mailing to someone who has asked not to receive solicitations;

- failure to include a valid postal address;

- ✪ omitting an opt-out procedure;

- ✪ failure to clearly mark the email as advertising; and,

- ✪ including sexual material without adequate warnings.

Some of the provisions contain criminal penalties as well as civil fines.

For more information on the CAN-SPAM Act, see **www.gigalaw.com/ canspam**. For text of the Act plus other spam laws around the world, see **www.spamlaws.com**.

HOME SOLICITATION LAWS

The Federal Trade Commission has rules governing door-to-door sales. In any such sale, it is a deceptive trade practice to fail to furnish a receipt explaining the sale (in the language of the presentation), as is failure to give notice that there is a right to back out of the contract within three days, known as a *right of rescission*. The notice must be supplied in duplicate, must be in at least ten-point type, and must be captioned either "Notice of Right to Cancel" or "Notice of Cancellation." The notice must be worded as the example on page 133 illustrates.

The seller must complete the notice and orally inform the buyer of the right to cancel. He or she cannot misrepresent the right to cancel, assign the contract until the fifth business day, or include a confession of judgment in the contract. For more specific details, see the rules contained in the Code of Federal Regulations, Title 16, Chapter I, Part 429.

NOTICE OF CANCELLATION

_____

Date

YOU MAY CANCEL THIS TRANSACTION, WITHOUT ANY PENALTY OR OBLIGATION, WITHIN THREE BUSINESS DAYS FROM THE ABOVE DATE.

IF YOU CANCEL, ANY PROPERTY TRADED IN, ANY PAYMENTS MADE BY YOU UNDER THE CONTRACT OR SALE, AND ANY NEGOTIABLE INSTRUMENT EXECUTED BY YOU WILL BE RETURNED TO YOU WITHIN 10 BUSINESS DAYS FOLLOWING RECEIPT BY THE SELLER OF YOUR CANCELLATION NOTICE, AND ANY SECURITY INTEREST ARISING OUT OF THE TRANSACTION WILL BE CANCELLED.

IF YOU CANCEL, YOU MUST MAKE AVAILABLE TO THE SELLER AT YOUR RESIDENCE, IN SUBSTANTIALLY AS GOOD CONDITION AS WHEN RECEIVED, ANY GOODS DELIVERED TO YOU UNDER THIS CONTRACT OR SALE; OR YOU MAY, IF YOU WISH, COMPLY WITH THE INSTRUCTIONS OF THE SELLER REGARDING THE RETURN SHIPMENT OF THE GOODS AT THE SELLER'S EXPENSE AND RISK.

IF YOU DO MAKE THE GOODS AVAILABLE TO THE SELLER AND THE SELLER DOES NOT PICK THEM UP WITHIN 20 DAYS OF THE DATE OF YOUR NOTICE OF CANCELLATION, YOU MAY RETAIN OR DISPOSE OF THE GOODS WITHOUT ANY FURTHER OBLIGATION. IF YOU FAIL TO MAKE THE GOODS AVAILABLE TO THE SELLER, OR IF YOU AGREE TO RETURN THE GOODS AND FAIL TO DO SO, THEN YOU REMAIN LIABLE FOR PERFORMANCE OF ALL OBLIGATIONS UNDER THE CONTRACT.

TO CANCEL THIS TRANSACTION, MAIL OR DELIVER A SIGNED AND DATED COPY OF THIS CANCELLATION NOTICE OR ANY OTHER WRITTEN NOTICE, OR SEND A TELEGRAM, TO _____(name of seller), AT _____(address of seller's place of business) NOT LATER THAN MIDNIGHT OF _____ (date).

I HEREBY CANCEL THIS TRANSACTION.

_____   _____
(Buyer's signature)   (Date)

Pennsylvania Law

Home solicitation sales are also addressed by the *Uniform Trade Practices and Consumer Protection Act*. If you call on a buyer at home and the sale you make is $25 or more, the person to whom you sold the goods may cancel the sale or contract with you within three business days following the date of the sale if he or she does so in writing. The buyer must return the goods to you in their original condition and you must return the full sales price.

NOTE: *The **mail box rule** applies here: if the consumer drops the notice of cancellation to you in the mail and it is postmarked three business days after the date the contract was signed, even though you may not receive the notice for a week, the notice is deemed timely because of the date of the postmark.*

All home solicitation sales contracts must be in the same principal language used in the sales presentation and in English as well. It must contain the date of the transaction, and the name and address of the seller, and be as close as possible to the line upon which the seller must sign his or her name. The example on pages 135–136 shows what the clause must say.

You must also include a duplicate form, that is attached to the contract and easily detachable (any reputable printer will have the appropriate paper to do this). It should be in boldfaced, ten-point type, in the same language as the rest of the contract.

BUYER'S RIGHT TO CANCEL

"YOU, THE BUYER, MAY CANCEL THIS TRANSACTION AT ANY TIME PRIOR TO MIDNIGHT OF THE THIRD BUSINESS DAY AFTER THE DATE OF THIS TRANSACTION. SEE THE ATTACHED NOTICE OF CANCELLATION FORM FOR AN EXPLANATION OF THIS RIGHT."

NOTICE OF CANCELLATION

[Enter date of transaction]

YOU MAY CANCEL THIS TRANSACTION, WITHOUT ANY PENALTY OR OBLIGATION, WITHIN THREE BUSINESS DAYS FROM THE ABOVE DATE.

IF YOU CANCEL, ANY PROPERTY TRADED IN, ANY PAYMENTS MADE BY YOU UNDER THE CONTRACT OR SALE, AND ANY NEGOTIABLE INSTRUMENT EXECUTED BY YOU WILL BE RETURNED WITHIN TEN BUSINESS DAYS FOLLOWING RECEIPT BY THE SELLER OF YOUR CANCELLATION NOTICE, AND ANY SECURITY INTEREST ARISING OUT OF THE TRANSACTION WILL BE CANCELLED.

IF YOU CANCEL, YOU MUST MAKE AVAILABLE TO THE SELLER AT YOUR RESIDENCE IN SUBSTANTIALLY AS GOOD CONDITION AS WHEN RECEIVED, ANY GOODS DELIVERED TO YOU UNDER THIS CONTRACT OR SALE; OR YOU MAY, IF YOU WISH, COMPLY WITH THE INSTRUCTIONS OF THE SELLER REGARDING THE RETURN SHIPMENT OF THE GOODS AT THE SELLER'S EXPENSE AND RISK.

IF YOU DO MAKE THE GOODS AVAILABLE TO THE SELLER AND THE SELLER DOES NOT PICK THEM UP WITHIN TWENTY DAYS OF THE DATE OF YOUR NOTICE OF CANCELLATION, YOU MAY RETAIN OR DISPOSE OF THE GOODS WITHOUT ANY FURTHER OBLIGATION. IF YOU FAIL TO MAKE THE GOODS AVAILABLE TO THE SELLER, OR IF YOU AGREE TO RETURN THE GOODS TO THE SELLER AND FAIL

TO DO SO, THEN YOU REMAIN LIABLE FOR PERFORMANCE OF ALL OBLIGATIONS UNDER THE CONTRACT.

TO CANCEL THIS TRANSACTION, MAIL OR DELIVER A SIGNED AND DATED COPY OF THIS CANCELLATION NOTICE OR ANY OTHER WRITTEN NOTICE, OR SEND A TELEGRAM, TO [name of seller], AT [address of seller's place of business] NOT LATER THAN MIDNIGHT OF [date].

I hereby cancel this transaction.

_____   _____
(Buyer's signature)   (Date)

Both copies of the notice must be completed by entering the name and address of the seller, the date of the transaction and the date by which the buyer may cancel the contract. The buyer must also be informed orally of his or her right to cancel the sale. The date on which the buyer is orally told of his or her right to cancel the contract and has been provided with his or her copy of the "Notice of Cancellation" is the date that controls when the buyer may legally cancel the sale.

Upon exercising his or her right to cancel the sales contract, the cancellation and refund must be honored by the seller within ten days, all goods must be returned to the seller within the same time period, and any negotiable instrument must be returned and cancelled. Any action necessary to terminate any security interest must also be taken.

TELEPHONE SOLICITATION LAWS

Telephone solicitations are governed by the *Telephone Consumer Protection Act* (47 U.S.C. Sec. 227) and the Federal Communications Commission rules implementing the Act (C.F.R., Title 47, Sec. 64.1200). Violators of the act can be sued for $500 damages by consumers and can be fined $10,000 by the FCC. Some of the requirements under the law include the following.

- ✪ Calls can only be made between 8 a.m. and 9 p.m.

- ✪ Solicitors must keep a *do not call* list and honor requests not to call.

- ✪ There must be a written policy that the parties called are told the name of the caller, the caller's business name and phone number or address, that the call is a sales call, and the nature of the goods or services.

- ✪ Personnel must be trained in the policies.

- ✪ Recorded messages cannot be used to call residences.

In 2003, the FCC introduced the national *Do Not Call Registry*, in which individuals could register their telephone numbers and prohibit certain telephone solicitors from calling the registered numbers. Once a person registers a telephone number, it remains on the registry for five years. Telemarketing firms can receive heavy fines for violating the registry statute, with fines ranging up to $11,000 per violation. Not all telephone solicitations are barred, however. The following solicitors may still contact a person whose telephone number has been entered in the registry:

- ✪ calls from companies with which the registered person has a prior business relationship;

- ✪ calls for which the recipient has given written consent;

- ✪ calls that do not include advertisements; and,

- ✪ calls from charitable organizations.

It is illegal under the Act to send advertising faxes to anyone who has not consented to receiving such faxes or is not an existing customer.

PRICING, WEIGHTS, AND LABELING

All food products are required to have labels displaying information on the product's nutritional values, such as calories, fat, and protein. For most products, the label must be in the required format so that consumers can easily compare products. However, if such a format will not fit on the product label, the information may be in another format that is easily readable.

Federal rules require metric measurement be included on products. Under these rules, metric measures do not have to be the first measurement on the container, but they must be included. Food items that are packaged as they are sold (such as delicatessen items) do not have to contain metric labels.

Pennsylvania Law   It is a second-degree misdemeanor (meaning a fine of up to $500 and up to sixty days in jail) to violate any of the following rules.

Misrepresenting quantity. You cannot misrepresent the quantity of goods offered for sale or goods purchased by wrapping the goods in such a way to mislead a consumer.

Misrepresenting price. You cannot misrepresent the price of any commodity or represent the price in any manner calculated to confuse. When a price includes a fraction of a cent, all elements of the fraction must be prominently displayed.

Method of price. Generally, products sold in liquid form must be sold by liquid measure. Products such as butter, margarine, flour, corn meal, grits, and potatoes must be sold by weight.

Information required on packages. Generally, all packages of commodities for sale must bear a conspicuous statement of:

- ✪ identity of commodity, unless it can be identified through wrapper;

- ✪ net quantity of contents in terms of weight, measure, or count;

○ for goods sold other than where they are packed, the name and place of business of the manufacturer, packer, or distributor; or,

○ the words "when packed" as a qualifier and the words "jumbo," "giant," "full," and "etc." cannot be used when describing the packaged quantity.

Declaration of unit price on random packages. In addition to the bulk sales requirements above, when goods are offered in packages of different weights, with the price stated on them, the price per single unit of weight must also be stated.

Advertising packages for sale. When a packaged commodity is advertised for sale with a price stated, the quantity must also be conspicuously stated.

Payment and Collection Laws

Depending on the business you are in, you may be paid by cash, checks, credit cards, or some sort of financing arrangement, such as a promissory note or mortgage. Both state and federal laws affect the type of payments you collect, and failure to follow the laws can cost you considerably.

CASH

Cash is probably the easiest form of payment and it is subject to few restrictions. The most important one is that you keep an accurate accounting of your cash transactions and that you report all of your cash income on your tax return. Recent efforts to stop the drug trade have resulted in some serious penalties for failing to report cash transactions and for money laundering. The laws are so sweeping that even if you deal in cash in an ordinary business, you may violate the law and face huge fines and imprisonment.

The most important law to be concerned with is the one requiring the filing of the *Report of Cash Payments over $10,000* (IRS form 8300). (A copy of form 8300 can be found at **www.irs.gov**.) If one person pays you with $10,000 or more in cash, you are required to file this form. A transaction does not have to happen in one day. If a person brings you smaller amounts of cash that add up to $10,000, and the government can construe them as one transaction, then the form must be filed. Under this law, *cash* also includes travelers' checks and money orders, but not cashiers' checks or bank checks.

Pennsylvania Law

Pennsylvania has the *Cash Consumer Protection Act*, which prohibits a merchant from refusing to sell goods or services to individuals who do not possess credit cards. You are permitted to demand and receive security before goods or services are provided, and that security can take the form of cash-on-account that is reasonably related to the value of the property (think of this as a *down payment* situation). Any violation of this Act carries with it a civil penalty of $1,000 for each violation. A person harmed by this can bring a private action for $100 or actual harm suffered, whichever is greater, and the court may award up to three times the actual damages sustained as a punitive measure.

CHECKS

It is important to accept checks in your business. While there is a small percentage that will be bad, most checks will be good, and you will be able to accommodate more customers. To avoid having problems with checks, you should comply with the following rules.

Credit Card Information Act

The *Credit Card Information Act* forbids a business from requiring a customer to provide a credit card number or expiration date in order to pay by cash or check. The business can request to see a card to establish that the customer is creditworthy or for additional identification, and can record the type of credit card and issuing company. The business cannot record the number of the card. The penalty for a violation is a fine of $250 for the first violation and $1,000 for each subsequent violation.

Refunds after Cashing a Check

A popular scam is for a person to purchase something by using a check, only to return the item the next day and demand a refund. After making the refund, the business discovers the initial payment check bounced. Do not make refunds until checks clear.

CREDIT CARDS

In our buy now, pay later society, charge cards can add greatly to your sales potential, especially with large, discretionary purchases. For MasterCard, Visa, and Discover, the fees businesses must pay to accept these cards are about 2%, and this amount is easily paid for by the extra purchases that the cards allow. American Express charges 4% to 5%. (You may decide this is not worth paying, since almost everyone who has an American Express card also has another card.)

For businesses that have a retail outlet, there is usually no problem getting merchant status. Most commercial banks can handle it. Discover can also set you up to accept their card as well as MasterCard and Visa, and they will wire the money into your bank account daily.

For mail order businesses, especially those operating out of the home, it is much harder to get merchant status because of the number of scams in which large amounts are charged, no products are shipped, and the company folds. Today, things are a little better. Some companies are even soliciting merchants. However, beware of those that charge exorbitant fees (such as $5 or $10 per order for "processing"). American Express will accept mail order companies operating out of the home. However, not as many people have their cards as others.

Some companies open a small storefront (or share one) to get merchant status, then process mostly mail orders. The processors usually do not want to accept you if you will do more than 50% mail order business; but if you do not have many complaints, you may be allowed to process mostly mail orders. Whatever you do, keep your charge customers happy so that they do not complain.

You might be tempted to try to run your charges through another business. This may be all right if you actually sell your products through the other businesses, but if you run your business charges through that account, the other business may lose its merchant status. People who bought a book by mail from you and then find a charge on their statement from a florist shop will probably call the credit card company saying that they never bought anything from the florist shop. If you have too many of these, the account will be closed.

A new money-making scheme by the credit card companies is to offer business credit cards that the merchants are charged a higher fee for accepting. To make these more profitable, the credit card companies are telling customers they are not allowed to use their personal credit cards for business purposes. To keep your processing fees down, you can tell your customers you prefer personal, not business, credit cards.

FINANCING LAWS

Some businesses can more easily make sales if they finance the purchases themselves. If the business has enough capital to do this, it can earn extra profits on the financing terms. Nonetheless, because of abuses, many consumer protection laws have been passed by both the federal and state governments.

Regulation Z   Two important federal laws regarding financing are called the *Truth in Lending Act* and the *Fair Credit Billing Act*. These are implemented by what is called *Regulation Z* (commonly known as *Reg. Z*), issued by the Board of Governors of the Federal Reserve System. (1 C.F.R., Vol. 12, p. 226.) This is a very complicated law, and some have said that no business can be sure to be in compliance with it.

The regulation covers all transactions in which four conditions are met:

1.   credit is offered;

2   the offering of credit is regularly done;

3.   there is a finance charge for the credit or there is a written agreement with more than four payments; and,

4.   the credit is for personal, family, or household purposes.

It also covers credit card transactions where only the first two conditions are met. It applies to leases if the consumer ends up paying the full value and keeping the item leased. It does not apply to the following transactions:

- ✪ transactions with businesses or agricultural purposes;

- ✪ transactions with organizations such as corporations or the government;

- ✪ transactions of over $25,000 that are not secured by the consumer's dwelling;

- ✪ credit involving public utilities;

- ✪ credit involving securities or commodities; and,

- ✪ home fuel budget plans.

The way for a small business to avoid Reg. Z violations is to avoid transactions that meet the conditions or to make sure all transactions fall under the exceptions. For many businesses, this is easy. Instead of extending credit to customers, accept credit cards and let the credit card company extend the credit. However, if your customers usually do not have credit cards or if you are in a business that often extends credit, such as used car sales, you should consult a lawyer knowledgeable about Reg. Z or get a copy for yourself at **www.cardreport.com/laws/tila/tila.html**.

Pennsylvania Laws

Pennsylvania also has laws regarding financing arrangements. Anyone engaged in retail installment selling must be licensed by the Pennsylvania Department of Banking. The law specifies what size type must be used in printed contracts, what notices must be included in them, and many other details. Anyone engaged in installment sales in Pennsylvania should carefully review the latest versions of the following statutes:

- ✪ *Goods and Services Installment Sales Act*;

- ✪ *Motor Vehicle Sales Finance Act*;

- ✪ *Home Improvement Finance Act*; and,

- ✪ *Insurance Premium Finance Company Act*.

USURY

Usury is the charging of an illegally high rate of interest on amounts of loans. In Pennsylvania, the usury laws are contained in the *Loan Interest and Protection Law*. According to the Act, the maximum lawful interest rate on the loan or use of money in an amount of $50,000 or less where there is no express contract for a lesser rate is capped at 6%. (If a contract is silent as to the interest rate amount, *with interest* shall be construed to refer to a rate of interest of 6%.) If the loan is in excess of $50,000, the maximum rate allowable is the amount of the monthly index of long-term government bond yields. There are specific rules that apply when the rate changes, and you are advised to read the Act regarding these changes. The only exception to this rule are residential mortgage interest rates, federally guaranteed loans, and commitments to enter into residential mortgages.

The penalty for charging in excess of the legal rate is that the borrower does not have to pay any interest and the lender has to repay triple the amounts received. However, this is limited to a four-year period of the contract.

COLLECTIONS

The *Fair Debt Collection Practices Act of 1977* bans the use of deception, harassment, and other unreasonable acts in the collection of debts. It has strict requirements whenever someone is collecting a debt for someone else. If you are in the collection business, you must get a copy of this law.

The Federal Trade Commission has issued some rules that prohibit deceptive representations, such as pretending to be in the motion picture industry, the government, or a credit bureau, or using questionnaires that do not say that they are for the purpose of collecting a debt. (C.F.R., Title 16, Ch. I, Part 237.)

Business Relations Laws

At both the federal and state levels, there exist many laws regarding how businesses relate to one another. Some of the more important ones are discussed in this chapter.

THE UNIFORM COMMERCIAL CODE

The *Uniform Commercial Code* (UCC) is a set of laws regulating numerous aspects of doing business. A national group drafted this set of uniform laws to avoid having a patchwork of different laws around the fifty states. Although some states modified some sections of the laws, the code is basically the same in most of the states. In Florida, the UCC is contained in Chapters 670 to 680 of the Florida Statutes. Each chapter is concerned with a different aspect of commercial relations, such as sales, warranties, bank deposits, commercial paper, and bulk transfers.

Businesses that wish to know their rights in all types of transactions should obtain a copy of the UCC and become familiar with it. It is especially useful in transactions between merchants. However, the meaning is not always clear from reading the statutes.

COMMERCIAL DISCRIMINATION

The *Robinson-Patman Act of 1936* prohibits businesses from injuring competition by offering the same goods at different prices to different buyers. This means that the large chain stores should not be getting a better price than your small shop. It also requires that promotional allowances must be made on proportionally the same terms to all buyers.

As a small business, you may be a victim of Robinson-Patman Act violation, but fighting a much larger company in court would probably be too expensive for you. Your best bet, if an actual violation has occurred, would be to see if you could get the government to prosecute it. For more information on what constitutes a violation, see the Federal Trade Commission and the Department of Justice's joint site at **www.ftc.gov/bc/compguide/index.htm**.

RESTRAINING TRADE

One of the earliest federal laws affecting business is the *Sherman Antitrust Act of 1890*. The purpose of the law was to protect competition in the marketplace by prohibiting monopolies.

Examples of some things that are prohibited are:

- ✪ agreements between competitors to sell at the same prices;

- ✪ agreements between competitors on how much will be sold or produced;

- ✪ agreements between competitors to divide up a market;

- ✪ refusing to sell one product without a second product; or,

- ✪ exchanging information among competitors, which results in similarity of prices.

As a small business, you will probably not be in a position to violate the Sherman Act, but you should be aware of it if a larger competitor tries to put you out of business. Fighting a much larger company in court would probably be too expensive for you, but if an actual violation has occurred, you might be able to get the government to prosecute it. For more information on what constitutes a violation, see the website by the Federal Trade Commission and the Department of Justice at **www.ftc.gov/bc/compguide**.

INTELLECTUAL PROPERTY PROTECTION

As a business owner, you should know enough about intellectual property law to protect your own creations and to keep from violating the rights of others. Intellectual property is the product of human creativity, such as writings, designs, inventions, melodies, and processes. They are things that can be stolen without being physically taken. For example, if you write a book, someone can steal the words from your book without stealing a physical copy of it.

As the Internet grows, intellectual property is becoming more valuable. Business owners should take the action necessary to protect their companies' intellectual property. Additionally, business owners should know intellectual property law to be sure that they do not violate the rights of others. Even an unknowing violation of the law can result in stiff fines and penalties.

The following are the types of intellectual property and the ways to protect them.

Patent A *patent* is protection given to new and useful inventions, discoveries, and designs. To be entitled to a patent, a work must be completely new and unobvious. A patent is granted to the first inventor who files for the patent. Once an invention is patented, no one else can make use of that invention, even if they discover it independently after a lifetime of research. A patent protects an invention for seventeen years; for designs, it is protected for three and one-half, seven, or fourteen years. Patents cannot be renewed. The patent application must clearly explain how to make the invention, so that when the patent expires, others will be able to freely make and use the invention. Patents are registered with the *United States Patent and Trademark Office* (PTO). Examples of things that would be patentable would be mechanical devices or new drug formulas.

In recent years, patents have been used to protect computer programs and things such as business methods, including Amazon's one click ordering. Few cases challenging these patents have gotten through the court system, so it is too early to tell if they will hold up. About half the patents that reach the Supreme Court are held to be invalid.

Copyright

A *copyright* is protection given to original works of authorship, such as written works, musical works, visual works, performance works, or computer software programs. A copyright exists from the moment of creation, but one cannot register a copyright until it has been fixed in tangible form. Also, one cannot copyright titles, names, or slogans. A copyright currently gives the author and his or her heirs exclusive right to the work for the life of the author plus seventy years.

Copyrights first registered before 1978 last for ninety-five years. (This was previously seventy-five years, but was extended twenty years to match the European system.) Copyrights are registered with the Register of Copyrights at the Library of Congress. Examples of works that would be copyrightable are books, paintings, songs, poems, plays, drawings, and films.

Trademark

A *trademark* is protection given to a name or symbol used to distinguish one person's goods or services from those of others. It can consist of letters, numerals, packaging, labeling, musical notes, colors, or a combination of these. If a trademark is used on services as opposed to goods, it is called a *service mark*.

A trademark lasts indefinitely if it is used continuously and renewed properly. Trademarks are registered with the United States Patent and Trademark Office and with individual states. (This is explained further in Chapter 3.) Examples of trademarks are the Chrysler name on automobiles, the red border on TIME magazine, and the shape of the Coca-Cola bottle.

Trade Secret

A *trade secret* is some information or process that provides a commercial advantage that is protected by keeping it a secret. Examples of trade secrets may be a list of successful distributors, the formula for Coca-Cola, or some unique source code in a computer program. Trade secrets are not registered anywhere—they are protected by the fact that they are not disclosed. They are protected only for as long as they are kept secret. If you independently discover the formula for Coca-Cola tomorrow, you can freely market it (but you cannot use the trademark "Coca-Cola" on your product to market it).

Unprotected Creations

Some things just cannot be protected—such things as ideas, systems, and discoveries are not allowed any protection under any law. If you have a great idea, such as selling packets of hangover medicine in bars, you cannot stop others from doing the same thing. If you invent a new medicine, you can patent it; if you pick a distinctive name for it, you can register it as a trademark; if you create a unique picture or instructions for the package, you can copyright them. However, you cannot stop others from using your basic business idea of marketing hangover medicine in bars.

Notice the subtle differences between the protective systems available. If you invent something two days after someone else does, you cannot even use it yourself if the other person has patented it. However, if you write the same poem as someone else and neither of you copied the other, both of you can copyright the poem. If you patent something, you can have the exclusive rights to it for the term of the patent, but you must disclose how others can make it after the patent expires. However, if you keep it a trade secret, you have exclusive rights as long as no one learns the secret.

Endless Laws

The state of Pennsylvania and the federal government have numerous laws and rules that apply to every aspect of every type of business. There are even laws governing such things as fence posts, hosiery, rabbit raising, refund policies, frozen desserts, and advertising. Every business is affected by at least one of these laws.

Some activities are covered by both state and federal laws. In such cases, you must obey the stricter of the rules. In addition, more than one agency of the state or federal government may have rules governing your business. Each of these may have the power to investigate violations and impose fines or other penalties.

Penalties for violations of these laws can range from a warning to a criminal fine and even jail time. In some cases, employees can sue for damages. Recently, employees have been given awards of millions of dollars from employers who violated the law. Since ignorance of the law is no excuse, it is your duty to learn which laws apply to your business or risk these penalties.

Very few people in business know the laws that apply to their businesses. If you take the time to learn them, you can become an expert in your field, and avoid problems with regulators. You can also fight back if one of your competitors uses some illegal method to compete with you.

The laws and rules that affect the most businesses are explained in this chapter, followed a list of more specialized laws. You should read through this list and see which ones may apply to your business. Then, go to your public library or law library and read them. Some may not apply to your phase of the business, but if any of them do apply, you should make copies to keep on hand.

No one could possibly know all the rules that affect business, much less comply with them all. (The Interstate Commerce Commission alone has forty trillion rates on its books telling the transportation industry what it should charge!) However, if you keep up with the important rules, you will stay out of trouble and have more chance of success.

FEDERAL LAWS

The federal laws that are most likely to affect small businesses are rules of the Federal Trade Commission (FTC). The FTC has some rules that affect many businesses, such as the rules about labeling, warranties, and mail order sales. Other rules affect only certain industries.

If you sell goods by mail, you should send for the FTC's booklet, *A Business Guide to the Federal Trade Commission's Mail Order Rule.* If you are going to be involved in a certain industry, such as those listed in this section, or using warranties or your own labeling, you should ask for their latest information on the subject. The address is:

Federal Trade Commission
600 Pennsylvania Avenue, NW
Washington, DC 20580

The rules of the FTC are contained in the Code of Federal Regulations (C.F.R.). Some of the industries covered are the following.

Industry	**Part**
Adhesive Compositions	235
Aerosol Products Used for Frosting Cocktail Glasses	417
Automobiles (New car fuel economy advertising)	259
Barber Equipment and Supplies	248
Binoculars	402
Business Opportunities and Franchises	436
Cigarettes	408
Decorative Wall Paneling	243
Dog and Cat Food	241
Dry Cell Batteries	403
Extension Ladders	418
Fallout Shelters	229
Feather and Down Products	253
Fiber Glass Curtains	413
Food (Games of Chance)	419
Funerals	453
Gasoline (Octane posting)	306
Gasoline	419
Greeting Cards	244
Home Entertainment Amplifiers	432
Home Insulation	460
Hosiery	22
Household Furniture	250
Jewelry	23
Ladies' Handbags	247
Law Books	256
Light Bulbs	409
Luggage and Related Products	24
Mail Order Insurance	234
Mail Order Merchandise	435
Men's and Boys' Tailored Clothing	412
Metallic Watch Band	19
Mirrors	21
Nursery	18
Ophthalmic Practices	456
Photographic Film and Film Processing	242
Private Vocational and Home Study Schools	254
Radiation Monitoring Instruments	232
Retail Food Stores (Advertising)	424
Shell Homes	230
Shoes	231
Sleeping Bags	400
Tablecloths and Related Products	404
Television Sets	410
Textile Wearing Apparel	423
Textiles	236
Tires	228
Used Automobile Parts	20
Used Lubricating Oil	406
Used Motor Vehicles	455
Waist Belts	405
Watches	245
Wigs and Hairpieces	252

Some other federal laws that affect businesses are as follows.

- ✪ *Alcohol Administration Act*

- ✪ *Child Protection and Toy Safety Act*

- ✪ *Clean Water Act*

- ✪ *Comprehensive Smokeless Tobacco Health Education Act*

- ✪ *Consumer Credit Protection Act*

- ✪ *Consumer Product Safety Act*

- ✪ *Energy Policy and Conservation Act*

- ✪ *Environmental Pesticide Control Act of 1972*

- ✪ *Fair Credit Reporting Act*

- ✪ *Fair Packaging and Labeling Act (1966)*

- ✪ *Flammable Fabrics Act*

- ✪ *Food, Drug, and Cosmetic Act*

- ✪ *Fur Products Labeling Act*

- ✪ *Hazardous Substances Act*

- ✪ *Hobby Protection Act*

- ✪ *Insecticide, Fungicide, and Rodenticide Act*

- ✪ *Magnuson-Moss Warranty Act*

- ✪ *Poison Prevention Packaging Act of 1970*

- ✪ *Solid Waste Disposal Act*

- ✪ *Textile Fiber Products Identification Act*

- ✪ *Toxic Substance Control Act*

- ✪ *Wool Products Labeling Act*

- ✪ *Nutrition Labeling and Education Act of 1990*

- ✪ *Food Safety Enforcement Enhancement Act of 1997*

PENNSYLVANIA LAWS

Pennsylvania has numerous laws regulating specific types of businesses or certain activities of businesses. The following is a list of those laws that are most likely to affect small businesses. Laws referred to as Acts (i.e., Act 118 of 1990) may be accessed through **www.legis.state.pa.us** and clicking on "Legislation Enacted since 1975," then on "Acts on general legislation approved." For Acts enacted prior to 1975, you should go to the website of the various departments to access Acts; for example, Act 691 of 1961 regulates Nursing Home Facilities. To obtain a copy of this act from your home computer, you should go to the Pennsylvania Department of Health website and search for the Act in the links provided. Laws cited as "Pa. Code" may be obtained through **www.pacode.com**. Laws cited as "Pa. C.S." are not officially online, and may only be obtained from your local library.

Laws Regulating Business in Pennsylvania

*Citations refer to Pennsylvania Consolidated Statutes (Pa.C.S.) or
Pennsylvania Administrative Code (Pa. Code). The symbol § stands
for "Sections."*

Adoption agencies	23 Pa.C.S. § 2101 et seq.
Adult congregate living facilities	Act 118 of 1990
Adult day care facilities	Act 118 of 1990
Adult foster home care	Act 118 of 1990
Ambulance service contracts	Act 293 of 1927
Animals	3 Pa.C.S.
Auctions and auctioneers	Act 85 of 1983
Banking	7 Pa.C.S. 10 Pa. Code
Boiler safety	Act 85 of 1998
Boxing and fighting	5 Pa.C.S. § 301 et seq.
Buildings, radon resistance standards	Act 75 of 1992
Burial contracts	9 Pa.C.S.
Cemeteries	9 Pa.C.S.
Charitable solicitation	10 Pa.C.S
Commissions merchants	Act 675 of 1857
Condominiums	Act 117 of 1963
Construction	1 Pa.C.S. § 1501
Consumer finance	Act 66 of 1937 Act 387 of 1968
Cooperatives	Act 21 of 1935
Cooperatives, Agricultural	15 Pa.C.S. § 7501 et seq.
Cooperatives, Electrical	15 Pa.C.S. § 7301 et seq.
Cooperatives, Mortgage	Act 21 of 1935
Cooperatives, Real Estate	68 Pa.C.S. § 4101 et seq.
Cooperatives, Worker's Corporation	15 Pa.C.S. § 7701 et seq.
Cosmetics	Act 86 of 1933
Credit cards	Act 36 of 1992 Act 150 of 1992

Credit service organizations	Act 150 of 1992
Dairies	3 Pa.C.S.
	Act 25 of 1885
Desserts, frozen	Act 215 of 1965
Drugs (Pharmaceuticals)	Act 699 of 1961
Dry cleaning	Act 214 of 1990
Eggs and poultry	Act 356 of 1919
	3 Pa.C.S.
Electrical	Act 75 of 1992
Elevators	Act 99 of 1895
Energy conservation standards	Act 222 of 1980
Explosives	Act 537 of 1937
	Act 362 of 1957
Factory-built housing	Act 192 of 1982
Fiduciary funds	Act 3 of 1995
Fireworks	Act 65 of 1939
Food	31 Pa.C.S.
Fruits and vegetables	Act 97 of 1929
Fuels, liquid	75 Pa.C.S. § 9401 et seq.
Gasoline and oil	58 Pa.C.S.
Glass (Glazing)	Act 5 of 1971
Hazardous substances	Act 165 of 1990
Hazardous waste clean-up	Act 108 of 1988
Health care	35 Pa.C.S.
	40 Pa.C.S.
Health clubs	Act 87 of 1989
Home health agencies	Act 48 of 1979
	Act 691 of 1961
Home improvement sales and financing	Act 62 of 1986
Honey	Act 184 of 1971
Horseracing	Act 135 of 1981
	Act 18 of 1993
Hospices	Act 19 of 1893
Hotels	Act 318 of 1913
	Act 509 of 1855
Household waste products	Act 155 of 1994
Housing codes, state minimum	Act 459 of 1949
Insurance and service plans	40 Pa.C.S.
	31 Pa. Code

Land sales	Act 9 of 1980
Legal services	37 Pa. Code
Liquor	47 Pa.C.S.
	40 Pa. Code
Livestock	3 Pa.C.S.
Lodging	48 Pa.C.S.
Lotteries	Act 91 of 1971
Meats	3 Pa.C.S.
Mental health	50 Pa.C.S.
Metal recyclers	Act 17 of 1984
Milk and milk products	Act 105 of 1937
Mining waste	Act 82 of 1955
Mobile homes	Act 261 of 1976
Money orders	Act 79 of 1996
Motion pictures	Act 42 of 1937
	Act 211 of 1935
Motor vehicle lemon law	Act 28 of 1984
Motor vehicles	75 Pa.C.S.
Multilevel marketing	Act 387 of 1968
Naval stores	Act 152 of 1925
Nonalcoholic beverages	Act 214 of 1937
Newsprint	45 Pa.C.S. §301 et seq.
Nursing homes	Act 691 of 1961
Oil	58 Pa.C.S.
Pest control	Act 251 of 1967
Pigeons, Racing and Carrier	Act 100 of 1965
Plumbing	Act 135 of 1895
Pyramid schemes	Act 387 of 1968
Radiation	Act 147 of 1984
Radio and television repairs	Act 173 of 1961
Real estate sales	Act 9 of 1980
Rental housing	66 Pa.C.S.
Restaurants	Act 35 of 1995
Secondhand dealers	Act 67 of 1927
Securities transactions	70 Pa.C.S.
	64 Pa. Code
Swimming and bathing places	Act 299 of 1931
Syrup	Act 8 of 1925
Television picture tubes	Act 173 of 1961

Timber and Lumber	Act 174 of 1876
Tobacco	3 Pa.C.S.
Tourist camps	Act 285 of 1953
Watches, Used	Act 100 of 1945
Weapons and firearms	18 Pa.C.S. § 6101 et seq.

Bookkeeping and Accounting

It is beyond the scope of this book to explain all the intricacies of setting up a business's bookkeeping and accounting system. However, it is important to realize that if you do not set up an understandable bookkeeping system, your business will undoubtedly fail.

Without accurate records of where your income is coming from and where it is going, you will be unable to increase your profits, lower your expenses, obtain needed financing, or make the right decisions in all areas of your business. The time to decide how you will handle your bookkeeping is when you open your business—not a year later when it is tax time.

INITIAL BOOKKEEPING

If you do not understand business taxation, you should pick up a good book on the subject, as well as the IRS tax guide for your type of business (proprietorship, partnership, corporation, or limited liability company).

The IRS tax book for small businesses is Publication 334, *Tax Guide for Small Businesses*. There are also instruction booklets for each type of business form, including Schedule C for proprietorships, Form 1120 or 1120S for C corporations and S corporations, and 1165 for partnerships and businesses that are taxed like partnerships (LLCs, LLPs).

Keep in mind that the IRS does not give you the best advice for saving on taxes and does not give you the other side of contested issues. For that, you need a private tax guide or advisor.

The most important thing to do is to set up your bookkeeping so that you can easily fill out your monthly, quarterly, and annual tax returns. The best way to do this is to get copies of the returns—not the totals that you will need to supply—and set up your bookkeeping system to group those totals.

For example, for a sole proprietorship, you will use Schedule C to report business income and expenses to the IRS at the end of the year. Use the categories on that form to sort your expenses. To make your job especially easy, every time you pay a bill, put the category number on the check.

ACCOUNTANTS

Most likely, your new business will not be able to afford hiring an accountant right away to handle your books. Do not be discouraged—doing them yourself will force you to learn about business accounting and taxation. The worst way to run a business is to know nothing about the tax laws and turn everything over to an accountant at the end of the year to find out what is due.

You should know the basics of tax law before making basic decisions, such as whether to buy or rent equipment or premises. You should understand accounting so you can time your financial affairs appropriately. If your business needs to buy supplies, inventory, or equipment, and provides goods or services throughout the year, you need to at least have a basic understanding of the system within which you are working.

Once you can afford an accountant, you should weigh the cost against your time and the risk that you will make an error. Even if you think you know enough to do your own corporate tax return, you should still take it to an accountant one year to see if you have been missing any deductions. You might decide that the money saved is worth the cost of the accountant's services.

COMPUTER PROGRAMS

Today, every business should keep its books by computer. There are inexpensive programs, such as Quicken, that can instantly provide you with reports of your income and expenses, as well as the right figures to plug into your tax returns.

Most programs even offer a tax program each year that will take all of your information and print it out on the current year's tax forms.

TAX TIPS

The following are a few tax tips for small businesses that will help you save money.

- ✪ Usually, when you buy equipment for a business, you must amortize the cost over several years. That is, you do not deduct it all when you buy it, but instead, take (for example) 25% of the cost off your taxes each year for four years. (The time is determined by the theoretical usefulness of the item.) However, small businesses are allowed to write off the entire cost of a limited amount of items under Internal Revenue Code (I.R.C.) Sec. 179. If you have income to shelter, use it.

- ✪ Owners of S corporations do not have to pay Social Security or Medicare taxes on the part of their profits that is not considered salary. As long as you pay yourself a reasonable salary, other money you take out is not subject to these taxes.

- ✪ You should not neglect to deposit withholding taxes for your own salary or profits. Besides being a large sum to come up with at once in April, there are penalties that must be paid for failure to do so.

- ✪ Do not fail to keep track of and remit your employees' withholding. You will be personally liable for them even if you are a corporation.

- ✪ If you keep track of the use of your car for business, you can deduct 44.5¢ per mile (this may go up or down each year—check with the IRS for current rates). If you use your car for business a considerable amount of the time, you may be able to depreciate it.

- ✪ If your business is a corporation and if you designate the stock as Section 1244 stock, then if the business fails, you are able to get a much better deduction for the loss.

- ✪ By setting up a retirement plan, you can exempt up to 20% of your salary from income tax. However, do not use money you might need later. There are penalties for taking it out of the retirement plan.

- ✪ When you buy things that will be resold or made into products that will be resold, you do not have to pay sales taxes on those purchases.

chapter 18

Paying Federal Taxes

As we all know, the federal government levies many different types of taxes on individuals and businesses. It is very important that you consult an accountant or attorney to properly comply with and take advantage of the incredibly complex federal tax code and regulations. This chapter discusses several of the most important federal taxes that will most likely affect your new business.

INCOME TAXES

The manner in which each type of business pays taxes is as follows.

Proprietorship   A proprietor reports profits and expenses on Schedule C attached to the usual Form 1040, and pays tax on all of the net income of the business. Each quarter, Form ES-1040 must be filed along with payment of one-quarter of the amount of income tax and Social Security taxes estimated to be due for the year.

Partnership   The partnership files a return showing the income and expenses, but pays no tax. Each partner is given a form showing his or her share of the profits or losses, and reports these on Schedule E of Form 1040.

Each quarter, Form ES-1040 must be filed by each partner, along with payment of one-quarter of the amount of income tax and Social Security taxes estimated to be due for the year.

C Corporation

A regular corporation is a separate taxpayer, and pays tax on its profits after deducting all expenses, including officers' salaries. If dividends are distributed, they are paid out of after-tax dollars, and the shareholders pay tax a second time when they receive the dividends. If a corporation needs to accumulate money for investment, it may be able to do so at lower tax rates than the shareholders. However, if all profits will be distributed to shareholders, the double-taxation may be excessive unless all income is paid as salaries. C corporations file Form 1120.

S Corporation

A small corporation has the option of being taxed like a partnership. If Form 2553 is filed by the corporation and accepted by the Internal Revenue Service, the S corporation will only file an informational return listing profits and expenses. Then, each shareholder will be taxed on a proportional share of the profits (or be able to deduct a proportional share of the losses). Unless a corporation will make a large profit that will not be distributed, S status is usually best in the beginning. An S corporation files Form 1120S and distributes Form K-1 to each shareholder. If any money is taken out by a shareholder that is not listed as wages subject to withholding, then the shareholder will usually have to file Form ES-1040 each quarter, along with payment of the estimated withholding on the withdrawals.

Limited Liability Companies and Partnerships

Limited liability companies and professional limited liability companies are allowed by the IRS to elect to be taxed either as a partnership or a corporation. To make this election, you file Form 8832, *Entity Classification Election,* with the IRS.

Tax Worksheets and Booklets

The IRS conducts workshops to inform businesses about the tax laws. For more information, call or write to the IRS at the following addresses:

Internal Revenue Service
Philadelphia, PA 19255
800-829-1040

For specific forms or questions, the following services are also available. Their lines are often busy, so you may have to keep trying.

Federal Tax Inquiries	800-829-1040
Problem Resolution	800-829-1040
Tax Forms and Publications	800-829-3676
Tele-Tax Service and Refund Information	800-829-4477
Tele-TIN (Telephone EIN)	215-574-2400

WITHHOLDING, SOCIAL SECURITY, AND MEDICARE TAXES

If you need basic information on business tax returns, the IRS publishes a rather large booklet that answers most questions and is available free of charge. Call or write them and ask for Publication No. 334. If you have any questions, look up their toll-free number in the phone book under "United States Government/Internal Revenue Service." If you want more creative answers and tax-saving information, you should find a good local accountant. To get started, you will need to be familiar with the following:

- employer identification number;

- Employee's Withholding Allowance Certificate;

- federal tax deposit coupons;

- electronic filing;

- Estimated Tax Payment Voucher;

- employer's quarterly tax return;

- Wage and Tax Statement;

✪   Form 1099 Miscellaneous; and,

✪   Earned Income Credit.

Employer Identification Number

If you are a sole proprietor with no employees, you can use your Social Security number for your business. If you are a corporation, a partnership, or a proprietorship with employees, you must obtain an employer identification number. This is done by filing the **APPLICATION FOR EMPLOYER IDENTIFICATION NUMBER (IRS FORM SS-4)**. (see form 5, p.231.) It usually takes a week or two to receive. You will need this number to open bank accounts for the business, so you should file this form a soon as you decide to go into business. The blank form with instructions is in Appendix C.

Employee's Withholding Allowance Certificate

You must have each employee fill out an **EMPLOYEE'S WITHHOLDING ALLOWANCE CERTIFICATE (IRS FORM W-4)** to calculate the amount of federal taxes to be deducted and to obtain their Social Security numbers. (see form 7, p.237.) (The number of allowances on this form is used with IRS Circular E, Publication 15, to figure out the exact deductions.)

Federal Tax Deposit Coupons

After taking withholdings from employees' wages, you must deposit them at a bank that is authorized to accept such funds. If at the end of any month you have over $1,000 in withheld taxes, including your contribution to FICA (Social Security and Medicare), you must make a deposit prior to the 15th of the following month. If on the 3rd, 7th, 11th, 15th, 19th, 22nd, or 25th of any month you have over $3,000 in withheld taxes, you must make a deposit within three banking days.

Electronic Filing

Each year, the IRS requires a few more forms to be filed electronically or over the telephone. When you receive your paper filing forms from the IRS, they will include your options for filing electronically or by telephone. In some cases, electronic filing may save time, but if your business is small and most of your numbers are zeros, it may be faster to mail in the paper forms.

Estimated Tax Payment Voucher

Sole proprietors and partners usually take draws from their businesses without the formality of withholding. However, they are still required to make deposits of income and FICA taxes each quarter. If more than $500 is due in April on a person's 1040 form, then not enough money was withheld each quarter and a penalty is assessed, unless the person falls into an exception. The quarterly withholding is submitted on form 1040-ES on January 15th, April 15th, June 15th, and September 15th each year. If these days fall on a weekend, the due date is the following Monday. The worksheet with Estimated Tax Payment Voucher (Form 1040-ES) can be used to determine the amount to pay.

> **NOTE:** *One of the exceptions to the rule is that if you withhold the same amount as last year's tax bill, then you do not have to pay a penalty. This is usually a lot easier than filling out the 1040-ES worksheet.*

Employer's Quarterly Tax Return

Each quarter, you must file Form 941, reporting your federal withholding and FICA taxes. If you owe more than $1,000 at the end of a quarter, you are required to make a deposit at the end of any month that you have $1,000 in withholding. The deposits are made to the Federal Reserve Bank or an authorized financial institution on Form 501. Most banks are authorized to accept deposits. If you owe more than $3,000 for any month, you must make a deposit at any point in the month in which you owe $3,000. After you file Form SS-4, the 941 forms will be sent to you automatically if you checked the box saying that you expect to have employees.

Wage and Tax Statement

At the end of each year, you are required to issue a W-2 Form to each employee. This form shows the amount of wages paid to the employee during the year, as well as the amounts withheld for taxes, Social Security, Medicare, and other purposes.

Form 1099 Miscellaneous

If you pay at least $600 to a person other than an employee (such as independent contractors), you are required to file a Form 1099-MISC for that person. Along with the 1099s, you must file a Form 1096, which is a summary sheet of all the 1099s you issued.

Many people are not aware of this law and fail to file these forms, but they are required for such things as services, royalties, rents, awards, and prizes that you pay to individuals (but not corporations). The rules for this are quite complicated, so you should either obtain Package 1099 from the IRS or consult your accountant.

Earned Income Credit

Persons who are not liable to pay income tax may have the right to a check from the government because of the Earned Income Credit. You are required to notify your employees of this. You can satisfy this requirement with one of the following:

- a W-2 Form with the notice on the back;

- a substitute for the W-2 Form with the notice on it;

- a copy of Notice 797; or,

- a written statement with the wording from Notice 797.

A Notice 797 can be downloaded from the IRS website at **www.irs.gov/pub/irs-pdf/n797.pdf**.

EXCISE TAXES

Excise taxes are taxes on certain activities or items. Some of the things that are subject to federal excise taxes are tobacco and alcohol, gasoline, tires and inner tubes, some trucks and trailers, firearms, ammunition, bows, arrows, fishing equipment, the use of highway vehicles of over 55,000 pounds, aircraft, wagering, telephone and tele-type services, coal, hazardous wastes, and vaccines. If you are involved with any of these, you should obtain from the IRS publication No. 510, *Information on Excise Taxes*.

UNEMPLOYMENT COMPENSATION TAXES

You must pay federal unemployment taxes if you paid wages of $1,500 in any quarter, or if you had at least one employee for twenty calendar weeks. The federal tax amount is 0.8% of the first $7,000 of wages paid each employee. If more than $100 is due by the end of any quarter (if you paid $12,500 in wages for the quarter), then Form 508 must be filed with an authorized financial institution or the Federal Reserve Bank in your area. You will receive Form 508 when you obtain your employer identification number.

At the end of each year, you must file Form 940 or Form 940EZ. This is your annual report of federal unemployment taxes. You will receive an original form from the IRS.

Paying Pennsylvania Taxes

Business tax information can be obtained from a variety of sources. Of course, you should speak to your tax professional about payment requirements and penalties, but you can familiarize yourself with the requirements and often make an application for your business online at **www.state.pa.us** or **www.paopen4business.state.pa.us**.

SALES AND USE TAXES

If you will be selling or renting goods or services at retail, you must collect Pennsylvania sales and use tax. Many items, such as drugs, some clothing apparel, dental products, and sanitary products, are exempt. For a list of exempt and nonexempt goods and services, obtain the pamphlet *Retailers' Information* from the Pennsylvania Department of Revenue by calling 717-787-8201.

To collect the sales and use tax, you first must obtain a tax number by filling out the **PENNSYLVANIA ENTERPRISE REGISTRATION (PA-100).** (see form 9, p.241.) This is a multipage form that covers registration of a business with various divisions of Pennsylvania government. A sample filled-in copy of the form is included in Appendix B, p.208. (Sections 14–17 and 19–22 do not necessarily apply to new businesses and do not appear in the sample.)

To order this form or any tax form twenty-four hours a day, call the Pennsylvania Department of Revenue at 800-362-2050, or if you are in the Harrisburg area or calling from out of state, 717-787-8094. You may also send written requests to:

Pennsylvania Department of Revenue
Tax Forms Distribution Unit
2850 Turnpike Industrial Drive
Middletown, PA 17057

Forms may also be obtained from their website at **www.revenue. state.pa.us**.

You are also advised to contact your county government to determine if there are any local taxes for which you may be responsible.

The sales and use tax returns are due for each month on the twentieth of the following month. You are allowed to deduct 1% of the tax as your reimbursement for collecting the tax if you remit on time, although the amount is usually not enough to compensate for the work. In some cases, if your sales are very limited (under $100 a quarter), you may be allowed to file returns quarterly.

Once you file your **Pennsylvania Enterprise Registration** form, you will have to start filing monthly returns whether you have any sales or not. If you do not file the return, even if you had no sales, you must pay a penalty of 5% with a minimum of $2. If you do not expect to have any sales for the first few months while you are setting up your business, you probably should wait before sending in the registration. Otherwise, you may forget to file the returns marked with zeros and end up paying the penalties.

One reason to get a tax number early is to exempt your purchases from tax. When you buy a product that you will resell or use as part of a product that you will sell, you are exempt from paying tax on it. To get the exemption, you need to submit a **Pennsylvania Exemption Certificate** to the seller. (see form 8, p.239.) This form must contain your sales and use tax registration number.

If you will only be selling items wholesale or out of state, you might think that you would not need a tax number or to submit returns. However, you will need to be registered to obtain the tax number to exempt your purchases.

If you have any sales before you get your monthly tax return forms, you should calculate the tax anyway and submit it. Otherwise, you will be charged a penalty even if it was not your fault that you did not have the forms.

Selling to Tax-Exempt Purchasers   You are required to collect sales and use taxes for all sales you make unless you have documentation on file proving that a purchase was exempt from the tax. The form to use for this is the **Pennsylvania Exemption Certificate**, which is included in Appendix C. In some cases, new businesses are required to post a bond to ensure taxes are paid.

MISCELLANEOUS BUSINESS TAXES

Although Pennsylvania taxes are some of the lowest in the nation, there are some additional taxes that must be paid that may or may not affect the type of business that you plan to open and where you plan to open it. For example, the City of Philadelphia and the County of Allegheny (including the City of Pittsburgh) must collect an additional 1% local sales and use tax. The Allegheny tax must be paid for any goods to be used in the county. This has caused much confusion, and some merchants require customers to produce their driver's licenses in order to determine whether the goods will be used in the county or not. Questions regarding the 1% local sales and use tax can be addressed by calling the Bureau of Business Tax Trust Fund at 717-783-5470. At this number, you may also obtain information regarding the Public Transportation Assistance Fund taxes.

The Miscellaneous Tax Division covers the Cigarette Tax (717-783-9374), the Malt Beverage Tax (717-783-9354), and the Small Games of Chance and Pari-Mutuel Tax (717-787-8275). You may qualify for a sales tax exemption depending on your business. Call 717-783-5473 to see if you may qualify.

Corporations also have several additional taxes placed upon them. The Bureau of Corporate Taxes at 717-783-6035 can help you with the Rate and Base Changes, the Capital Stock/Franchise Tax, and the Corporate Loans Tax. Information about prepayment requirements can be found at 717-787-1808.

The Employer Withholding Division can help you with your withholding requirements for your employees. Contact them at 717-787-1586.

There are also several taxes relating to transportation: the Motor Carriers Road Tax, the Liquid Fuels Tax, the Diesel Fuels Tax (for usage), and the Oil Franchise Tax. Contact the Bureau of Motor Fuels Tax at 717-783-9191.

PERSONAL PROPERTY TAXES

Personal property taxes are levied against tangible and intangible property. Examples of intangible property are *holdings*, such as stocks and bonds. The personal property tax is administered on the county level, and varies from county to county across the state. You are encouraged to contact your county tax assessment office.

UNEMPLOYMENT COMPENSATION TAXES

Employers in Pennsylvania are responsible for contributing to the Unemployment Compensation Fund. This fund provides benefits to employees who are separated from their service through no fault of their own. Situations where a discharged employee can receive their benefits include layoffs due to decrease in work and natural disasters that prevent a business from operating. Situations where an employee may *not* collect unemployment compensation include being fired and voluntarily quitting the position. To determine how much an employer needs to contribute to the fund, the assigned contribution rate (determined annually by the Department of Labor and Industry) is multiplied by the wages paid to an employee.

The assigned contribution rate is determined by considering such factors as the number of employees and past employment history. The assigned contribution rate varies from employer to employer. You may be liable to contribute to the Unemployment Compensation Fund if you employ at least one other person. You may be liable for the unemployment compensation tax as well.

To obtain more information and an application, call 800-362-2050 or go to **www.revenue.state.pa.us** and request a **PENNSYLVANIA ENTERPRISE REGISTRATION (PA-100) FORM**. (see form 9, p.241.) You may also register online at **www.paopen4business.state.pa.us**.

INCOME TAXES

Pennsylvania taxes corporations. The type of business and its structure determine any taxes for which that business is obligated to pay. You are encouraged to seek information from the Pennsylvania Department of Revenue at 717-783-6035, or direct your inquiries to:

Pennsylvania Department of Revenue
1131 Strawberry Square
Harrisburg, PA 17128
www.revenue.state.pa.us

The Department of Revenue also publishes the *Pennsylvania Tax Update*, to which you may subscribe. Inquiries may be emailed to **parev@revenue.state.pa.us**.

Out-of-State Taxes

While paying federal and Pennsylvania taxes are probably expected by the new business owner, the realization that taxes may also have to be paid to other states and governments often escape the new business owner. However, depending on your contact with these other states, which can come from unexpected ways, a tax obligation will probably arise and need to be paid.

STATE SALES TAXES

In 1992, the United States Supreme Court struck a blow for the rights of small businesses by ruling that state tax authorities cannot force them to collect sales taxes on interstate mail orders (*Quill Corporation v. North Dakota*). Unfortunately, the court left open the possibility that Congress could allow interstate taxation of mail order sales, and since then several bills have been introduced that would do so.

At present, companies are only required to collect sales taxes for states in which they *do business*. Exactly what business is enough to trigger taxation is a legal question, and some states try to define it as broadly as possible.

If you have an office in a state, you are doing business there, and any goods shipped to consumers in that state are subject to sales taxes. If you have a full-time employee working in the state much of the year, many states will consider you doing business there. In some states, attending a two-day trade show is enough business to trigger taxation for the entire year for every order shipped to the state. One loophole that often works is to be represented at shows by persons who are not your employees.

Because the laws are different in each state, you will have to do some research on a state-by-state basis to find out how much business you can do in a state without being subject to their taxation. You can request a state's rules from its department of revenue, but keep in mind that what a department of revenue wants the law to be is not always what the courts will rule that it is.

BUSINESS TAXES

Be wary of being subject to a state's income or other business taxes. For example, California charges every company doing business in the state a minimum $800 a year fee and charges income tax on a portion of the company's worldwide income. Doing a small amount of business in the state is clearly not worth getting mired in California taxation. For this reason, some trade shows have been moved from the state. This has resulted in a review of the tax policies and some *safe-harbor* guidelines to advise companies on what they can do without becoming subject to taxation.

Write to the department of revenue of any state with which you have business contacts to see what might trigger your taxation.

INTERNET TAXES

State revenue departments are eager to tax commerce on the Internet. Theories have already been proposed that websites available to state residents mean a company is doing business in a state. Fortunately, Congress has passed a moratorium on taxation of Internet business.

CANADIAN TAXES

The Canadian government expects American companies that sell goods by mail order to Canadians to collect taxes for them and file returns with Revenue Canada, their tax department. Those companies that receive an occasional unsolicited order are not expected to register, and Canadian customers who order things from the U.S. pay the tax plus a $5 fee upon receipt of the goods. Companies that solicit Canadian orders are expected to be registered if their worldwide income is $30,000 or more per year. In some cases, a company may be required to post a bond and to pay for the cost of Canadian auditors visiting its premises and auditing its books. For these reasons, you may notice that some companies decline to accept orders from Canada.

The End...
and the Beginning

If you have read through this whole book, you know more about the rules and laws for operating a Pennsylvania business than most people in business today. However, after learning about all the governmental regulations, you may become discouraged. You are probably wondering how you can keep track of all the laws and how you will have any time left to make money after complying with the laws. Do not worry—people are starting businesses every day, and they are making lots of money.

The laws and regulations (and especially the registration fees) can seem confusing, conflicting, and outrageous. Remember—prior to reading this book, you faced an uphill struggle against an unknown, sometimes adversarial bureaucracy, but now you have all the knowledge to proceed with your dream of starting your own business and succeeding. There is a system in place that you must go through to start your business and two things can happen—the system can work you or you can work the system. By reading this book, there is no reason why you cannot make the system work for you, so *go for it*. No doubt, you will encounter some problems along the way even though you are empowered with the knowledge in this book. If you feel you are treated unfairly or differently, or do not understand an explanation given to you, speak up. You are entitled to know all the answers to all your questions, and you are entitled to be treated with respect and dignity. If you are ever dissatisfied, seek help up the ladder and contact your legislator. Most legislators have knowledgeable staffs that can assist you in any registration or certification requirement that you must fulfill. Your taxes and your vote support your legislator, so do not be afraid to make use of their services.

One way to avoid problems with the government is to keep a low profile and avoid open confrontation. For a lawyer, it can be fun going to appeals court over an unfair parking ticket or making a federal case out of a $25 fine, but for most people, the expenses of a fight with the government are unbearable. If you start a mass protest against the IRS or OSHA, they will have to make an example of you so that no one else gets any ideas.

BUSINESS RESOURCES

The attitude of employees of the government business in Pennsylvania has changed radically since this book was first published. Bureaucratic red tape that plagued business owners and hindered business development in the state is mostly gone. Although a few forms still must be filed with the state and local governments in hard copy, most *business for doing business* is streamlined, and can be handled swiftly and securely via the Internet.

Every person planning to start a business—no matter how small or large—should take advantage of the wealth of resources available to them. After reading this book, go to **www.state.pa.us**, known as *PA Power Port*. The PA Power Port is the main gateway to government in Pennsylvania. Not only should you take a look around this site—especially via the hyperlink to doing business in the state—but you should also access the specific laws that affect your business through the appropriate department.

Additionally, financing may be obtained through the Department of Community and Economic Development for your business if you meet certain qualifications and guidelines. Many grants are available as well. It would be worth your while to research the many options that may be available to you through the Department of Community and Economic Development's Center for Entrepreneurial Assistance at **www.inventpa.com**. There are also programs and low-interest or no-interest loans available to upgrade equipment of certain businesses. In some cases, tax credits may apply to your business.

Not all resources offer free or low- or no-cost financing, but that does not make these resources any less valuable to your business. For example, the Area Loan Organization certified by the Department of Community and Economic Development will help you apply for a loan by assisting you in evaluating and packaging your loan application.

Advocacy programs also exist, and although you may never need their advocacy services, these commissions and programs can provide a wealth of information to which you can refer. Among these advocacy agencies are the Pennsylvania Chamber of Business and Industry at **www.pachamber.org**; Pennsylvania Economic Development Association at **www.peda.org**; the Office of Small Business Advocate at **www.dced.state.pa.us**, and, the Pennsylvania Commission for Women at **www.pcw.state.pa.us**.

The important thing is that you know the laws and the penalties for violations before making your decision. Knowing the laws will also allow you to use the loopholes in the laws to avoid violations.

Congratulations on deciding to start a business in Pennsylvania.

Glossary

A

acceptance. Agreeing to the terms of an offer and creating a contract.

affirmative action. Hiring an employee to achieve a balance in the workplace and avoid existing or continuing discrimination based on minority status.

alien. A person who is not a citizen of the country in which he or she lives and works.

articles of incorporation. The document that sets forth the organization of a corporation.

B

bait advertising. Offering a product for sale with the intention of selling another product.

bulk sales. Selling substantially all of a company's inventory.

C

C corporation. A corporation that pays taxes on its profits.

collections. The collection of money owed to a business.

common law. Laws that are determined in court cases rather than statutes.

consideration. The exchange of value or promises in a contract.

contract. An agreement between two or more parties.

copyright. Legal protection given to original works of authorship.

corporation. An artificial person that is set up to conduct a business owned by shareholders and run by officers and directors.

D

deceptive pricing. Pricing goods or services in a manner intended to deceive the customers.

discrimination. The choosing among various options based on their characteristics.

domain name. The address of a website.

E

employee. Person who works for another under that person's control and direction.

endorsements. Positive statements about goods or services.

excise tax. A tax paid on the sale or consumption of goods or services.

express warranty. A specific guarantee of a product or service.

F

fictitious name. A name used by a business that is not its personal or legal name.

G

general partnership. A business that is owned by two or more persons.

goods. Items of personal property.

guarantee. A promise of quality of a good or service.

I

implied warranty. A guarantee of a product or service that is not specifically made, but can be implied from the circumstances of the sale.

independent contractor. Person who works for another as a separate business, not as an employee.

intangible property. Personal property that does not have physical presence, such as the ownership interest in a corporation.

intellectual property. Legal rights to the products of the mind, such as writings, musical compositions, formulas, and designs.

L

liability. The legal responsibility to pay for an injury.

limited liability company. An entity recognized as a legal "person" that is set up to conduct a business owned and run by members.

limited liability partnership. An entity recognized as a legal "person" that is set up to conduct a business owned and run by members that is set up for professionals such as attorneys or doctors.

limited partnership. A business that is owned by two or more persons, of which one or more is liable for the debts of the business and one or more has no liability for the debts.

limited warranty. A guarantee covering certain aspects of a good or service.

M

merchant. A person who is in business.

merchant's firm offer. An offer by a business made under specific terms.

N

nonprofit corporation. An entity recognized as a legal "person" that is set up to run an operation in which none of the profits are distributed to controlling members.

O

occupational license. A government-issued permit to transact business.

offer. A proposal to enter into a contract.

overtime. Hours worked in excess of forty hours in one week, or eight hours in one day.

P

partnership. A business formed by two or more persons.

patent. Protection given to inventions, discoveries, and designs.

personal property. Any type of property other than land and the structures attached to it.

pierce the corporate veil. When a court ignores the structure of a corporation, and holds its owners responsible for its debts or liabilities.

professional association. An entity recognized as a legal "person" that is set up to conduct a business of professionals such as attorneys or doctors.

proprietorship. A business that is owned by one person.

R

real property. Land and the structures attached to it.

resident alien. A person who is not a citizen of the country, but who may legally reside and work there.

S

S corporation. A corporation in which the profits are taxed to the shareholders.

sale on approval. Selling an item with the agreement that it may be brought back and the sale cancelled.

sale or return. An agreement whereby goods are to be purchased or returned to the vendor.

securities. Interests in a business, such as stocks or bonds.

sexual harassment. Activity that causes an employee to feel or be sexually threatened.

shares. Units of stock in a corporation.

statute of frauds. Law that requires certain contracts to be in writing.

stock. Ownership interests in a corporation.

sublease. An agreement to rent premises from an existing tenant.

T

tangible property. Physical personal property, such as desks and tables.

trade secret. Commercially valuable information or process that is protected by being kept a secret.

trademark. A name or symbol used to identify the source of goods or services.

U

unemployment compensation. Payments to a former employee who was terminated from a job for a reason not based on his or her fault.

usury. Charging an interest rate higher than that allowed by law.

W

withholding. Money taken out of an employee's salary and remitted to the government.

workers compensation. Insurance program to cover injuries or deaths of employees.

Business Start-Up Checklist

Use the business start-up checklist on the following page to make sure you follow all the necessary steps in establishing your new business.

BUSINESS START-UP CHECKLIST

❏ Make your plan
- ❏ Obtain and read all relevant publications on your type of business
- ❏ Obtain and read all laws and regulations affecting your business
- ❏ Calculate whether your plan will produce a profit
- ❏ Plan your sources of capital
- ❏ Plan your sources of goods or services
- ❏ Plan your marketing efforts

❏ Choose your business name
- ❏ Check other business names and trademarks
- ❏ Register your name, trademark, etc.

❏ Choose the business form
- ❏ Prepare and file organizational papers
- ❏ Prepare and file fictitious name if necessary

❏ Choose the location
- ❏ Check competitors
- ❏ Check zoning

❏ Obtain necessary licenses
- ❏ City
- ❏ County
- ❏ State
- ❏ Federal

❏ Choose a bank
- ❏ Checking
- ❏ Credit card processing
- ❏ Loans

❏ Obtain necessary insurance
- ❏ Workers' Comp
- ❏ Liability
- ❏ Hazard
- ❏ Automobile
- ❏ Health
- ❏ Life/Disability

❏ File necessary federal tax registrations

❏ File necessary state tax registrations

❏ Set up a bookkeeping system

❏ Plan your hiring
- ❏ Obtain required posters
- ❏ Obtain or prepare employment application
- ❏ Obtain new hire tax forms
- ❏ Prepare employment policies
- ❏ Determine compliance with health and safety laws

❏ Plan your opening
- ❏ Obtain all necessary equipment and supplies
- ❏ Obtain all necessary inventory
- ❏ Do all necessary marketing and publicity
- ❏ Obtain all necessary forms and agreements
- ❏ Prepare your company policies on refunds, exchanges, and returns

Sample, Filled-In Forms

The following forms are selected filled-in forms for demonstration purposes. Most have a corresponding blank form in Appendix C. The form numbers in this appendix correspond to the form numbers in Appendix C. If there is no blank for a particular form, it is because you must obtain it from a government agency. If you need instructions for these forms as you follow how they are filled out, they can be found in Appendix C, or in the chapters that discuss those forms. Please note that these samples show only the information relevant to the greatest number of businesses. You may need to fill out more parts of certain forms, depending on your particular business. For example, only the first ten sections of the lengthy Pennsylvania Enterprise Registration form appear here, although the form appears in its entirety in Appendix C

**PENNSYLVANIA DEPARTMENT OF STATE
CORPORATION BUREAU**

Application for Registration of Fictitious Name
54 Pa.C.S. § 311

Name Jane Roe Address 789 Back Street City Harrisburg State PA Zip Code 00000	**Document will be returned to the name and address you enter to the left.** ⇐

Fee: $70

In compliance with the requirements of 54 Pa.C.S. § 311 (relating to registration), the undersigned entity(ies) desiring to register a fictitious name under 54 Pa.C.S. Ch. 3 (relating to fictitious names), hereby state(s) that:

1. The fictitious name is: **Acme Printing**

2. A brief statement of the character or nature of the business or other activity to be carried on under or through the fictitious name is: The printing and reproduction of personal documents

3. The address, including number and street, if any, of the principal place of business (P.O. Box alone is **not** acceptable):

456 Main Street	Harrisburg	PA	00000	
Number and street	City	State	Zip	County

4. The name and address, including number and street, if any, of each individual interested in the business is:

Name	Number and Street	City	State
None			

DSCB:54-311-2

---

5. Each entity, other than an individual, interested in such business is (are):

| Name | Form of Organization | Organizing Jurisdiction |

Principal Office Address

PA Registered Office, if any

| Name | Form of Organization | Organizing Jurisdiction |

Principal Office Address

PA Registered Office, if any

---

6. The applicant is familiar with the provisions of 54 Pa.C.S. § 332 (relating to effect of registration) and understands that filing under the Fictitious Names Act does not create any exclusive or other right in the fictitious name.

---

7. Optional): The name(s) of the agent(s), if any, any one of whom is authorized to execute amendments to, withdrawals from or cancellation of this registration in behalf of all then existing parties to the registration, is (are):

IN TESTIMONY WHEREOF, the undersigned have caused this Application for Registration of Fictitious Name to be executed this

__23rd__ day of __May__ , __2007__.

_____	_Jane Roe_____
Individual Signature	Individual Signature
_____	_____
Individual Signature	Individual Signature
_____	_____
Entity Name	Entity Name
_____	_____
Signature	Signature
_____	_____
Title	Title

Department of State
Corporation Bureau
P.O. Box 8722
Harrisburg, PA 17105-8722
(717) 787-1057
Web site: www.dos.state.pa.us/corps

Instructions for Completion of Form:

A. Typewritten is preferred. If not, the form shall be completed in black or blue-black ink in order to permit reproduction. The filing fee for this form is $70 made payable to the Department of State.

B. Under 15 Pa.C.S. § 135(c) (relating to addresses) an actual street or rural route box number must be used as an address, and the Department of State is required to refuse to receive or file any document that sets forth only a post office box address.

C. The following, in addition to the filing fee, shall accompany this form:

   (1) Any necessary copies of form DSCB:17.2.3 (Consent to Appropriation or Use of Similar Name).

   (2) An necessary governmental approvals.

D. For general instructions relating to fictitious name registration see 19 Pa. Code Subch. 17C (relating to fictitious names). These instructions relate to such matters as voluntary and mandatory registration, general restrictions on name availability, use of corporate designators, agent for effecting amendments, etc., execution, official advertising when an individual is a party to the registration, and effect of registration and non-registration.

E. The name of a commercial registered office provider may not be used in Paragraph 3 in lieu of an address.

F. Insert in Paragraph 5 for each entity which is not an individual the following information: (i) the name of the entity and a statement of its form of organization, e.g., corporation, general partnership, limited partnership, business trust, (ii) the name of the jurisdiction under the laws of which it is organized, (iii) the address, including street and number, if any, of its principal office under the laws of its domiciliary jurisdiction and (iv) the address, including street and number, if any, of its registered office, if any, in this Commonwealth. If any of the entities has an association which has designated the name of a commercial registered office provider in lieu of a registered office address as permitted by 15 Pa.C.S. § 109, the name of the provider and the venue county should be inserted in the last column.

G. Every individual whose name appears in Paragraph 4 of the form **must sign** the form exactly as the name is set forth in Paragraph 4. The name of every other entity listed in Paragraph 5 shall be signed on its behalf by an officer, trustee or other authorized person. See 19 Pa. Code § 13.8(b) (relating to execution), which permits execution pursuant to power of attorney. A copy of the underlying power of attorney or other authorization should not be submitted to, and will not be received by or filed in, the Department.

H. If an individual is a party to the registration, the parties are required by 54 Pa.C.S. § 311(g) to advertise their intention to file or the filing of an application for registration of fictitious name. Proofs of publication of such advertising should not be submitted to the Department, and will not be received by or filed in the Department, but should be kept with the permanent records of the business.

I. This form and all accompanying documents shall be mailed to the address stated above.

DSCB: PCF3
Corporation Bureau
Pennsylvania Dept. of State

COUNTER - CORPORATE CERTIFICATION & SEARCH REQUEST FORM

ENTITY NAME: _Acme Printing_

DOCUMENT REQUESTED:

_____ Good Standing (Subsistence) Certificate

_____ Certified Copy of Corporate Index

_____ Great Seal Certificate attesting to _____

_____

_____ Certified Copy of _____

_____ Plain Copy of _____

__X___ Corporate Record Search or Plain Copy of Index

_____ Name Reservation

COMMENTS:

REQUESTER NAME: _Jane Doe_

REQUESTER ADDRESS: _789 Back Street_

Harrisburg, PA 00000

Mail this order when complete. _to above address_

The undersigned agrees to pay all statutory fees with respect to this request in advance.

SIGNATURE OF REQUESTING PARTY _Jane Doe_

__X___ Will pay by check.

_____ Deduct fees from Account# _____.

Total Due: $_12.00_____ 0

PENNSYLVANIA DEPARTMENT OF STATE
CORPORATION BUREAU

Application for Registration of Mark
(54 Pa.C.S. § 1112)

Name	**Document will be returned to the name and address you enter to the left.**
John Q. Public	⇐
Address	
123 Main Street	
City State Zip Code	
Harrisburg, PA 17000	

Fee: $50

In compliance with the requirements of the 54 Pa.C.S. § 1112 (relating to application for registration), the undersigned, having adopted and used a trade mark or service mark in this Commonwealth and desiring to register such mark, hereby states that:

1. The name of the applicant is *(see instruction A)*:

   Acme Lighting Supply, Inc. (a Pennsylvania corporation)

2. The residence, location or place of business of the applicant is:

123 Main Street	Harrisburg	PA	17000	Dauphin
Number and street	City	State	Zip	County

3. The name and description of the mark is *(a facsimile of the mark to be registered accompanies this application as Exhibit A and is incorporated herein by reference)*:

   The mark is a blue bulls-eye on a light blue background.

4. General class in which such goods or services fall is *(use only one of the classifications as set forth in the general classes of goods and services established by the United States Patent and Trademark Office attached)*:
   Goods (54 PaCS § 1103(ii))

DSCB:54-1112– 2

5. The goods or services in connection with which the mark is used and the mode and manner in which the mark is used in connection with such goods or services are:

Lighting installations, parts and service

6. The date when the mark was first used anywhere is:

1-1-00

7. The date when the mark was first used in this Commonwealth by the applicant or the predecessor in interest is:

1-1-00

8. The date, if any, an application to register the mark, or portions or a composite thereof, was filed by the applicant or a predecessor in interest in the United States Patent and Trademark Office. Also provide filing date and serial number of each application, the status thereof and, if any application was finally refused registration, or has otherwise not resulted in a registration, the reasons therefore. *(Please attach 8½ x 11 sheet(s) if more space is needed.)*

9. Applicant is the owner of the mark, that the mark is in use and that, to the applicant's knowledge, no other person has registered, either federally or in this Commonwealth or has the right to use such mark, either in the identical form thereof or in such near resemblance thereto as to be likely, when applied to the goods or services of such other person, to cause confusion, or to cause mistake, or to deceive.

IN TESTIMONY WHEREOF, the undersigned person has caused this Application for Registration of Mark to be executed this 5th day of May 2007.

John Q. Public
Name of Applicant

John Q. Public
Signature

President and CEO of Acme Lighting Supply
Title

Department of Homeland Security
U.S. Citizenship and Immigration Services

OMB No. 1615-0047; Expires 03/31/07

Employment Eligibility Verification

Please read instructions carefully before completing this form. The instructions must be available during completion of this form. **ANTI-DISCRIMINATION NOTICE:** It is illegal to discriminate against work eligible individuals. Employers CANNOT specify which document(s) they will accept from an employee. The refusal to hire an individual because of a future expiration date may also constitute illegal discrimination.

Section 1. Employee Information and Verification. To be completed and signed by employee at the time employment begins.

Print Name: Last	First	Middle Initial	Maiden Name
REDDENBACHER	MARY	J.	HASSENFUSS

Address (Street Name and Number)	Apt. #	Date of Birth (month/day/year)
1234 LIBERTY LANE		1/26/69

City	State	Zip Code	Social Security #
ALLENTOWN	PA	17110	123-45-6789

I am aware that federal law provides for imprisonment and/or fines for false statements or use of false documents in connection with the completion of this form.

I attest, under penalty of perjury, that I am (check one of the following):
- ☐ A citizen or national of the United States
- ☐ A Lawful Permanent Resident (Alien #) A _____
- ☐ An alien authorized to work until _____
  (Alien # or Admission #) _____

Employee's Signature	Date (month/day/year)
Mary Reddenbacher	8/21/06

Preparer and/or Translator Certification. *(To be completed and signed if Section 1 is prepared by a person other than the employee.) I attest, under penalty of perjury, that I have assisted in the completion of this form and that to the best of my knowledge the information is true and correct.*

Preparer's/Translator's Signature	Print Name

Address (Street Name and Number, City, State, Zip Code)	Date (month/day/year)

Section 2. Employer Review and Verification. To be completed and signed by employer. Examine one document from List A OR examine one document from List B and one from List C, as listed on the reverse of this form, and record the title, number and expiration date, if any, of the document(s).

	List A	OR	List B	AND	List C
Document title:					
Issuing authority:					
Document #:					
Expiration Date (if any):					
Document #:					
Expiration Date (if any):					

CERTIFICATION - I attest, under penalty of perjury, that I have examined the document(s) presented by the above-named employee, that the above-listed document(s) appear to be genuine and to relate to the employee named, that the employee began employment on *(month/day/year)* _____ and that to the best of my knowledge the employee is eligible to work in the United States. (State employment agencies may omit the date the employee began employment.)

Signature of Employer or Authorized Representative	Print Name	Title
Jeff Schmoe	Jeff Schmoe	owner

Business or Organization Name	Address (Street Name and Number, City, State, Zip Code)	Date (month/day/year)
Jeff's Motorcycles	5432 Rocket Ave, Speedy, PA, 12345	8/21/06

Section 3. Updating and Reverification. To be completed and signed by employer.

A. New Name (if applicable)	B. Date of Rehire (month/day/year) (if applicable)

C. If employee's previous grant of work authorization has expired, provide the information below for the document that establishes current employment eligibility.

Document Title:	Document #:	Expiration Date (if any):

I attest, under penalty of perjury, that to the best of my knowledge, this employee is eligible to work in the United States, and if the employee presented document(s), the document(s) I have examined appear to be genuine and to relate to the individual.

Signature of Employer or Authorized Representative	Date (month/day/year)

NOTE: This is the 1991 edition of the Form I-9 that has been rebranded with a current printing date to reflect the recent transition from the INS to DHS and its components.

Form I-9 (Rev. 05/31/05)Y Page 2

Form **SS-4**
(Rev. February 2000)
Department of the Treasury
Internal Revenue Service

Application for Employer Identification Number

(For use by employers, corporations, partnerships, trusts, estates, churches, government agencies, Indian tribal entities, certain individuals, and others.)

▶ See separate instructions for each line.   ▶ Keep a copy for your records.

OMB No. 1545-0003

EIN

1 Legal name of entity (or individual) for whom the EIN is being requested	
Doe Company	

2 Trade name of business (if different from name on line 1)	**3** Executor, administrator, trustee, "care of" name

4a Mailing address (room, apt., suite no. and street, or P.O. box)	**5a** Street address (if different) (Do not enter a P.O. box.)
123 Main Street	
4b City, state, and ZIP code	**5b** City, state, and ZIP code
Harrisburg, PA 17000	

6 County and state where principal business is located
Dauphin, Pennsylvania

7a Name of principal officer, general partner, grantor, owner, or trustor	**7b** SSN, ITIN, or EIN
John Doe	

8a **Type of entity** (check only one box)

- [X] Sole proprietor (SSN) _____
- [ ] Partnership
- [ ] Corporation (enter form number to be filed) ▶ _____
- [ ] Personal service corporation
- [ ] Church or church-controlled organization
- [ ] Other nonprofit organization (specify) ▶ _____
- [ ] Other (specify) ▶

- [ ] Estate (SSN of decedent) _____
- [ ] Plan administrator (SSN) _____
- [ ] Trust (SSN of grantor) _____
- [ ] National Guard   [ ] State/local government
- [ ] Farmers' cooperative [ ] Federal government/military
- [ ] REMIC   [ ] Indian tribal governments/enterprises
- Group Exemption Number (GEN) ▶ _____

8b If a corporation, name the state or foreign country (if applicable) where incorporated

State	Foreign country

9 **Reason for applying** (check only one box)

- [X] Started new business (specify type) ▶ _____
  clothing manufacturing
- [ ] Hired employees (Check the box and see line 12.)
- [ ] Compliance with IRS withholding regulations
- [ ] Other (specify) ▶

- [ ] Banking purpose (specify purpose) ▶ _____
- [ ] Changed type of organization (specify new type) ▶ _____
- [ ] Purchased going business
- [ ] Created a trust (specify type) ▶ _____
- [ ] Created a pension plan (specify type) ▶ _____

10 Date business started or acquired (month, day, year). See instructions.	**11** Closing month of accounting year
10-15-2007	December

12 First date wages or annuities were paid (month, day, year). **Note.** If applicant is a withholding agent, enter date income will first be paid to nonresident alien. (month, day, year) . . . . ▶ 10-22-2007

13 Highest number of employees expected in the next 12 months (enter -0- if none). 3

Do you expect to have $1,000 or less in employment tax liability for the calendar year? [ ] **Yes** [ ] **No.** (If you expect to pay $4,000 or less in wages, you can mark yes.)

Agricultural	Household	Other

14 Check **one** box that best describes the principal activity of your business.

- [ ] Construction [ ] Rental & leasing [ ] Transportation & warehousing
- [ ] Real estate   [ ] Manufacturing   [ ] Finance & insurance

- [ ] Health care & social assistance [ ] Wholesale–agent/broker
- [ ] Accommodation & food service   [ ] Wholesale–other   [ ] Retail
- [ ] Other (specify) fabric

15 Indicate principal line of merchandise sold, specific construction work done, products produced, or services provided.
clothing manufacturing

16a Has the applicant ever applied for an employer identification number for this or any other business? . . . . [ ] Yes [X] No
Note. If "Yes," please complete lines 16b and 16c.

16b If you checked "Yes" on line 16a, give applicant's legal name and trade name shown on prior application if different from line 1 or 2 above.
Legal name ▶ _____   Trade name ▶ _____

16c Approximate date when, and city and state where, the application was filed. Enter previous employer identification number if known.

Approximate date when filed (mo., day, year)	City and state where filed	Previous EIN

Third Party Designee	Complete this section **only** if you want to authorize the named individual to receive the entity's EIN and answer questions about the completion of this form.	
	Designee's name	Designee's telephone number (include area code) ( )
	Address and ZIP code	Designee's fax number (include area code) ( )

Under penalties of perjury, I declare that I have examined this application, and to the best of my knowledge and belief, it is true, correct, and complete.

Name and title (type or print clearly) ▶ John Doe, Partner

Applicant's telephone number (include area code) ( )

Signature ▶ *John Doe*   Date ▶ 10/15/2007

Applicant's fax number (include area code) ( )

For Privacy Act and Paperwork Reduction Act Notice, see separate instructions.   Cat. No. 16055N   Form **SS-4** (Rev. 2-2006)

Form W-4 (2006)

Purpose. Complete Form W-4 so that your employer can withhold the correct federal income tax from your pay. Because your tax situation may change, you may want to refigure your withholding each year.

Exemption from withholding. If you are exempt, complete only lines 1, 2, 3, 4, and 7 and sign the form to validate it. Your exemption for 2006 expires February 16, 2007. See Pub. 505, Tax Withholding and Estimated Tax.

Note. You cannot claim exemption from withholding if (a) your income exceeds $850 and includes more than $300 of unearned income (for example, interest and dividends) and (b) another person can claim you as a dependent on their tax return.

Basic instructions. If you are not exempt, complete the **Personal Allowances Worksheet** below. The worksheets on page 2 adjust your withholding allowances based on itemized deductions, certain credits, adjustments to income, or two-earner/two-job situations. Complete all worksheets that apply. However, you may claim fewer (or zero) allowances.

Head of household. Generally, you may claim head of household filing status on your tax return only if you are unmarried and pay more than 50% of the costs of keeping up a home for yourself and your dependent(s) or other qualifying individuals. See line **E** below.

Tax credits. You can take projected tax credits into account in figuring your allowable number of withholding allowances. Credits for child or dependent care expenses and the child tax credit may be claimed using the **Personal Allowances Worksheet** below. See Pub. 919, How Do I Adjust My Tax Withholding, for information on converting your other credits into withholding allowances.

Nonwage income. If you have a large amount of nonwage income, such as interest or dividends, consider making estimated tax payments using Form 1040-ES, Estimated Tax for Individuals. Otherwise, you may owe additional tax.

Two earners/two jobs. If you have a working spouse or more than one job, figure the total number of allowances you are entitled to claim on all jobs using worksheets from only one Form W-4. Your withholding usually will be most accurate when all allowances are claimed on the Form W-4 for the highest paying job and zero allowances are claimed on the others.

Nonresident alien. If you are a nonresident alien, see the Instructions for Form 8233 before completing this Form W-4.

Check your withholding. After your Form W-4 takes effect, use Pub. 919 to see how the dollar amount you are having withheld compares to your projected total tax for 2006. See Pub. 919, especially if your earnings exceed $130,000 (Single) or $180,000 (Married).

Recent name change? If your name on line 1 differs from that shown on your social security card, call 1-800-772-1213 to initiate a name change and obtain a social security card showing your correct name.

Personal Allowances Worksheet (Keep for your records.)

A Enter "1" for **yourself** if no one else can claim you as a dependent . . . . **A** _1_

B Enter "1" if:
- You are single and have only one job; or
- You are married, have only one job, and your spouse does not work; or
- Your wages from a second job or your spouse's wages (or the total of both) are $1,000 or less.

. . **B** _1_

C Enter "1" for your **spouse**. But, you may choose to enter "-0-" if you are married and have either a working spouse or more than one job. (Entering "-0-" may help you avoid having too little tax withheld.) . . . . **C** _0_

D Enter number of **dependents** (other than your spouse or yourself) you will claim on your tax return . . . . . . **D** _1_

E Enter "1" if you will file as **head of household** on your tax return (see conditions under **Head of household** above) . **E** _____

F Enter "1" if you have at least $1,500 of **child or dependent care expenses** for which you plan to claim a credit . . **F** _____
(**Note.** Do **not** include child support payments. See **Pub. 503,** Child and Dependent Care Expenses, for details.)

G **Child Tax Credit** (including additional child tax credit):
- If your total income will be less than $55,000 ($82,000 if married), enter "2" for each eligible child.
- If your total income will be between $55,000 and $84,000 ($82,000 and $119,000 if married), enter "1" for each eligible child plus "1" **additional** if you have four or more eligible children. **G** _____

H Add lines A through G and enter total here. (**Note.** This may be different from the number of exemptions you claim on your tax return.) ▶ **H** _____

For accuracy, complete all worksheets that apply.
- If you plan to **itemize or claim adjustments to income** and want to reduce your withholding, see the **Deductions and Adjustments Worksheet** on page 2.
- If you have **more than one job** or are **married and you and your spouse both work** and the combined earnings from all jobs exceed $35,000 ($25,000 if married) see the **Two-Earner/Two-Job Worksheet** on page 2 to avoid having too little tax withheld.
- If **neither** of the above situations applies, **stop here** and enter the number from line H on line 5 of Form W-4 below.

Cut here and give Form W-4 to your employer. Keep the top part for your records.

Form **W-4**

Department of the Treasury
Internal Revenue Service

Employee's Withholding Allowance Certificate

▶ Whether you are entitled to claim a certain number of allowances or exemption from withholding is subject to review by the IRS. Your employer may be required to send a copy of this form to the IRS.

OMB No. 1545-0074

2006

1 Type or print your first name and middle initial.	Last name	2 Your social security number
George H.	Smith	345 67 8900

Home address (number and street or rural route)
4567 Paris Street

City or town, state, and ZIP code
Allentown, PA 17000

3 ☒ Single ☐ Married ☐ Married, but withhold at higher Single rate.
Note. If married, but legally separated, or spouse is a nonresident alien, check the "Single" box.

4 If your last name differs from that shown on your social security card, check here. You must call 1-800-772-1213 for a new card. ▶ ☐

5 Total number of allowances you are claiming (from line **H** above **or** from the applicable worksheet on page 2) **5** _3_

6 Additional amount, if any, you want withheld from each paycheck . . . . **6** $ _0_

7 I claim exemption from withholding for 2006, and I certify that I meet **both** of the following conditions for exemption.
- Last year I had a right to a refund of **all** federal income tax withheld because I had **no** tax liability **and**
- This year I expect a refund of **all** federal income tax withheld because I expect to have **no** tax liability.

If you meet both conditions, write "Exempt" here . . . . ▶ **7** _____

Under penalties of perjury, I declare that I have examined this certificate and to the best of my knowledge and belief, it is true, correct, and complete.

Employee's signature
(Form is not valid unless you sign it.) ▶ *George H. Smith*

Date ▶ *November 6   2006*

8 Employer's name and address (Employer: Complete lines 8 and 10 only if sending to the IRS.)	9 Office code (optional)	10 Employer identification number (EIN)

For Privacy Act and Paperwork Reduction Act Notice, see page 2.   Cat. No. 10220Q   Form **W-4** (2006)

PA-100 (1) 6-03

MAIL COMPLETED APPLICATION TO:
DEPARTMENT OF REVENUE
BUREAU OF BUSINESS TRUST FUND TAXES
DEPT. 280901
HARRISBURG, PA 17128-0901

COMMONWEALTH OF PENNSYLVANIA
PA ENTERPRISE REGISTRATION FORM

DEPARTMENT USE ONLY

RECEIVED DATE

DEPARTMENT OF REVENUE &
DEPARTMENT OF LABOR AND INDUSTRY

TYPE OR PRINT LEGIBLY, USE BLACK INK

SECTION 1 – REASON FOR THIS REGISTRATION

REFER TO THE INSTRUCTIONS (PAGE 18) AND CHECK THE APPLICABLE BOX(ES) TO INDICATE THE REASON(S) FOR THIS REGISTRATION.

1. ☐ NEW REGISTRATION
2. ☐ ADDING TAX(ES) & SERVICE(S)
3. ☐ REACTIVATING TAX(ES) & SERVICE(S)
4. ☐ ADDING ESTABLISHMENT(S)
5. ☐ INFORMATION UPDATE

6. DID THIS ENTERPRISE:
   ☐ YES ☐ NO ACQUIRE ALL OR PART OF ANOTHER BUSINESS?
   ☐ YES ☐ NO RESULT FROM A CHANGE IN LEGAL STRUCTURE (FOR EXAMPLE, FROM INDIVIDUAL PROPRIETOR TO CORPORATION, PARTNERSHIP TO CORPORATION, CORPORATION TO LIMITED LIABILITY COMPANY, ETC)?
   ☐ YES ☐ NO UNDERGO A MERGER, CONSOLIDATION, DISSOLUTION, OR OTHER RESTRUCTURING?

SECTION 2 – ENTERPRISE INFORMATION

1. DATE OF FIRST OPERATIONS	2. DATE OF FIRST OPERATIONS IN PA	3. ENTERPRISE FISCAL YEAR END
1-1-98	1-1-01	12-31-07

4. ENTERPRISE LEGAL NAME	5. FEDERAL EMPLOYER IDENTIFICATION NUMBER (EIN)
Superior Flooring, Inc.	00-0000

6. ENTERPRISE TRADE NAME (if different than legal name)	7. ENTERPRISE TELEPHONE NUMBER
Superior Flooring, Inc.	(789) 555-4321

8. ENTERPRISE STREET ADDRESS (do not use PO Box)	CITY/TOWN	COUNTY	STATE	ZIP CODE + 4
123 Main Street	Anytown	Capitol	PA	10000-1234

9. ENTERPRISE MAILING ADDRESS (if different than street address)	CITY/TOWN	STATE	ZIP CODE + 4
same	same	same	same

10. LOCATION OF ENTERPRISE RECORDS (street address)	CITY/TOWN	STATE	ZIP CODE + 4
123 Main St.	Anytown	PA	10000-1234

11. ESTABLISHMENT NAME (doing business as)	12. NUMBER OF ESTABLISHMENTS *	13. SCHOOL DISTRICT	14. MUNICIPALITY
		same	

* Enterprises with more than one establishment as defined in the general instructions must complete Section 17.

SECTION 3 – TAXES AND SERVICES

ALL REGISTRANTS MUST CHECK THE APPLICABLE BOX(ES) TO INDICATE THE TAX(ES) AND SERVICE(S) REQUESTED FOR THIS REGISTRATION AND COMPLETE THE CORRESPONDING SECTIONS INDICATED ON PAGES 2 AND 3. IF REACTIVATING ANY PREVIOUS ACCOUNT(S), LIST THE ACCOUNT NUMBER(S) IN THE SPACE PROVIDED.

	PREVIOUS ACCOUNT NBR.		PREVIOUS ACCOUNT NBR.
☐ CIGARETTE DEALER'S LICENSE		☐ SALES TAX EXEMPT STATUS	
☐ CORPORATION TAXES		☐ SALES, USE, HOTEL OCCUPANCY TAX LICENSE	
☐ EMPLOYER WITHHOLDING TAX		☒ SMALL GAMES OF CHANCE LIC./CERT.	
☐ FUELS TAX PERMIT		☐ TRANSIENT VENDOR CERTIFICATE	
☐ LIQUID FUELS TAX PERMIT		☐ UNEMPLOYMENT COMPENSATION	
☐ LOCAL SALES, USE, HOTEL OCCUPANCY TAX		☐ USE TAX	
☐ MOTOR CARRIERS ROAD TAX/IFTA		☐ VEHICLE RENTAL TAX	
☐ PROMOTER LICENSE		☐ WHOLESALER CERTIFICATE	
☐ PUBLIC TRANSPORTATION ASSISTANCE TAX LICENSE		☐ WORKERS' COMPENSATION COVERAGE	

SECTION 4 – AUTHORIZED SIGNATURE

I, (WE) THE UNDERSIGNED, DECLARE UNDER THE PENALTIES OF PERJURY THAT THE STATEMENTS CONTAINED HEREIN ARE TRUE, CORRECT, AND COMPLETE.

AUTHORIZED SIGNATURE (ATTACH POWER OF ATTORNEY IF APPLICABLE)	DAYTIME TELEPHONE NUMBER	TITLE Chief Executive Officer
Janet A. Doe	( )	
TYPE OR PRINT NAME	E-MAIL ADDRESS	DATE
Janet A. Doe		1-1-07

TYPE OR PRINT PREPARER'S NAME		TITLE
Michael B. Roe		Accountant
DAYTIME TELEPHONE NUMBER	E-MAIL ADDRESS	DATE
(717 555 1212		1-1-07

4

PA-100 8-01

ENTERPRISE NAME

DEPARTMENT USE ONLY

SECTION 5 – BUSINESS STRUCTURE

CHECK THE APPROPRIATE BOX FOR QUESTIONS 1, 2 & 3. IN ADDITION TO SECTIONS 1 THROUGH 10, COMPLETE THE SECTION(S) INDICATED.

1. ☐ SOLE PROPRIETORSHIP (INDIVIDUAL)   ☐ GENERAL PARTNERSHIP   ☐ ASSOCIATION   ☐ LIMITED LIABILITY COMPANY

   ☐ CORPORATION (Sec. 11)   ☐ LIMITED PARTNERSHIP   ☐ BUSINESS TRUST   *STATE WHERE CHARTERED* _____

   ☐ GOVERNMENT (Sec. 13)   ☐ LIMITED LIABILITY PARTNERSHIP   ☐ ESTATE   ☐ RESTRICTED PROFESSIONAL COMPANY

   ☐ JOINT VENTURE PARTNERSHIP   *STATE WHERE CHARTERED* _____

2. ☒ PROFIT   ☐ NON-PROFIT   IS THE ENTERPRISE ORGANIZED FOR PROFIT OR NON-PROFIT?

3. ☐ YES   ☒ NO   IS THE ENTERPRISE EXEMPT FROM TAXATION UNDER INTERNAL REVENUE CODE SECTION 501(C)(3)? IF YES, PROVIDE A COPY OF THE ENTERPRISE'S EXEMPTION AUTHORIZATION LETTER FROM THE INTERNAL REVENUE SERVICE.

SECTION 6 – OWNERS, PARTNERS, SHAREHOLDERS, OFFICERS, AND RESPONSIBLE PARTY INFORMATION

PROVIDE THE FOLLOWING FOR **ALL** INDIVIDUAL AND/OR ENTERPRISE OWNERS, PARTNERS, SHAREHOLDERS, OFFICERS, AND RESPONSIBLE PARTIES. IF STOCK IS PUBLICLY TRADED, **PROVIDE THE FOLLOWING FOR ANY SHAREHOLDER WITH AN EQUITY POSITION OF 5% OR MORE.** *ADDITIONAL SPACE IS AVAILABLE IN SECTION 6A, PAGE 11.*

1. NAME	2. SOCIAL SECURITY NUMBER	3. DATE OF BIRTH *	4. FEDERAL EIN
Janet Doe	123-45-6789	1-2-34	00-00000

5. ☒ OWNER ☐ OFFICER ☐ PARTNER ☐ SHAREHOLDER ☐ RESPONSIBLE PARTY	6. TITLE	7. EFFECTIVE DATE OF TITLE	8. PERCENTAGE OF OWNERSHIP 51 %	9. EFFECTIVE DATE OF OWNERSHIP 1-1-07

10. HOME ADDRESS (street)	CITY/TOWN	COUNTY	STATE	ZIP CODE + 4
345 First Ave	Anytown	Capitol	PA	10001-1234

11. THIS PERSON IS RESPONSIBLE TO REMIT/MAINTAIN: ☐ SALES TAX   ☐ EMPLOYER WITHHOLDING TAX   ☐ MOTOR FUEL TAXES

   ☐ WORKERS' COMPENSATION COVERAGE

* DATE OF BIRTH REQUIRED ONLY IF APPLYING FOR A CIGARETTE WHOLESALE DEALER'S LICENSE, A SMALL GAMES OF CHANCE DISTRIBUTOR LICENSE, OR A SMALL GAMES OF CHANCE MANUFACTURER CERTIFICATE.

SECTION 7 – ESTABLISHMENT BUSINESS ACTIVITY INFORMATION

REFER TO THE INSTRUCTIONS TO COMPLETE THIS SECTION. COMPLETE SECTION 17 FOR MULTIPLE ESTABLISHMENTS.

1. ENTER THE PERCENTAGE THAT EACH **PA** BUSINESS ACTIVITY REPRESENTS OF THE TOTAL RECEIPTS OR REVENUES AT THIS ESTABLISHMENT. LIST ALL PRODUCTS OR SERVICES ASSOCIATED WITH EACH BUSINESS ACTIVITY. ENTER THE PERCENTAGE THAT THE PRODUCTS OR SERVICES REPRESENT OF THE TOTAL RECEIPTS OR REVENUES AT THIS ESTABLISHMENT.

PA BUSINESS ACTIVITY	%	PRODUCTS OR SERVICES	%	ADDITIONAL PRODUCTS OR SERVICES	%
Accommodation & Food Services					
Agriculture, Forestry, Fishing, & Hunting					
Art, Entertainment, & Recreation Services					
Communications/Information					
Construction (must complete question 3)					
Domestics (Private Households)					
Educational Services					
Finance					
Health Care Services					
Insurance					
Management of Companies & Enterprises					
Manufacturing					
Mining, Quarrying, & Oil/Gas Extraction					
Other Services					
Professional, Scientific, & Technical Services					
Public Administration					
Real Estate					
Retail Trade					
Sanitary Service	70	flooring/paneling			
Social Assistance Services					
Transportation					
Utilities					
Warehousing					
Wholesale Trade	30	flooring/paneling			
TOTAL	100%				

2. ENTER THE PERCENTAGE THAT THIS ESTABLISHMENT'S RECEIPTS OR REVENUES REPRESENT OF THE TOTAL PA RECEIPTS OR REVENUES OF THE ENTERPRISE.
_____ %

3. ESTABLISHMENTS ENGAGED IN CONSTRUCTION **MUST** ENTER THE PERCENTAGE OF CONSTRUCTION ACTIVITY THAT IS NEW AND/OR RENOVATIVE AND THE PERCENTAGE OF CONSTRUCTION ACTIVITY THAT IS RESIDENTIAL AND/OR COMMERCIAL.

_____ % NEW   +   _____ % RENOVATIVE = 100%

_____ % RESIDENTIAL   +   _____ % COMMERCIAL = 100%

5

PA-100 6-03

ENTERPRISE NAME **Superior Flooring, Inc.**

SECTION 8 – ESTABLISHMENT SALES INFORMATION

1. ☐ YES ☐ NO IS THIS ESTABLISHMENT SELLING TAXABLE PRODUCTS OR OFFERING TAXABLE SERVICES TO CONSUMERS FROM A LOCATION **IN PENNSYLVANIA**? IF YES, COMPLETE SECTION 18.

2. ☐ YES ☐ NO IS THIS ESTABLISHMENT SELLING CIGARETTES **IN PENNSYLVANIA**? IF YES, COMPLETE SECTIONS 18 AND 19.

3. LIST EACH COUNTY **IN PENNSYLVANIA** WHERE THIS ESTABLISHMENT IS CONDUCTING TAXABLE SALES ACTIVITY(IES).

COUNTY **Capitol**   COUNTY _____   COUNTY _____

COUNTY _____   COUNTY _____   COUNTY _____

ATTACH ADDITIONAL 8 1/2 X 11 SHEETS IF NECESSARY.

SECTION 9 – ESTABLISHMENT EMPLOYMENT INFORMATION

PART 1

1. ☒ YES ☐ NO DOES THIS ESTABLISHMENT EMPLOY INDIVIDUALS WHO **WORK IN PENNSYLVANIA?** IF YES, INDICATE:
   - a. DATE WAGES FIRST **PAID** (MM/DD/YYYY) **1-1-07**
   - b. DATE WAGES RESUMED FOLLOWING A BREAK IN EMPLOYMENT .... _____
   - c. TOTAL NUMBER OF EMPLOYEES .... _____
   - d. NUMBER OF EMPLOYEES PRIMARILY WORKING IN NEW BUILDING OR INFRASTRUCTURE **3**
   - e. NUMBER OF EMPLOYEES PRIMARILY WORKING IN REMODELING CONSTRUCTION **0**
   - f. ESTIMATED GROSS WAGES PER QUARTER .... $ **3,000** .00
   - g. NAME OF WORKERS' COMPENSATION INSURANCE COMPANY _____
     - 1. POLICY NUMBER _____ EFFECTIVE START DATE _____ END DATE _____
     - 2. AGENCY NAME _____ DAYTIME TELEPHONE NUMBER ( )
       MAILING ADDRESS _____ CITY/TOWN _____ STATE ___ ZIP CODE + 4 _____
     - 3. IF THIS ENTERPRISE DOES NOT HAVE WORKERS' COMPENSATION INSURANCE, CHECK ONE:
       - a. THIS ESTABLISHMENT EMPLOYS ONLY EXCLUDED WORKERS .... _____ ☐
       - b. THIS ESTABLISHMENT HAS ZERO EMPLOYEES .... _____ ☐
       - c. THIS ESTABLISHMENT RECEIVED APPROVAL TO SELF-INSURE BY THE PA BUREAU OF WORKERS' COMPENSATION .... _____ ☐
         IF ITEM 3c. IS CHECKED, PROVIDE PA WORKERS' COMPENSATION BUREAU CODE _____

2. ☐ YES ☒ NO DOES THIS ESTABLISHMENT EMPLOY PA RESIDENTS WHO **WORK OUTSIDE OF PENNSYLVANIA?** IF YES, INDICATE:
   - a. DATE WAGES FIRST **PAID** (MM/DD/YYYY) .... _____
   - b. DATE WAGES RESUMED FOLLOWING A BREAK IN EMPLOYMENT .... _____
   - c. ESTIMATED GROSS WAGES PER QUARTER. .... $ _____ .00

3. ☐ YES ☐ NO DOES THIS ESTABLISHMENT PAY REMUNERATION FOR SERVICES TO PERSONS YOU DO NOT CONSIDER EMPLOYEES? IF YES, EXPLAIN THE SERVICES PERFORMED _____

PART 2

1. ☐ YES ☒ NO IS THIS REGISTRATION A RESULT OF A TAXABLE DISTRIBUTION FROM A BENEFIT TRUST, DEFERRED PAYMENT, OR RETIREMENT PLAN FOR PA RESIDENTS? IF YES, INDICATE:
   - a. DATE BENEFITS FIRST **PAID** (MM/DD/YYYY) .... _____
   - b. ESTIMATED BENEFITS PAID PER QUARTER .... $ _____ .00

SECTION 10 – BULK SALE/TRANSFER INFORMATION

IF ASSETS WERE ACQUIRED IN BULK FROM MORE THAN ONE ENTERPRISE, PHOTOCOPY THIS SECTION AND PROVIDE THE FOLLOWING INFORMATION ABOUT EACH SELLER/TRANSFEROR.

1. ☐ YES ☒ NO DID THE ENTERPRISE ACQUIRE 51% OR MORE OF **ANY CLASS** OF THE **PA ASSETS** OF ANOTHER ENTERPRISE? SEE THE CLASS OF ASSETS LISTED BELOW.

2. ☐ YES ☒ NO DID THE ENTERPRISE ACQUIRE 51% OR MORE OF THE **TOTAL ASSETS** OF ANOTHER ENTERPRISE?

IF THE ANSWER TO EITHER QUESTION IS YES, PROVIDE THE FOLLOWING INFORMATION ABOUT THE **SELLER/TRANSFEROR.**

3. SELLER/TRANSFEROR NAME			4. FEDERAL EIN	
N/A			N/A	
5. SELLER/TRANSFEROR STREET ADDRESS	CITY/TOWN		STATE	ZIP CODE + 4
N/A	N/A		N/A	N/A

6. DATE ASSETS ACQUIRED	7. ASSETS ACQUIRED:		
	☐ ACCOUNTS RECEIVABLE	☐ FIXTURES	☐ MACHINERY
	☐ CONTRACTS	☐ FURNITURE	☐ NAME AND/OR GOODWILL
N/A	☐ CUSTOMERS/CLIENTS	☐ INVENTORY	☐ REAL ESTATE
	☐ EQUIPMENT	☐ LEASES	☐ OTHER _____ N/A

IMPORTANT: IF, IN ADDITION TO ACQUIRING ASSETS IN BULK, THE ENTERPRISE ALSO ACQUIRED ALL OR PART OF A PREDECESSOR'S BUSINESS, SECTION 14 MUST BE COMPLETED.

Blank Forms

The following forms may be photocopied or removed from this book and used immediately. Some of the tax forms explained in this book are not included here because you should use original returns provided by the IRS (940, 941) or the Pennsylvania Department of Revenue (Quarterly Unemployment Compensation Form).

NOTE: *If a form has instructions that are provided by the government, they are on the pages that immediately follow the blank form.*

Table of Forms

Tax Timetable

	Pennsylvania			Federal			
	Sales	Unemployment	Corp. Income	Est. Payment	Annual Return	Form 941*	Misc.
JAN.	20th	6th	15th	15th		31st	31st 940 W-2 508 1099
FEB.	20th	3rd	15th				
MAR.	20th	3rd	15th		15th Corp. & Partnership		
APR.	20th	5th	15th	15th	15th Personal	30th	30th 508
MAY	20th	5th	15th				
JUN.	20th	3rd	15th	15th			
JUL.	20th	6th	15th			31st	31st 508
AUG.	20th	4th	15th				
SEP.	20th	3rd	15th	15th			
OCT.	20th	5th	15th			31st	31st 508
NOV.	20th	3rd	15th				
DEC.	20th	3rd	15th				

*In addition to form 941, deposits must be made regularly if withholding exceeds $500 in any month

This page intentionally left blank.

PENNSYLVANIA DEPARTMENT OF STATE
CORPORATION BUREAU

Application for Registration of Fictitious Name
54 Pa.C.S. § 311

Name
Address
City   State   Zip Code

Document will be returned to the name and address you enter to the left.
⇐

Fee: $70

In compliance with the requirements of 54 Pa.C.S. § 311 (relating to registration), the undersigned entity(ies) desiring to register a fictitious name under 54 Pa.C.S. Ch. 3 (relating to fictitious names), hereby state(s) that:

1. The fictitious name is:

2. A brief statement of the character or nature of the business or other activity to be carried on under or through the fictitious name is:

3. The address, including number and street, if any, of the principal place of business (P.O. Box alone is **not** acceptable):

   Number and street   City   State   Zip   County

4. The name and address, including number and street, if any, of each individual interested in the business is:
   Name   Number and Street   City   State

DSCB:54-311-2

5. Each entity, other than an individual, interested in such business is (are):

| Name | Form of Organization | Organizing Jurisdiction |

Principal Office Address

PA Registered Office, if any

| Name | Form of Organization | Organizing Jurisdiction |

Principal Office Address

PA Registered Office, if any

6. The applicant is familiar with the provisions of 54 Pa.C.S. § 332 (relating to effect of registration) and understands that filing under the Fictitious Names Act does not create any exclusive or other right in the fictitious name.

7. Optional): The name(s) of the agent(s), if any, any one of whom is authorized to execute amendments to, withdrawals from or cancellation of this registration in behalf of all then existing parties to the registration, is (are):

IN TESTIMONY WHEREOF, the undersigned have caused this Application for Registration of Fictitious Name to be executed this

_____ day of _____,_____.

_____
Individual Signature

_____
Individual Signature

_____
Individual Signature

_____
Individual Signature

_____
Entity Name

_____
Entity Name

_____
Signature

_____
Signature

_____
Title

_____
Title

Department of State
Corporation Bureau
P.O. Box 8722
Harrisburg, PA 17105-8722
(717) 787-1057
Web site: www.dos.state.pa.us/corps

Instructions for Completion of Form:

A. Typewritten is preferred. If not, the form shall be completed in black or blue-black ink in order to permit reproduction. The filing fee for this form is $70 made payable to the Department of State.

B. Under 15 Pa.C.S. § 135(c) (relating to addresses) an actual street or rural route box number must be used as an address, and the Department of State is required to refuse to receive or file any document that sets forth only a post office box address.

C. The following, in addition to the filing fee, shall accompany this form:

   (1) Any necessary copies of form DSCB:17.2.3 (Consent to Appropriation or Use of Similar Name).

   (2) An necessary governmental approvals.

D. For general instructions relating to fictitious name registration see 19 Pa. Code Subch. 17C (relating to fictitious names). These instructions relate to such matters as voluntary and mandatory registration, general restrictions on name availability, use of corporate designators, agent for effecting amendments, etc., execution, official advertising when an individual is a party to the registration, and effect of registration and non-registration.

E. The name of a commercial registered office provider may not be used in Paragraph 3 in lieu of an address.

F. Insert in Paragraph 5 for each entity which is not an individual the following information: (i) the name of the entity and a statement of its form of organization, e.g., corporation, general partnership, limited partnership, business trust, (ii) the name of the jurisdiction under the laws of which it is organized, (iii) the address, including street and number, if any, of its principal office under the laws of its domiciliary jurisdiction and (iv) the address, including street and number, if any, of its registered office, if any, in this Commonwealth. If any of the entities has an association which has designated the name of a commercial registered office provider in lieu of a registered office address as permitted by 15 Pa.C.S. § 109, the name of the provider and the venue county should be inserted in the last column.

G. Every individual whose name appears in Paragraph 4 of the form **must sign** the form exactly as the name is set forth in Paragraph 4. The name of every other entity listed in Paragraph 5 shall be signed on its behalf by an officer, trustee or other authorized person. See 19 Pa. Code § 13.8(b) (relating to execution), which permits execution pursuant to power of attorney. A copy of the underlying power of attorney or other authorization should not be submitted to, and will not be received by or filed in, the Department.

H. If an individual is a party to the registration, the parties are required by 54 Pa.C.S. § 311(g) to advertise their intention to file or the filing of an application for registration of fictitious name. Proofs of publication of such advertising should not be submitted to the Department, and will not be received by or filed in the Department, but should be kept with the permanent records of the business.

I. This form and all accompanying documents shall be mailed to the address stated above.

This page intentionally left blank.

DSCB: PCF3
Corporation Bureau
Pennsylvania Dept. of State

COUNTER - CORPORATE CERTIFICATION & SEARCH REQUEST FORM

ENTITY NAME: _____

_____

_____

_____

_____

DOCUMENT REQUESTED:

_____ Good Standing (Subsistence) Certificate

_____ Certified Copy of Corporate Index

_____ Great Seal Certificate attesting to _____

_____

_____ Certified Copy of _____

_____ Plain Copy of _____

_____ Corporate Record Search or Plain Copy of Index

_____ Name Reservation

COMMENTS:

REQUESTER NAME: _____

REQUESTER ADDRESS: _____

_____

Mail this order when complete. _____

The undersigned agrees to pay all statutory fees with respect to this request in advance.

SIGNATURE OF REQUESTING PARTY: _____

_____ Will pay by check.

_____ Deduct fees from Account# _____.

Total Due: $_____

This page intentionally left blank.

PENNSYLVANIA DEPARTMENT OF STATE
CORPORATION BUREAU

Application for Registration of Mark
(54 Pa.C.S. § 1112)

Name
Address
City   State   Zip Code

Document will be returned to the name and address you enter to the left.
⇐

Fee: $50

    In compliance with the requirements of the 54 Pa.C.S. § 1112 (relating to application for registration), the undersigned, having adopted and used a trade mark or service mark in this Commonwealth and desiring to register such mark, hereby states that:

1. The name of the applicant is *(see instruction A)*:

_____

2. The residence, location or place of business of the applicant is:

_____

    Number and street   City   State   Zip   County

3. The name and description of the mark is *(a facsimile of the mark to be registered accompanies this application as Exhibit A and is incorporated herein by reference)*:

_____

_____

4. General class in which such goods or services fall is *(use only one of the classifications as set forth in the general classes of goods and services established by the United States Patent and Trademark Office attached)*:

_____

DSCB:54-1112– 2

5. The goods or services in connection with which the mark is used and the mode and manner in which the mark is used in connection with such goods or services are:

_____

6. The date when the mark was first used anywhere is:

_____

7. The date when the mark was first used in this Commonwealth by the applicant or the predecessor in interest is:

_____

8. The date, if any, an application to register the mark, or portions or a composite thereof, was filed by the applicant or a predecessor in interest in the United States Patent and Trademark Office. Also provide filing date and serial number of each application, the status thereof and, if any application was finally refused registration, or has otherwise not resulted in a registration, the reasons therefore. *(Please attach 8½ x 11 sheet(s) if more space is needed.)*

_____

_____

9. Applicant is the owner of the mark, that the mark is in use and that, to the applicant's knowledge, no other person has registered, either federally or in this Commonwealth or has the right to use such mark, either in the identical form thereof or in such near resemblance thereto as to be likely, when applied to the goods or services of such other person, to cause confusion, or to cause mistake, or to deceive.

IN TESTIMONY WHEREOF, the undersigned person has caused this Application for Registration of Mark to be executed this_____ day of _____,_____.

_____
Name of Applicant

_____
Signature

_____
Title

DSCB:54-1112-3

Department of State
Corporation Bureau
P.O. Box 8722
Harrisburg, PA 17105-8722
(717) 787-1057
web site: www.dos.state.pa.us/corps

Instructions for Completion of Form:

A. If a corporation, set forth the name in Paragraph 1 and also give jurisdiction of incorporation. If a partnership, set forth the name in Paragraph 1 and also give the jurisdiction in which the partnership is organized and the names of the general partners.

B. Typewritten is preferred. If not, the form must be completed in black ink in order to permit reproduction. The filing fee for this form is $50 made payable to the Department of State.

C. The name of a commercial registered office provider may not be used in Paragraph 2 in lieu of an address.

D. An application for registration of a mark is limited to a single general class of goods or services, but a mark may be made the subject of multiple registrations in two or more general classes. (See general classes of goods and services established by the United States Patent and Trademark Office in accordance with the International Classification System attached).

E. This registration is effective for a term of five years from the date of registration. Application to renew for a similar term must be made on form DSCB:54-1114 (Application for Renewal of Registration of Mark) within six months prior to the expiration of such term.

F. This form and all accompanying documents shall be mailed to the address listed above.

Schedule of classes of goods and services.

GOODS

1. Chemical products used in industry, science, photography, agriculture, horticulture, forestry; artificial and synthetic resins; plastics in the form of powders, liquids or pastes, for industrial use; manures (natural and artificial); fire extinguishing compositions; tempering substances and chemical preparations for soldering; chemical substances for preserving foodstuffs; tanning substances; adhesive substances used in industry.
2. Paints, varnishes, lacquers; preservatives against rust and against deterioration of wood; coloring matters, dyestuffs; mordants; natural resins metals in foil and powder form for painters and decorators.
3. Bleaching preparations and other substances for laundry use; cleaning, polishing, scouring and abrasive preparations; soaps; perfumery, essential oils, cosmetics, hair lotions; dentifrices.
4. Industrial oils and greases (other than edible oils and fats and essential oils); lubricants; dust laying and absorbing compositions; fuels (including motor spirit) and illuminants; candles, tapers, night-lights and wicks.
5. Pharmaceutical, veterinary and sanitary substances; infants' and invalids' foods; plasters, material for bandaging; material for stopping teeth, dental wax; disinfectants; preparations for killing weeds and destroying vermin.
6. Unwrought and partly wrought common metals and their alloys; anchors, anvils, bells, rolled and cast building materials; rails and other metallic materials for railway tracks; chains (except driving chains for vehicles); cables and wires (non-electric); locksmiths' work; metallic pipes and tubes; safes and cash boxes; steel balls; horseshoes; nails and screws; other goods in nonprecious metal not included in other classes; ores.
7. Machines and machine tools; motors (except for land vehicles); machine couplings and belting (except for land vehicles); large size agricultural implements; incubators.
8. Hand tools and instruments; cutlery, forks and spoons; side arms.
9. Scientific, nautical, surveying and electrical apparatus and instruments (including wireless), photographic, cinematographic, optical, weighing, measuring, signaling, checking (supervision), lifesaving and teaching apparatus and instruments; coin or counter-fed apparatus; talking machines; cash registers; calculating machines; fire extinguishing apparatus.
10. Surgical, medical, dental and veterinary instruments and apparatus (including artificial limbs, eyes and teeth).
11. Installations for lighting, heating, steam generating, cooking, refrigerating, drying, ventilating, water supply and sanitary purposes.
12. Vehicles; apparatus for locomotion by land, air or water.
13. Firearms; ammunition and projectiles; explosive substances; fireworks.
14. Precious metals and their alloys and goods in precious metals or coated therewith (except cutlery, forks and spoons); jewelry, precious stones, horological and other chronometric instruments.
15. Musical instruments (other than talking machines and wireless apparatus).
16. Paper and paper articles, cardboard and cardboard articles; printed matter, newspapers and periodicals, books; bookbinding material; photographs, stationery, adhesive materials (stationery); artists' materials; paint brushes; typewriters and office requisites (other than furniture); instructional and teaching material (other than apparatus); playing cards; printers' type and cliches (stereotype).
17. Gutta-percha, India rubber, balata and substitutes, articles made from these substances and not included in other classes; plastics in the form of sheets, blocks and rods, being for use in manufacture; materials for packing, stopping or insulating; asbestos, mica and their products; hose pipes (nonmetallic).
18. Leather and imitations of leather, and articles made from these materials and not included in other classes; skins, hides; trunks and traveling bags; umbrellas, parasols and walking sticks, whips, harness and saddlery.
19. Building materials, natural and artificial stone, cement, lime, mortar, plaster and gravel; pipes of earthenware or cement; road-making materials; asphalt, pitch and bitumen; portable buildings; stone monuments; chimney pots.
20. Furniture, mirrors, picture frames; articles (not included in other classes) of wood, cork, reeds, cane, wicker, horn, bone, ivory, whalebone, shell, amber, mother-of-pearl, meerschaum, celluloid, substitutes for all these materials, or of plastics.
21. Small domestic utensils and containers (not of precious metal or coated therewith); combs and sponges; brushes (other than paint brushes); brush-making materials; instruments and material for cleaning purposes; steel wool; glassware, porcelain and earthenware, not included in other classes.
22. Ropes, string, nets, tents, awnings, tarpaulins, sails, sacks; padding and stuffing materials (hair, capoc, feathers, seaweed, etc.); raw fibrous textile materials.
23. Yarns, threads.
24. Tissues (piece goods); bed and table covers; textile articles not included in other classes.
25. Clothing, including boots, shoes and slippers.
26. Lace and embroidery, ribbons and braid; buttons, press buttons, hooks and eyes, pins and needles; artificial flowers.
27. Carpets, rugs, mats and matting; linoleums and other materials for covering floors; wall hangings (nontextile).
28. Games and playthings; gymnastic and sporting articles (except clothing); ornaments and decorations for Christmas trees.

29. Meat, fish, poultry and game; meat extracts; preserved, dried and cooked fruits and vegetables; jellies, jams; eggs, milk and other dairy products; edible oils and fats; preserves, pickles.
30. Coffee, tea, cocoa, sugar, rice, tapioca, sago, coffee substitutes; flour and preparations made from cereals; bread, biscuits,

cakes, pastry and confectionery, ices, honey, treacle; yeast, baking powder; salt, mustard; pepper, vinegar, sauces, spices; ice.

31. Agricultural, horticultural and forestry products and grains not included in other classes; living animals; fresh fruits and vegetables; seeds; live plants and flowers; foodstuffs for animals, malt.

32. Beer, ale and porter; mineral and aerated waters and other nonalcoholic drinks; syrups and other preparations for making beverages.

33. Wines, spirits and liqueurs.

34. Tobacco, raw or manufactured; smokers' articles; matches.

SERVICES

35. Advertising and business.
36. Insurance and financial.
37. Construction and repair.
38. Communication.
39. Transportation and storage.
40. Material treatment.
41. Education and entertainment.
42. Computer, scientific and legal
43. Hotels and restaurants
44. Medical, beauty and agricultural
45. Personal

This page intentionally left blank.

Department of Homeland Security
U.S. Citizenship and Immigration Services

OMB No. 1615-0047; Expires 03/31/07

Employment Eligibility Verification

Please read instructions carefully before completing this form. The instructions must be available during completion of this form. **ANTI-DISCRIMINATION NOTICE:** It is illegal to discriminate against work eligible individuals. Employers **CANNOT** specify which document(s) they will accept from an employee. The refusal to hire an individual because of a future expiration date may also constitute illegal discrimination.

Section 1. Employee Information and Verification. To be completed and signed by employee at the time employment begins.

Print Name: Last	First	Middle Initial	Maiden Name

Address (Street Name and Number)		Apt. #	Date of Birth (month/day/year)

City	State	Zip Code	Social Security #

I am aware that federal law provides for imprisonment and/or fines for false statements or use of false documents in connection with the completion of this form.

I attest, under penalty of perjury, that I am (check one of the following):

☐ A citizen or national of the United States
☐ A Lawful Permanent Resident (Alien #) A _____
☐ An alien authorized to work until _____
(Alien # or Admission #) _____

Employee's Signature	Date (month/day/year)

Preparer and/or Translator Certification. (To be completed and signed if Section 1 is prepared by a person other than the employee.) I attest, under penalty of perjury, that I have assisted in the completion of this form and that to the best of my knowledge the information is true and correct.

Preparer's/Translator's Signature	Print Name

Address (Street Name and Number, City, State, Zip Code)	Date (month/day/year)

Section 2. Employer Review and Verification. To be completed and signed by employer. Examine one document from List A OR examine one document from List B and one from List C, as listed on the reverse of this form, and record the title, number and expiration date, if any, of the document(s).

List A	OR	List B	AND	List C
Document title: _____		_____		_____
Issuing authority: _____		_____		_____
Document #: _____		_____		_____
Expiration Date (if any): _____		_____		_____
Document #: _____				
Expiration Date (if any): _____				

CERTIFICATION - Iattest, under penalty of perjury, that I have examined the document(s) presented by the above-named employee, that the above-listed document(s) appear to be genuine and to relate to the employee named, that the employee began employment on (month/day/year) _____ and that to the best of my knowledge the employee is eligible to work in the United States. (State employment agencies may omit the date the employee began employment.)

Signature of Employer or Authorized Representative	Print Name	Title

Business or Organization Name	Address (Street Name and Number, City, State, Zip Code)	Date (month/day/year)

Section 3. Updating and Reverification. To be completed and signed by employer.

A. New Name (if applicable)	B. Date of Rehire (month/day/year) (if applicable)

C. If employee's previous grant of work authorization has expired, provide the information below for the document that establishes current employment eligibility.

Document Title: _____   Document #: _____   Expiration Date (if any): _____

I attest, under penalty of perjury, that to the best of my knowledge, this employee is eligible to work in the United States, and if the employee presented document(s), the document(s) I have examined appear to be genuine and to relate to the individual.

Signature of Employer or Authorized Representative	Date (month/day/year)

NOTE: This is the 1991 edition of the Form I-9 that has been rebranded with a current printing date to reflect the recent transition from the INS to DHS and its components.

Form I-9 (Rev. 05/31/05)Y Page 2

Department of Homeland Security
U.S. Citizenship and Immigration Services

OMB No. 1615-0047; Expires 03/31/07

Employment Eligibility Verification

INSTRUCTIONS
PLEASE READ ALL INSTRUCTIONS CAREFULLY BEFORE COMPLETING THIS FORM.

Anti-Discrimination Notice. It is illegal to discriminate against any individual (other than an alien not authorized to work in the U.S.) in hiring, discharging, or recruiting or referring for a fee because of that individual's national origin or citizenship status. It is illegal to discriminate against work eligible individuals. Employers **CANNOT** specify which document(s) they will accept from an employee. The refusal to hire an individual because of a future expiration date may also constitute illegal discrimination.

Section 1- Employee. All employees, citizens and noncitizens, hired after November 6, 1986, must complete Section 1 of this form at the time of hire, which is the actual beginning of employment. **The employer is responsible for ensuring that Section 1 is timely and properly completed.**

Preparer/Translator Certification. The Preparer/Translator Certification must be completed if Section 1 is prepared by a person other than the employee. A preparer/translator may be used only when the employee is unable to complete Section 1 on his/her own. However, the employee must still sign Section 1 personally.

Section 2 - Employer. For the purpose of completing this form, the term "employer" includes those recruiters and referrers for a fee who are agricultural associations, agricultural employers or farm labor contractors.

Employers must complete Section 2 by examining evidence of identity and employment eligibility within three (3) business days of the date employment begins. If employees are authorized to work, but are unable to present the required document(s) within three business days, they must present a receipt for the application of the document(s) within three business days and the actual document(s) within ninety (90) days. However, if employers hire individuals for a duration of less than three business days, Section 2 must be completed at the time employment begins. **Employers must record: 1)** document title; **2)** issuing authority; **3)** document number, **4)** expiration date, if any; and **5)** the date employment begins. Employers must sign and date the certification. Employees must present original documents. Employers may, but are not required to, photocopy the document(s) presented. These photocopies may only be used for the verification process and must be retained with the I-9. **However, employers are still responsible for completing the I-9.**

Section 3 - Updating and Reverification. Employers must complete Section 3 when updating and/or reverifying the I-9. Employers must reverify employment eligibility of their employees on or before the expiration date recorded in Section 1. Employers **CANNOT** specify which document(s) they will accept from an employee.

- If an employee's name has changed at the time this form is being updated/reverified, complete Block A.

- If an employee is rehired within three (3) years of the date this form was originally completed and the employee is still eligible to be employed on the same basis as previously indicated on this form (updating), complete Block B and the signature block.

- If an employee is rehired within three (3) years of the date this form was originally completed and the employee's work authorization has expired **or** if a current employee's work authorization is about to expire (reverification), complete Block B and:

- examine any document that reflects that the employee is authorized to work in the U.S. (see List A **or** C),

- record the document title, document number and expiration date (if any) in Block C, and

- complete the signature block.

Photocopying and Retaining Form I-9. A blank I-9 may be reproduced, provided both sides are copied. The Instructions must be available to all employees completing this form. Employers must retain completed I-9s for three (3) years after the date of hire or one (1) year after the date employment ends, whichever is later.

For more detailed information, you may refer to the Department of Homeland Security (DHS) Handbook for Employers, (Form M-274). You may obtain the handbook at your local U.S. Citizenship and Immigration Services (USCIS) office.

Privacy Act Notice. The authority for collecting this information is the Immigration Reform and Control Act of 1986, Pub. L. 99-603 (8 USC 1324a).

This information is for employers to verify the eligibility of individuals for employment to preclude the unlawful hiring, or recruiting or referring for a fee, of aliens who are not authorized to work in the United States.

This information will be used by employers as a record of their basis for determining eligibility of an employee to work in the United States. The form will be kept by the employer and made available for inspection by officials of the U.S. Immigration and Customs Enforcement, Department of Labor and Office of Special Counsel for Immigration Related Unfair Employment Practices.

Submission of the information required in this form is voluntary. However, an individual may not begin employment unless this form is completed, since employers are subject to civil or criminal penalties if they do not comply with the Immigration Reform and Control Act of 1986.

Reporting Burden. We try to create forms and instructions that are accurate, can be easily understood and which impose the least possible burden on you to provide us with information. Often this is difficult because some immigration laws are very complex. Accordingly, the reporting burden for this collection of information is computed as follows: **1)** learning about this form, 5 minutes; **2)** completing the form, 5 minutes; and **3)** assembling and filing (recordkeeping) the form, 5 minutes, for an average of 15 minutes per response. If you have comments regarding the accuracy of this burden estimate, or suggestions for making this form simpler, you can write to U.S. Citizenship and Immigration Services, Regulatory Management Division, 111 Massachuetts Avenue, N.W., Washington, DC 20529. OMB No. 1615-0047.

NOTE: This is the 1991 edition of the Form I-9 that has been rebranded with a current printing date to reflect the recent transition from the INS to DHS and its components.

EMPLOYERS MUST RETAIN COMPLETED FORM I-9
PLEASE DO NOT MAIL COMPLETED FORM I-9 TO ICE OR USCIS

Form I-9 (Rev. 05/31/05)Y

LISTS OF ACCEPTABLE DOCUMENTS

LIST A		**LIST B**		**LIST C**
Documents that Establish Both Identity and Employment Eligibility	**OR**	**Documents that Establish Identity**	**AND**	**Documents that Establish Employment Eligibility**

LIST A

Documents that Establish Both Identity and Employment Eligibility

1. U.S. Passport (unexpired or expired)

2. Certificate of U.S. Citizenship *(Form N-560 or N-561)*

3. Certificate of Naturalization *(Form N-550 or N-570)*

4. Unexpired foreign passport, with *I-551 stamp or* attached *Form I-94* indicating unexpired employment authorization

5. Permanent Resident Card or Alien Registration Receipt Card with photograph *(Form I-151 or I-551)*

6. Unexpired Temporary Resident Card *(Form I-688)*

7. Unexpired Employment Authorization Card *(Form I-688A)*

8. Unexpired Reentry Permit *(Form I-327)*

9. Unexpired Refugee Travel Document *(Form 1-571)*

10. Unexpired Employment Authorization Document issued by DHS that contains a photograph *(Form I-688B)*

OR

LIST B

Documents that Establish Identity

1. Driver's license or ID card issued by a state or outlying possession of the United States provided it contains a photograph or information such as name, date of birth, gender, height, eye color and address

2. ID card issued by federal, state or local government agencies or entities, provided it contains a photograph or information such as name, date of birth, gender, height, eye color and address

3. School ID card with a photograph

4. Voter's registration card

5. U.S. Military card or draft record

6. Military dependent's ID card

7. U.S. Coast Guard Merchant Mariner Card

8. Native American tribal document

9. Driver's license issued by a Canadian government authority

For persons under age 18 who are unable to present a document listed above:

10. School record or report card

11. Clinic, doctor or hospital record

12. Day-care or nursery school record

AND

LIST C

Documents that Establish Employment Eligibility

1. U.S. social security card issued by the Social Security Administration *(other than a card stating it is not valid for employment)*

2. Certification of Birth Abroad issued by the Department of State *(Form FS-545 or Form DS-1350)*

3. Original or certified copy of a birth certificate issued by a state, county, municipal authority or outlying possession of the United States bearing an official seal

4. Native American tribal document

5. U.S. Citizen ID Card *(Form I-197)*

6. ID Card for use of Resident Citizen in the United States *(Form I-179)*

7. Unexpired employment authorization document issued by DHS *(other than those listed under List A)*

Illustrations of many of these documents appear in Part 8 of the Handbook for Employers (M-274)

This page intentionally left blank.

Form **SS-4**
(Rev. February 2006)
Department of the Treasury
Internal Revenue Service

Application for Employer Identification Number

(For use by employers, corporations, partnerships, trusts, estates, churches, government agencies, Indian tribal entities, certain individuals, and others.)

▶ See separate instructions for each line.   ▶ Keep a copy for your records.

OMB No. 1545-0003

EIN

Type or print clearly.	**1** Legal name of entity (or individual) for whom the EIN is being requested

2 Trade name of business (if different from name on line 1)	**3** Executor, administrator, trustee, "care of" name
4a Mailing address (room, apt., suite no. and street, or P.O. box)	**5a** Street address (if different) (Do not enter a P.O. box.)
4b City, state, and ZIP code	**5b** City, state, and ZIP code

6 County and state where principal business is located

7a Name of principal officer, general partner, grantor, owner, or trustor	**7b** SSN, ITIN, or EIN

8a **Type of entity** (check only one box)

☐ Sole proprietor (SSN) _____
☐ Partnership
☐ Corporation (enter form number to be filed) ▶ _____
☐ Personal service corporation
☐ Church or church-controlled organization
☐ Other nonprofit organization (specify) ▶ _____
☐ Other (specify) ▶

☐ Estate (SSN of decedent) _____
☐ Plan administrator (SSN) _____
☐ Trust (SSN of grantor) _____
☐ National Guard   ☐ State/local government
☐ Farmers' cooperative   ☐ Federal government/military
☐ REMIC   ☐ Indian tribal governments/enterprises
Group Exemption Number (GEN) ▶ _____

8b If a corporation, name the state or foreign country (if applicable) where incorporated

State	Foreign country

9 **Reason for applying** (check only one box)

☐ Started new business (specify type) ▶ _____
☐ Hired employees (Check the box and see line 12.)
☐ Compliance with IRS withholding regulations
☐ Other (specify) ▶

☐ Banking purpose (specify purpose) ▶ _____
☐ Changed type of organization (specify new type) ▶ _____
☐ Purchased going business
☐ Created a trust (specify type) ▶ _____
☐ Created a pension plan (specify type) ▶ _____

10 Date business started or acquired (month, day, year). See instructions.	**11** Closing month of accounting year

12 First date wages or annuities were paid (month, day, year). **Note.** If applicant is a withholding agent, enter date income will first be paid to nonresident alien. (month, day, year) . . . . ▶

13 Highest number of employees expected in the next 12 months (enter -0- if none).

	Agricultural	Household	Other

Do you expect to have $1,000 or less in employment tax liability for the calendar year? ☐ **Yes** ☐ **No.** (If you expect to pay $4,000 or less in wages, you can mark yes.)

14 Check **one** box that best describes the principal activity of your business.

☐ Construction ☐ Rental & leasing ☐ Transportation & warehousing ☐ Health care & social assistance ☐ Wholesale–agent/broker
☐ Real estate   ☐ Manufacturing   ☐ Finance & insurance   ☐ Accommodation & food service   ☐ Wholesale–other   ☐ Retail
                                    ☐ Other (specify)

15 Indicate principal line of merchandise sold, specific construction work done, products produced, or services provided.

16a Has the applicant ever applied for an employer identification number for this or any other business? . . . . ☐ **Yes** ☐ **No**
Note. If "Yes," please complete lines 16b and 16c.

16b If you checked "Yes" on line 16a, give applicant's legal name and trade name shown on prior application if different from line 1 or 2 above.
Legal name ▶   Trade name ▶

16c Approximate date when, and city and state where, the application was filed. Enter previous employer identification number if known.

Approximate date when filed (mo., day, year)	City and state where filed	Previous EIN

Third Party Designee	Complete this section **only** if you want to authorize the named individual to receive the entity's EIN and answer questions about the completion of this form.
	Designee's name	Designee's telephone number (include area code) ( )
	Address and ZIP code	Designee's fax number (include area code) ( )

Under penalties of perjury, I declare that I have examined this application, and to the best of my knowledge and belief, it is true, correct, and complete.

Name and title (type or print clearly) ▶

Applicant's telephone number (include area code) ( )

Signature ▶   Date ▶

Applicant's fax number (include area code) ( )

For Privacy Act and Paperwork Reduction Act Notice, see separate instructions.   Cat. No. 16055N   Form **SS-4** (Rev. 2-2006)

Do I Need an EIN?

File Form SS-4 if the applicant entity does not already have an EIN but is required to show an EIN on any return, statement, or other document.[1] See also the separate instructions for each line on Form SS-4.

IF the applicant...	AND...	THEN...
Started a new business	Does not currently have (nor expect to have) employees	Complete lines 1, 2, 4a–8a, 8b (if applicable), and 9–16c.
Hired (or will hire) employees, including household employees	Does not already have an EIN	Complete lines 1, 2, 4a–6, 7a–b (if applicable), 8a, 8b (if applicable), and 9–16c.
Opened a bank account	Needs an EIN for banking purposes only	Complete lines 1–5b, 7a–b (if applicable), 8a, 9, and 16a–c.
Changed type of organization	Either the legal character of the organization or its ownership changed (for example, you incorporate a sole proprietorship or form a partnership)[2]	Complete lines 1–16c (as applicable).
Purchased a going business[3]	Does not already have an EIN	Complete lines 1–16c (as applicable).
Created a trust	The trust is other than a grantor trust or an IRA trust[4]	Complete lines 1–16c (as applicable).
Created a pension plan as a plan administrator[5]	Needs an EIN for reporting purposes	Complete lines 1, 3, 4a–b, 8a, 9, and 16a–c.
Is a foreign person needing an EIN to comply with IRS withholding regulations	Needs an EIN to complete a Form W-8 (other than Form W-8ECI), avoid withholding on portfolio assets, or claim tax treaty benefits[6]	Complete lines 1–5b, 7a–b (SSN or ITIN optional), 8a–9, and 16a–c.
Is administering an estate	Needs an EIN to report estate income on Form 1041	Complete lines 1, 2, 3, 4a–6, 8a, 9-11, 12-15 (if applicable), and 16a–c.
Is a withholding agent for taxes on non-wage income paid to an alien (i.e., individual, corporation, or partnership, etc.)	Is an agent, broker, fiduciary, manager, tenant, or spouse who is required to file Form 1042, Annual Withholding Tax Return for U.S. Source Income of Foreign Persons	Complete lines 1, 2, 3 (if applicable), 4a–5b, 7a–b (if applicable), 8a, 9, and 16a–c.
Is a state or local agency	Serves as a tax reporting agent for public assistance recipients under Rev. Proc. 80-4, 1980-1 C.B. 581[7]	Complete lines 1, 2, 4a–5b, 8a, 9, and 16a–c.
Is a single-member LLC	Needs an EIN to file Form 8832, Entity Classification Election, for filing employment tax returns, **or** for state reporting purposes[8]	Complete lines 1–16c (as applicable).
Is an S corporation	Needs an EIN to file Form 2553, Election by a Small Business Corporation[9]	Complete lines 1–16c (as applicable).

[1] For example, a sole proprietorship or self-employed farmer who establishes a qualified retirement plan, or is required to file excise, employment, alcohol, tobacco, or firearms returns, must have an EIN. A partnership, corporation, REMIC (real estate mortgage investment conduit), nonprofit organization (church, club, etc.), or farmers' cooperative must use an EIN for any tax-related purpose even if the entity does not have employees.

[2] However, do not apply for a new EIN if the existing entity only (a) changed its business name, (b) elected on Form 8832 to change the way it is taxed (or is covered by the default rules), or (c) terminated its partnership status because at least 50% of the total interests in partnership capital and profits were sold or exchanged within a 12-month period. The EIN of the terminated partnership should continue to be used. See Regulations section 301.6109-1(d)(2)(iii).

[3] Do not use the EIN of the prior business unless you became the "owner" of a corporation by acquiring its stock.

[4] However, grantor trusts that do not file using Optional Method 1 and IRA trusts that are required to file Form 990-T, Exempt Organization Business Income Tax Return, must have an EIN. For more information on grantor trusts, see the Instructions for Form 1041.

[5] A plan administrator is the person or group of persons specified as the administrator by the instrument under which the plan is operated.

[6] Entities applying to be a Qualified Intermediary (QI) need a QI-EIN even if they already have an EIN. See Rev. Proc. 2000-12.

[7] See also *Household employer* on page 3. **Note.** State or local agencies may need an EIN for other reasons, for example, hired employees.

[8] Most LLCs do not need to file Form 8832. See *Limited liability company (LLC)* on page 4 for details on completing Form SS-4 for an LLC.

[9] An existing corporation that is electing or revoking S corporation status should use its previously-assigned EIN.

Form SS-8
(Rev. June 2003)
Department of the Treasury
Internal Revenue Service

Determination of Worker Status
for Purposes of Federal Employment Taxes
and Income Tax Withholding

OMB No. 1545-0004

Name of firm (or person) for whom the worker performed services	Worker's name

Firm's address (include street address, apt. or suite no., city, state, and ZIP code)	Worker's address (include street address, apt. or suite no., city, state, and ZIP code)

Trade name	Telephone number (include area code) ( )	Worker's social security number

Telephone number (include area code) ( )	Firm's employer identification number	Worker's employer identification number (if any)

If the worker is paid by a firm other than the one listed on this form for these services, enter the name, address, and employer identification number of the payer.

Important Information Needed To Process Your Request

We must have your permission to disclose your name and the information on this form and any attachments to other parties involved with this request. **Do we have your permission to disclose this information?** . . . . ☐ **Yes** ☐ **No**
If you answered "No" or did not mark a box, we will not process your request and will not issue a determination.

You must answer ALL items OR mark them "Unknown" or "Does not apply." If you need more space, attach another sheet.

A This form is being completed by: ☐ Firm ☐ Worker; for services performed _____ to _____ .
(beginning date)   (ending date)

B Explain your reason(s) for filing this form (e.g., you received a bill from the IRS, you believe you received a Form 1099 or Form W-2 erroneously, you are unable to get worker's compensation benefits, you were audited or are being audited by the IRS). ----------------------
----

C Total number of workers who performed or are performing the same or similar services _____ .
D How did the worker obtain the job? ☐ Application ☐ Bid ☐ Employment Agency ☐ Other (specify) _____ .

E Attach copies of all supporting documentation (contracts, invoices, memos, Forms W-2, Forms 1099, IRS closing agreements, IRS rulings, etc.). In addition, please inform us of any current or past litigation concerning the worker's status. If no income reporting forms (Form 1099-MISC or W-2) were furnished to the worker, enter the amount of income earned for the year(s) at issue $ _____ .
F Describe the firm's business. --

G Describe the work done by the worker and provide the worker's job title. ----------------------
----

H Explain why you believe the worker is an employee or an independent contractor. ----------------------
----

I Did the worker perform services for the firm before getting this position? . . . . ☐ **Yes** ☐ **No** ☐ **N/A**
If "Yes," what were the dates of the prior service? --
If "Yes," explain the differences, if any, between the current and prior service. ----------------------
----

J If the work is done under a written agreement between the firm and the worker, attach a copy (preferably signed by both parties). Describe the terms and conditions of the work arrangement. --
----

For Privacy Act and Paperwork Reduction Act Notice, see page 5.   Cat. No. 16106T   Form **SS-8** (Rev. 6-2003)

Page **2**

Part I **Behavioral Control**

1. What specific training and/or instruction is the worker given by the firm? ....

2. How does the worker receive work assignments? ....

3. Who determines the methods by which the assignments are performed? ....

4. Who is the worker required to contact if problems or complaints arise and who is responsible for their resolution? ....

5. What types of reports are required from the worker? Attach examples. ....

6. Describe the worker's daily routine (i.e., schedule, hours, etc.). ....

7. At what location(s) does the worker perform services (e.g., firm's premises, own shop or office, home, customer's location, etc.)? ....

8. Describe any meetings the worker is required to attend and any penalties for not attending (e.g., sales meetings, monthly meetings, staff meetings, etc.). ....

9. Is the worker required to provide the services personally? . . . . ☐ **Yes** ☐ **No**

10. If substitutes or helpers are needed, who hires them? ....

11. If the worker hires the substitutes or helpers, is approval required? . . . . ☐ **Yes** ☐ **No**
    If "Yes," by whom? ....

12. Who pays the substitutes or helpers? ....

13. Is the worker reimbursed if the worker pays the substitutes or helpers? . . . . ☐ **Yes** ☐ **No**
    If "Yes," by whom? ....

Part II **Financial Control**

1. List the supplies, equipment, materials, and property provided by each party:
   The firm ....
   The worker ....
   Other party ....

2. Does the worker lease equipment? . . . . ☐ **Yes** ☐ **No**
   If "Yes," what are the terms of the lease? (Attach a copy or explanatory statement.) ....

3. What expenses are incurred by the worker in the performance of services for the firm? ....

4. Specify which, if any, expenses are reimbursed by:
   The firm ....
   Other party ....

5. Type of pay the worker receives: ☐ Salary ☐ Commission ☐ Hourly Wage ☐ Piece Work
   ☐ Lump Sum ☐ Other (specify) ....
   If type of pay is commission, and the firm guarantees a minimum amount of pay, specify amount $ _____ .

6. Is the worker allowed a drawing account for advances? . . . . ☐ **Yes** ☐ **No**
   If "Yes," how often? ....
   Specify any restrictions. ....

7. Whom does the customer pay? . . . . ☐ Firm ☐ Worker
   If worker, does the worker pay the total amount to the firm? ☐ **Yes** ☐ **No** If "No," explain. ....

8. Does the firm carry worker's compensation insurance on the worker? . . . . ☐ **Yes** ☐ **No**

9. What economic loss or financial risk, if any, can the worker incur beyond the normal loss of salary (e.g., loss or damage of equipment, material, etc.)? ....

Form SS-8 (Rev. 6-2003)   Page **3**

Part III   Relationship of the Worker and Firm

1   List the benefits available to the worker (e.g., paid vacations, sick pay, pensions, bonuses). ------------------------------
----

2   Can the relationship be terminated by either party without incurring liability or penalty?   . . . .   ☐ **Yes**   ☐ **No**
    If "No," explain your answer. --
----

3   Does the worker perform similar services for others?   . . . .   ☐ **Yes**   ☐ **No**
    If "Yes," is the worker required to get approval from the firm?   . . . .   ☐ **Yes**   ☐ **No**

4   Describe any agreements prohibiting competition between the worker and the firm while the worker is performing services or during any later period. Attach any available documentation. ---
----

5   Is the worker a member of a union?   . . . .   ☐ **Yes**   ☐ **No**

6   What type of advertising, if any, does the worker do (e.g., a business listing in a directory, business cards, etc.)? Provide copies, if applicable.
----

7   If the worker assembles or processes a product at home, who provides the materials and instructions or pattern? ----------------
----

8   What does the worker do with the finished product (e.g., return it to the firm, provide it to another party, or sell it)? --------------
----

9   How does the firm represent the worker to its customers (e.g., employee, partner, representative, or contractor)? --------------
----

10   If the worker no longer performs services for the firm, how did the relationship end? --
----

Part IV   For Service Providers or Salespersons—Complete this part if the worker provided a service directly to customers or is a salesperson.

1   What are the worker's responsibilities in soliciting new customers? --
----

2   Who provides the worker with leads to prospective customers? ---

3   Describe any reporting requirements pertaining to the leads. ---
----

4   What terms and conditions of sale, if any, are required by the firm? --

5   Are orders submitted to and subject to approval by the firm?   . . . .   ☐ **Yes**   ☐ **No**

6   Who determines the worker's territory? ---

7   Did the worker pay for the privilege of serving customers on the route or in the territory?   . . . .   ☐ **Yes**   ☐ **No**
    If "Yes," whom did the worker pay? --
    If "Yes," how much did the worker pay?   . . . . $ _____ .

8   Where does the worker sell the product (e.g., in a home, retail establishment, etc.)? --
----

9   List the product and/or services distributed by the worker (e.g., meat, vegetables, fruit, bakery products, beverages, or laundry or dry cleaning services). If more than one type of product and/or service is distributed, specify the principal one. -------------------------------
----

10   Does the worker sell life insurance full time?   . . . .   ☐ **Yes**   ☐ **No**

11   Does the worker sell other types of insurance for the firm?   . . . .   ☐ **Yes**   ☐ **No**
    If "Yes," enter the percentage of the worker's total working time spent in selling other types of insurance.   . . .   _____ %

12   If the worker solicits orders from wholesalers, retailers, contractors, or operators of hotels, restaurants, or other similar establishments, enter the percentage of the worker's time spent in the solicitation.   . . . .   _____ %

13   Is the merchandise purchased by the customers for resale or use in their business operations?   . . . .   ☐ **Yes**   ☐ **No**
    Describe the merchandise and state whether it is equipment installed on the customers' premises. ----------------------------
----

Part V   Signature (see page 4)

Under penalties of perjury, I declare that I have examined this request, including accompanying documents, and to the best of my knowledge and belief, the facts presented are true, correct, and complete.

Signature ▶ _____   Title ▶ _____   Date ▶ _____
                 (Type or print name below)

Time for filing a claim for refund. Generally, you must file your claim for a credit or refund within 3 years from the date your original return was filed or within 2 years from the date the tax was paid, whichever is later.

Filing Form SS-8 does not prevent the expiration of the time in which a claim for a refund must be filed. If you are concerned about a refund, and the statute of limitations for filing a claim for refund for the year(s) at issue has not yet expired, you should file **Form 1040X,** Amended U.S. Individual Income Tax Return, to protect your statute of limitations. File a separate Form 1040X for each year.

On the Form 1040X you file, do not complete lines 1 through 24 on the form. Write "Protective Claim" at the top of the form, sign and date it. In addition, you should enter the following statement in Part II, Explanation of Changes to Income, Deductions, and Credits: "Filed Form SS-8 with the Internal Revenue Service Office in (Holtsville, NY; Newport, VT; or Washington, DC; as appropriate). By filing this protective claim, I reserve the right to file a claim for any refund that may be due after a determination of my employment tax status has been completed."

Filing Form SS-8 does not alter the requirement to timely file an income tax return. Do not delay filing your tax return in anticipation of an answer to your SS-8 request. In addition, if applicable, do not delay in responding to a request for payment while waiting for a determination of your worker status.

Instructions for Firms

If a **worker** has requested a determination of his or her status while working for you, you will receive a request from the IRS to complete a Form SS-8. In cases of this type, the IRS usually gives each party an opportunity to present a statement of the facts because any decision will affect the employment tax status of the parties. Failure to respond to this request will not prevent the IRS from issuing a determination letter based on the information he or she has made available so that the worker may fulfill his or her Federal tax obligations. However, the information that you provide is extremely valuable in determining the status of the worker.

If **you** are requesting a determination for a particular class of worker, complete the form for **one** individual who is representative of the class of workers whose status is in question. If you want a written determination for more than one class of workers, complete a separate Form SS-8 for one worker from each class whose status is typical of that class. A written determination for any worker will apply to other workers of the same class if the facts are not materially different for these workers. Please provide a list of names and addresses of all workers potentially affected by this determination.

If you have a reasonable basis for not treating a worker as an employee, you may be relieved from having to pay employment taxes for that worker under section 530 of the 1978 Revenue Act. However, this relief provision cannot be considered in conjunction with a Form SS-8 determination because the determination does not constitute an examination of any tax return. For more information regarding section 530 of the 1978 Revenue Act and to determine if you qualify for relief under this section, you may visit the IRS website at **www.irs.gov**.

Privacy Act and Paperwork Reduction Act Notice. We ask for the information on this form to carry out the Internal Revenue laws of the United States. This information will be used to determine the employment status of the worker(s) described on the form. Subtitle C, Employment Taxes, of the Internal Revenue Code imposes employment taxes on wages. Sections 3121(d), 3306(a), and 3401(c) and (d) and the related regulations define employee and employer for purposes of employment taxes imposed under Subtitle C. Section 6001 authorizes the IRS to request information needed to determine if a worker(s) or firm is subject to these taxes. Section 6109 requires you to provide your taxpayer identification number. Neither workers nor firms are required to request a status determination, but if you choose to do so, you must provide the information requested on this form. Failure to provide the requested information may prevent us from making a status determination. If any worker or the firm has requested a status determination and you are being asked to provide information for use in that determination, you are not required to provide the requested information. However, failure to provide such information will prevent the IRS from considering it in making the status determination. Providing false or fraudulent information may subject you to penalties. Routine uses of this information include providing it to the Department of Justice for use in civil and criminal litigation, to the Social Security Administration for the administration of social security programs, and to cities, states, and the District of Columbia for the administration of their tax laws. We may also disclose this information to Federal and state agencies to enforce Federal nontax criminal laws and to combat terrorism. We may provide this information to the affected worker(s) or the firm as part of the status determination process.

You are not required to provide the information requested on a form that is subject to the Paperwork Reduction Act unless the form displays a valid OMB control number. Books or records relating to a form or its instructions must be retained as long as their contents may become material in the administration of any Internal Revenue law. Generally, tax returns and return information are confidential, as required by section 6103.

The time needed to complete and file this form will vary depending on individual circumstances. The estimated average time is: **Recordkeeping,** 22 hrs.; **Learning about the law or the form,** 47 min.; and **Preparing and sending the form to the IRS,** 1 hr., 11 min. If you have comments concerning the accuracy of these time estimates or suggestions for making this form simpler, we would be happy to hear from you. You can write to the Tax Products Coordinating Committee, Western Area Distribution Center, Rancho Cordova, CA 95743-0001. **Do not** send the tax form to this address. Instead, see **Where To File** on page 4.

Form W-4 (2006)

Purpose. Complete Form W-4 so that your employer can withhold the correct federal income tax from your pay. Because your tax situation may change, you may want to refigure your withholding each year.

Exemption from withholding. If you are exempt, complete only lines 1, 2, 3, 4, and 7 and sign the form to validate it. Your exemption for 2006 expires February 16, 2007. See Pub. 505, Tax Withholding and Estimated Tax.

Note. You cannot claim exemption from withholding if (a) your income exceeds $850 and includes more than $300 of unearned income (for example, interest and dividends) and (b) another person can claim you as a dependent on their tax return.

Basic instructions. If you are not exempt, complete the **Personal Allowances Worksheet** below. The worksheets on page 2 adjust your withholding allowances based on itemized deductions, certain credits, adjustments to income, or two-earner/two-job situations. Complete all worksheets that apply. However, you may claim fewer (or zero) allowances.

Head of household. Generally, you may claim head of household filing status on your tax return only if you are unmarried and pay more than 50% of the costs of keeping up a home for yourself and your dependent(s) or other qualifying individuals. See line **E** below.

Tax credits. You can take projected tax credits into account in figuring your allowable number of withholding allowances. Credits for child or dependent care expenses and the child tax credit may be claimed using the **Personal Allowances Worksheet** below. See Pub. 919, How Do I Adjust My Tax Withholding, for information on converting your other credits into withholding allowances.

Nonwage income. If you have a large amount of nonwage income, such as interest or dividends, consider making estimated tax payments using Form 1040-ES, Estimated Tax for Individuals. Otherwise, you may owe additional tax.

Two earners/two jobs. If you have a working spouse or more than one job, figure the total number of allowances you are entitled to claim on all jobs using worksheets from only one Form W-4. Your withholding usually will be most accurate when all allowances are claimed on the Form W-4 for the highest paying job and zero allowances are claimed on the others.

Nonresident alien. If you are a nonresident alien, see the Instructions for Form 8233 before completing this Form W-4.

Check your withholding. After your Form W-4 takes effect, use Pub. 919 to see how the dollar amount you are having withheld compares to your projected total tax for 2006. See Pub. 919, especially if your earnings exceed $130,000 (Single) or $180,000 (Married).

Recent name change? If your name on line 1 differs from that shown on your social security card, call 1-800-772-1213 to initiate a name change and obtain a social security card showing your correct name.

Personal Allowances Worksheet (Keep for your records.)

A Enter "1" for **yourself** if no one else can claim you as a dependent . . . . **A** _____

B Enter "1" if:
- You are single and have only one job; or
- You are married, have only one job, and your spouse does not work; or
- Your wages from a second job or your spouse's wages (or the total of both) are $1,000 or less.

B _____

C Enter "1" for your **spouse.** But, you may choose to enter "-0-" if you are married and have either a working spouse or more than one job. (Entering "-0-" may help you avoid having too little tax withheld.) . . . . **C** _____

D Enter number of **dependents** (other than your spouse or yourself) you will claim on your tax return . . . . . . **D** _____

E Enter "1" if you will file as **head of household** on your tax return (see conditions under **Head of household** above) . **E** _____

F Enter "1" if you have at least $1,500 of **child or dependent care expenses** for which you plan to claim a credit . . **F** _____
(**Note.** Do **not** include child support payments. See **Pub. 503,** Child and Dependent Care Expenses, for details.)

G **Child Tax Credit** (including additional child tax credit):
- If your total income will be less than $55,000 ($82,000 if married), enter "2" for each eligible child.
- If your total income will be between $55,000 and $84,000 ($82,000 and $119,000 if married), enter "1" for each eligible child plus "1" **additional** if you have four or more eligible children.

G _____

H Add lines A through G and enter total here. (**Note.** This may be different from the number of exemptions you claim on your tax return.) ▶ **H** _____

For accuracy, complete all worksheets that apply.
- If you plan to **itemize or claim adjustments to income** and want to reduce your withholding, see the **Deductions and Adjustments Worksheet** on page 2.
- If you have **more than one job** or are **married and you and your spouse both work** and the combined earnings from all jobs exceed $35,000 ($25,000 if married) see the **Two-Earner/Two-Job Worksheet** on page 2 to avoid having too little tax withheld.
- If **neither** of the above situations applies, **stop here** and enter the number from line H on line 5 of Form W-4 below.

Cut here and give Form W-4 to your employer. Keep the top part for your records.

Form **W-4**
Department of the Treasury
Internal Revenue Service

Employee's Withholding Allowance Certificate

▶ Whether you are entitled to claim a certain number of allowances or exemption from withholding is subject to review by the IRS. Your employer may be required to send a copy of this form to the IRS.

OMB No. 1545-0074

2006

1 Type or print your first name and middle initial.	Last name	**2** Your social security number

Home address (number and street or rural route)

3 ☐ Single ☐ Married ☐ Married, but withhold at higher Single rate.
Note. If married, but legally separated, or spouse is a nonresident alien, check the "Single" box.

City or town, state, and ZIP code

4 If your last name differs from that shown on your social security card, check here. You must call 1-800-772-1213 for a new card. ▶ ☐

5 Total number of allowances you are claiming (from line **H** above **or** from the applicable worksheet on page 2) | **5** |

6 Additional amount, if any, you want withheld from each paycheck . . . . | **6** $ |

7 I claim exemption from withholding for 2006, and I certify that I meet **both** of the following conditions for exemption.
- Last year I had a right to a refund of **all** federal income tax withheld because I had **no** tax liability **and**
- This year I expect a refund of **all** federal income tax withheld because I expect to have **no** tax liability.

If you meet both conditions, write "Exempt" here . . . . ▶ | **7** |

Under penalties of perjury, I declare that I have examined this certificate and to the best of my knowledge and belief, it is true, correct, and complete.

Employee's signature
(Form is not valid unless you sign it.) ▶

Date ▶

8 Employer's name and address (Employer: Complete lines 8 and 10 only if sending to the IRS.)	**9** Office code (optional)	**10** Employer identification number (EIN)

For Privacy Act and Paperwork Reduction Act Notice, see page 2.   Cat. No. 10220Q   Form **W-4** (2006)

Deductions and Adjustments Worksheet

Note. Use this worksheet *only* if you plan to itemize deductions, claim certain credits, or claim adjustments to income on your 2006 tax return.

1 Enter an estimate of your 2006 itemized deductions. These include qualifying home mortgage interest, charitable contributions, state and local taxes, medical expenses in excess of 7.5% of your income, and miscellaneous deductions. (For 2006, you may have to reduce your itemized deductions if your income is over $150,500 ($75,250 if married filing separately). See *Worksheet 3* in Pub. 919 for details.) . . .   **1** $ _____

2 Enter: { $10,300 if married filing jointly or qualifying widow(er)
             $ 7,550 if head of household
             $ 5,150 if single or married filing separately } . . . . . .   **2** $ _____

3 **Subtract** line 2 from line 1. If line 2 is greater than line 1, enter "-0-" . . . . . .   **3** $ _____

4 Enter an estimate of your 2006 adjustments to income, including alimony, deductible IRA contributions, and student loan interest   **4** $ _____

5 **Add** lines 3 and 4 and enter the total. (Include any amount for credits from *Worksheet 7* in Pub. 919) .   **5** $ _____

6 Enter an estimate of your 2006 nonwage income (such as dividends or interest) . . . .   **6** $ _____

7 **Subtract** line 6 from line 5. Enter the result, but not less than "-0-" . . . . .   **7** $ _____

8 **Divide** the amount on line 7 by $3,300 and enter the result here. Drop any fraction . . . . . .   **8** _____

9 Enter the number from the **Personal Allowances Worksheet,** line H, page 1 . . . . . .   **9** _____

10 **Add** lines 8 and 9 and enter the total here. If you plan to use the **Two-Earner/Two-Job Worksheet,** also enter this total on line 1 below. Otherwise, **stop here** and enter this total on Form W-4, line 5, page 1 .   **10** _____

Two-Earner/Two-Job Worksheet (See *Two earners/two jobs* on page 1.)

Note. Use this worksheet *only* if the instructions under line H on page 1 direct you here.

1 Enter the number from line H, page 1 (or from line 10 above if you used the **Deductions and Adjustments Worksheet**)   **1** _____

2 Find the number in **Table 1** below that applies to the **LOWEST** paying job and enter it here . . . .   **2** _____

3 If line 1 is **more than or equal to** line 2, subtract line 2 from line 1. Enter the result here (if zero, enter "-0-") and on Form W-4, line 5, page 1. **Do not** use the rest of this worksheet . . . .   **3** _____

Note. If line 1 is *less than* line 2, enter "-0-" on Form W-4, line 5, page 1. Complete lines 4–9 below to calculate the additional withholding amount necessary to avoid a year-end tax bill.

4 Enter the number from line 2 of this worksheet . . . .   **4** _____

5 Enter the number from line 1 of this worksheet . . . .   **5** _____

6 **Subtract** line 5 from line 4 . . . .   **6** _____

7 Find the amount in **Table 2** below that applies to the **HIGHEST** paying job and enter it here . . . .   **7** $ _____

8 **Multiply** line 7 by line 6 and enter the result here. This is the additional annual withholding needed . .   **8** $ _____

9 Divide line 8 by the number of pay periods remaining in 2006. For example, divide by 26 if you are paid every two weeks and you complete this form in December 2005. Enter the result here and on Form W-4, line 6, page 1. This is the additional amount to be withheld from each paycheck . . . .   **9** $ _____

Table 1: Two-Earner/Two-Job Worksheet

Married Filing Jointly						All Others	
If wages from **HIGHEST** paying job are—	AND, wages from **LOWEST** paying job are—	Enter on line 2 above	If wages from **HIGHEST** paying job are—	AND, wages from **LOWEST** paying job are—	Enter on line 2 above	If wages from **LOWEST** paying job are—	Enter on line 2 above
$0 - $42,000	$0 - $4,500	0	$42,001 and over	32,001 - 38,000	6	$0 - $6,000	0
	4,501 - 9,000	1		38,001 - 46,000	7	6,001 - 12,000	1
	9,001 - 18,000	2		46,001 - 55,000	8	12,001 - 19,000	2
	18,001 and over	3		55,001 - 60,000	9	19,001 - 26,000	3
$42,001 and over	$0 - $4,500	0		60,001 - 65,000	10	26,001 - 35,000	4
	4,501 - 9,000	1		65,001 - 75,000	11	35,001 - 50,000	5
	9,001 - 18,000	2		75,001 - 95,000	12	50,001 - 65,000	6
	18,001 - 22,000	3		95,001 - 105,000	13	65,001 - 80,000	7
	22,001 - 26,000	4		105,001 - 120,000	14	80,001 - 90,000	8
	26,001 - 32,000	5		120,001 and over	15	90,001 - 120,000	9
						120,001 and over	10

Table 2: Two-Earner/Two-Job Worksheet

Married Filing Jointly		All Others	
If wages from **HIGHEST** paying job are—	Enter on line 7 above	If wages from **HIGHEST** paying job are—	Enter on line 7 above
$0 - $60,000	$500	$0 - $30,000	$500
60,001 - 115,000	830	30,001 - 75,000	830
115,001 - 165,000	920	75,001 - 145,000	920
165,001 - 290,000	1,090	145,001 - 330,000	1,090
290,001 and over	1,160	330,001 and over	1,160

 Printed on recycled paper

REV-1220 AS + (10-05)

COMMONWEALTH OF PENNSYLVANIA
DEPARTMENT OF REVENUE
BUREAU OF BUSINESS TRUST FUND TAXES
PO BOX 280901
HARRISBURG, PA 17128-0901

PENNSYLVANIA EXEMPTION
CERTIFICATE

CHECK ONE:

☐ STATE OR LOCAL SALES AND USE TAX
☐ STATE OR LOCAL HOTEL OCCUPANCY TAX
☐ PUBLIC TRANSPORTATION ASSISTANCE TAXES AND FEES (PTA)
☐ PASSENGER CAR RENTAL TAX (PCRT)

(Please Print or Type)

> **This form cannot be used to obtain a Sales Tax License Number, PTA License Number or Exempt Status.**

**Read Instructions
On Reverse Carefully**

THIS FORM MAY BE PHOTOCOPIED – VOID UNLESS COMPLETE INFORMATION IS SUPPLIED

CHECK ONE: ☐ **PENNSYLVANIA TAX UNIT EXEMPTION CERTIFICATE** (USE FOR ONE TRANSACTION)

☐ **PENNSYLVANIA TAX BLANKET EXEMPTION CERTIFICATE** (USE FOR MULTIPLE TRANSACTIONS)

Name of Seller, Vendor, or Lessor

Street	City	State	Zip Code

Property and services purchased or leased using this certificate **are exempt** from tax because: (Select the appropriate paragraph from the back of this form, check the corresponding block below and insert information requested.)

☐ 1. Property or services will be used directly by purchaser in performing purchaser's operation of:

☐ 2. Purchaser is a/an: _____

☐ 3. Property will be resold under License Number _____ (If purchaser does not have a PA Sales Tax License Number, include a statement under Number 7 explaining why a number is not required.)

☐ 4. Purchaser is a/an: _____ holding Exemption Number _____

☐ 5. Property or services will be used directly by purchaser performing a public utility service. (Complete Part 5 on Reverse.)

☐ 6. Exempt wrapping supplies, License Number _____ . (If purchaser does not have a PA Sales Tax License Number, include a statement under Number 7 explaining why a number is not required.)

☐ 7. Other _____
(Explain in detail. Additional space on reverse side.)

I am authorized to execute this Certificate and claim this exemption. Misuse of this Certificate by seller, lessor, buyer, lessee, or their representative is punishable by fine and imprisonment.

Name of Purchaser or Lessee	Signature	Date

Street	City	State	Zip Code

---

1. ACCEPTANCE AND VALIDITY:

For this certificate to be valid, the seller/lessor shall exercise good faith in accepting this certificate, which includes: (1) the certificate shall be completed properly; (2) the certificate shall be in the seller/lessor's possession within sixty days from the date of sale/lease; (3) the certificate does not contain information which is knowingly false; and (4) the property or service is consistent with the exemption to which the customer is entitled. For more information, refer to Exemption Certificates, Title 61 PA Code §32.2. An invalid certificate may subject the seller/lessor to the tax.

2. REPRODUCTION OF FORM:

This form may be reproduced but shall contain the same information as appears on this form.

3. RETENTION

The seller or lessor must retain this certificate for at least four years from the date of the exempt sale to which the certificate applies. **DO NOT RETURN THIS FORM TO THE PA DEPARTMENT OF REVENUE.**

4. EXEMPT ORGANIZATIONS:

This form may be used in conjunction with form REV-1715, Exempt Organization Declaration of Sales Tax Exemption, when a purchase of $200 or more is made by an organization which is registered with the PA Department of Revenue as an exempt organization. These organizations are assigned an exemption number, beginning with the two digits 75 (example: 75-00000-0).

GENERAL INSTRUCTIONS

Those purchasers set forth below may use this form in connection with the claim for exemption for the following taxes:

   a. State and Local Sales and Use Tax;
   b. PTA rental fee or tax on leases of motor vehicles;
   c. Hotel Occupancy Tax if referenced with the symbol (●);
   d. PTA fee on the purchase of tires if referenced with the symbol (+);
   e. Passenger Car Rental Tax

EXEMPTION REASONS

1.) Property and/or services will be used directly by purchaser in performing purchaser's operation of:

A. Manufacturing   B. Mining   C. Dairying   D. Processing   E. Farming   F. Shipbuilding

This exemption is not valid for property or services which are used in: (a) constructing, repairing, or remodeling of real property, other than real property which is used directly in exempt operations; or (b) maintenance, managerial, administrative, supervisory, sales, delivery, warehousing or other nonoperational activities. Effective October 1, 1991, this exemption does not apply to certain services and PTA tire fee.

2.) Purchaser is a/an:

   + A. Instrumentality of the Commonwealth.
   + B. Political subdivision of the Commonwealth.
   + ● C. Municipal Authority created under the "Municipal Authority Acts of 1935 or 1945."
   + ● D. Electric Co-operative Corporation created under the "Electric Co-operative Law of 1990."
   ● E. Co-operative Agricultural Association required to pay Corporate Net Income Tax under the Act of May 23, 1945, P.L. 893, as amended (exemption not valid for registered vehicles).
   + ● F. Credit Unions organized under "Federal Credit Union Act" or State "Credit Union Act".
   + ● G. Federal Instrumentality
   ● H. Federal employee on official business (Exemption limited to Hotel Occupancy Tax only. A copy of orders or statement from supervisor must be attached to this certificate.)
   I. School Bus Operator (This Exemption Certificate is limited to the purchase of parts, repairs or maintenance services upon vehicles licensed as school buses by the PA Department of Transportation. For purchase of school buses, see NOTE below.)

3.) Property and/or services will be resold or rented in the ordinary course of purchaser's business. If purchaser does not have a PA Sales Tax License Number, complete Number 7 explaining why such number is not required. This Exemption is valid for property or services to be resold: (1) in original form; or (2) as an ingredient or component of other property.

4.)

Renewable Entities beginning with the two numbers 75.	**Permanent Exemptions beginning with the two numbers 76**	**Special Exemptions**
A. Religious Organization	+ E. School District	F. Direct Pay Permit Holder
B. Volunteer Firemen's Organization		+ ● G. Individual Holding Diplomatic ID
C. Nonprofit Educational Institution		H. Keystone Opportunity Zone
D. Charitable Organization		I. Tourist Promotion Agency

Exemption limited to purchase of tangible personal property or services for use and not for sale. The exemption shall not be used by a contractor performing services to real property. An exempt organization or institution shall have an exemption number assigned by the PA Department of Revenue and diplomats shall have an identification card assigned by the Federal Government. The exemption for categories "A, B, C and D" are not valid for property used for the following: (1) construction, improvement, repair or maintenance or any real property, except supplies and materials used for routine repair or maintenance of the real property; (2) any unrelated activities or operation of a public trade or business; or (3) equipment used to maintain real property.

5.) Property or services will be used directly by purchaser in the production, delivery, or rendition of public utility services as defined by the PA Utility Code.

   ☐ PA Public Utility Commission and/or   ☐ Interstate Commerce Commission

This Exemption is not valid for property or services used for the following: (1) construction, improvement, repair or maintenance of real property, other than real property which is used directly in rendering the public utility services; or (2) managerial, administrative, supervisor, sales or other nonoperational activities; or (3) tools and equipment used but not installed in maintenance of facilities or direct use equipment. Tools and equipment used to repair "direct use" property are exempt from tax.

6.) Vendor/Seller purchasing wrapping supplies and nonreturnable containers used to wrap property which is sold to others.

7.) Other (Attach a separate sheet of paper if more space is required.) _____

_____

_____

NOTE: Do not use this form for claiming an exemption on the registration of a vehicle. To claim an exemption from tax for a motor vehicle, trailer, semi-trailer or tractor with the PA Department of Transportation, Bureau of Motor Vehicles and Licensing, use **FORM MV-1**, "Application for Certificate of Title", for "first time" registrations and **FORM MV-4ST**, "Vehicle Sales and Use Tax Return/Application for Registration", for all other registrations.

PA-100 (1) 6-03

MAIL COMPLETED APPLICATION TO:
DEPARTMENT OF REVENUE
BUREAU OF BUSINESS TRUST FUND TAXES
DEPT. 280901
HARRISBURG, PA 17128-0901

COMMONWEALTH OF PENNSYLVANIA

PA ENTERPRISE REGISTRATION FORM

DEPARTMENT USE ONLY

RECEIVED DATE

DEPARTMENT OF REVENUE &
DEPARTMENT OF LABOR AND INDUSTRY

TYPE OR PRINT LEGIBLY, USE BLACK INK

SECTION 1 – REASON FOR THIS REGISTRATION

REFER TO THE INSTRUCTIONS (PAGE 18) AND CHECK THE APPLICABLE BOX(ES) TO INDICATE THE REASON(S) FOR THIS REGISTRATION.

1. ☐ NEW REGISTRATION
2. ☐ ADDING TAX(ES) & SERVICE(S)
3. ☐ REACTIVATING TAX(ES) & SERVICE(S)
4. ☐ ADDING ESTABLISHMENT(S)
5. ☐ INFORMATION UPDATE

6. DID THIS ENTERPRISE:

☐ YES ☐ NO ACQUIRE ALL OR PART OF ANOTHER BUSINESS?

☐ YES ☐ NO RESULT FROM A CHANGE IN LEGAL STRUCTURE (FOR EXAMPLE, FROM INDIVIDUAL PROPRIETOR TO CORPORATION, PARTNERSHIP TO CORPORATION, CORPORATION TO LIMITED LIABILITY COMPANY, ETC)?

☐ YES ☐ NO UNDERGO A MERGER, CONSOLIDATION, DISSOLUTION, OR OTHER RESTRUCTURING?

SECTION 2 – ENTERPRISE INFORMATION

1. DATE OF FIRST OPERATIONS	2. DATE OF FIRST OPERATIONS IN PA	3. ENTERPRISE FISCAL YEAR END		
4. ENTERPRISE LEGAL NAME		5. FEDERAL EMPLOYER IDENTIFICATION NUMBER (EIN)		
6. ENTERPRISE TRADE NAME (if different than legal name)		7. ENTERPRISE TELEPHONE NUMBER ( )		
8. ENTERPRISE STREET ADDRESS (do not use PO Box)	CITY/TOWN	COUNTY	STATE	ZIP CODE + 4
9. ENTERPRISE MAILING ADDRESS (if different than street address)	CITY/TOWN		STATE	ZIP CODE + 4
10. LOCATION OF ENTERPRISE RECORDS (street address)	CITY/TOWN		STATE	ZIP CODE + 4
11. ESTABLISHMENT NAME (doing business as)	12. NUMBER OF ESTABLISHMENTS *	13. SCHOOL DISTRICT	14. MUNICIPALITY	

* Enterprises with more than one establishment as defined in the general instructions must complete Section 17.

SECTION 3 – TAXES AND SERVICES

ALL REGISTRANTS MUST CHECK THE APPLICABLE BOX(ES) TO INDICATE THE TAX(ES) AND SERVICE(S) REQUESTED FOR THIS REGISTRATION AND COMPLETE THE CORRESPONDING SECTIONS INDICATED ON PAGES 2 AND 3. IF REACTIVATING ANY PREVIOUS ACCOUNT(S), LIST THE ACCOUNT NUMBER(S) IN THE SPACE PROVIDED.

	PREVIOUS ACCOUNT NBR.		PREVIOUS ACCOUNT NBR.
☐ CIGARETTE DEALER'S LICENSE	_____	☐ SALES TAX EXEMPT STATUS	_____
☐ CORPORATION TAXES	_____	☐ SALES, USE, HOTEL OCCUPANCY TAX LICENSE	_____
☐ EMPLOYER WITHHOLDING TAX	_____	☐ SMALL GAMES OF CHANCE LIC./CERT.	_____
☐ FUELS TAX PERMIT	_____	☐ TRANSIENT VENDOR CERTIFICATE	_____
☐ LIQUID FUELS TAX PERMIT	_____	☐ UNEMPLOYMENT COMPENSATION	_____
☐ LOCAL SALES, USE, HOTEL OCCUPANCY TAX	_____	☐ USE TAX	_____
☐ MOTOR CARRIERS ROAD TAX/IFTA	_____	☐ VEHICLE RENTAL TAX	_____
☐ PROMOTER LICENSE	_____	☐ WHOLESALER CERTIFICATE	_____
☐ PUBLIC TRANSPORTATION ASSISTANCE TAX LICENSE	_____	☐ WORKERS' COMPENSATION COVERAGE	_____

SECTION 4 – AUTHORIZED SIGNATURE

I, (WE) THE UNDERSIGNED, DECLARE UNDER THE PENALTIES OF PERJURY THAT THE STATEMENTS CONTAINED HEREIN ARE TRUE, CORRECT, AND COMPLETE.

AUTHORIZED SIGNATURE (ATTACH POWER OF ATTORNEY IF APPLICABLE)	DAYTIME TELEPHONE NUMBER ( )	TITLE
TYPE OR PRINT NAME	E-MAIL ADDRESS	DATE
TYPE OR PRINT PREPARER'S NAME		TITLE
DAYTIME TELEPHONE NUMBER ( )	E-MAIL ADDRESS	DATE

4

PA-100 8-01

ENTERPRISE NAME	DEPARTMENT USE ONLY

SECTION 5 – BUSINESS STRUCTURE

CHECK THE APPROPRIATE BOX FOR QUESTIONS 1, 2 & 3. IN ADDITION TO SECTIONS 1 THROUGH 10, COMPLETE THE SECTION(S) INDICATED.

1. ☐ SOLE PROPRIETORSHIP (INDIVIDUAL)　☐ GENERAL PARTNERSHIP　☐ ASSOCIATION　☐ LIMITED LIABILITY COMPANY
　 ☐ CORPORATION (Sec. 11)　☐ LIMITED PARTNERSHIP　☐ BUSINESS TRUST　　*STATE WHERE CHARTERED* _____
　 ☐ GOVERNMENT (Sec. 13)　☐ LIMITED LIABILITY PARTNERSHIP　☐ ESTATE　☐ RESTRICTED PROFESSIONAL COMPANY
　　　　　　　　　　　　　☐ JOINT VENTURE PARTNERSHIP　　　　　　*STATE WHERE CHARTERED* _____

2. ☐ PROFIT　　☐ NON-PROFIT　　IS THE ENTERPRISE ORGANIZED FOR PROFIT OR NON-PROFIT?

3. ☐ YES　　☐ NO　　IS THE ENTERPRISE EXEMPT FROM TAXATION UNDER INTERNAL REVENUE CODE SECTION 501(C)(3)? IF YES, PROVIDE A COPY OF THE ENTERPRISE'S EXEMPTION AUTHORIZATION LETTER FROM THE INTERNAL REVENUE SERVICE.

SECTION 6 – OWNERS, PARTNERS, SHAREHOLDERS, OFFICERS, AND RESPONSIBLE PARTY INFORMATION

PROVIDE THE FOLLOWING FOR **ALL** INDIVIDUAL AND/OR ENTERPRISE OWNERS, PARTNERS, SHAREHOLDERS, OFFICERS, AND RESPONSIBLE PARTIES. IF STOCK IS PUBLICLY TRADED, **PROVIDE THE FOLLOWING FOR ANY SHAREHOLDER WITH AN EQUITY POSITION OF 5% OR MORE.** *ADDITIONAL SPACE IS AVAILABLE IN SECTION 6A, PAGE 11.*

1. NAME		2. SOCIAL SECURITY NUMBER	3. DATE OF BIRTH *	4. FEDERAL EIN
5. ☐ OWNER　☐ OFFICER ☐ PARTNER　☐ SHAREHOLDER ☐ RESPONSIBLE PARTY	6. TITLE	7. EFFECTIVE DATE OF TITLE	8. PERCENTAGE OF OWNERSHIP ___%	9. EFFECTIVE DATE OF OWNERSHIP
10. HOME ADDRESS (street)	CITY/TOWN	COUNTY	STATE	ZIP CODE + 4

11. THIS PERSON IS RESPONSIBLE TO REMIT/MAINTAIN:　☐ SALES TAX　☐ EMPLOYER WITHHOLDING TAX　☐ MOTOR FUEL TAXES

　　　　　　　　　　　　　　　　　　　　　☐ WORKERS' COMPENSATION COVERAGE

* DATE OF BIRTH REQUIRED ONLY IF APPLYING FOR A CIGARETTE WHOLESALE DEALER'S LICENSE, A SMALL GAMES OF CHANCE DISTRIBUTOR LICENSE, OR A SMALL GAMES OF CHANCE MANUFACTURER CERTIFICATE.

SECTION 7 – ESTABLISHMENT BUSINESS ACTIVITY INFORMATION

REFER TO THE INSTRUCTIONS TO COMPLETE THIS SECTION. COMPLETE SECTION 17 FOR MULTIPLE ESTABLISHMENTS.

1. ENTER THE PERCENTAGE THAT EACH **PA** BUSINESS ACTIVITY REPRESENTS OF THE TOTAL RECEIPTS OR REVENUES AT THIS ESTABLISHMENT. LIST ALL PRODUCTS OR SERVICES ASSOCIATED WITH EACH BUSINESS ACTIVITY. ENTER THE PERCENTAGE THAT THE PRODUCTS OR SERVICES REPRESENT OF THE TOTAL RECEIPTS OR REVENUES AT THIS ESTABLISHMENT.

PA BUSINESS ACTIVITY	%	PRODUCTS OR SERVICES	%	ADDITIONAL PRODUCTS OR SERVICES	%
Accommodation & Food Services					
Agriculture, Forestry, Fishing, & Hunting					
Art, Entertainment, & Recreation Services					
Communications/Information					
Construction (must complete question 3)					
Domestics (Private Households)					
Educational Services					
Finance					
Health Care Services					
Insurance					
Management of Companies & Enterprises					
Manufacturing					
Mining, Quarrying, & Oil/Gas Extraction					
Other Services					
Professional, Scientific, & Technical Services					
Public Administration					
Real Estate					
Retail Trade					
Sanitary Service					
Social Assistance Services					
Transportation					
Utilities					
Warehousing					
Wholesale Trade					
TOTAL	100%				

2. ENTER THE PERCENTAGE THAT THIS ESTABLISHMENT'S RECEIPTS OR REVENUES REPRESENT OF THE TOTAL PA RECEIPTS OR REVENUES OF THE ENTERPRISE.

_____ %

3. ESTABLISHMENTS ENGAGED IN CONSTRUCTION *MUST* ENTER THE PERCENTAGE OF CONSTRUCTION ACTIVITY THAT IS NEW AND/OR RENOVATIVE AND THE PERCENTAGE OF CONSTRUCTION ACTIVITY THAT IS RESIDENTIAL AND/OR COMMERCIAL.

_____ % NEW　　+　_____ % RENOVATIVE　= 100%
_____ % RESIDENTIAL　+　_____ % COMMERCIAL　= 100%

PA-100 6-03

ENTERPRISE NAME

DEPARTMENT USE ONLY

SECTION 8 – ESTABLISHMENT SALES INFORMATION

1. ☐ YES ☐ NO IS THIS ESTABLISHMENT SELLING TAXABLE PRODUCTS OR OFFERING TAXABLE SERVICES TO CONSUMERS FROM A LOCATION **IN PENNSYLVANIA**? IF YES, COMPLETE SECTION 18.

2. ☐ YES ☐ NO IS THIS ESTABLISHMENT SELLING CIGARETTES **IN PENNSYLVANIA**? IF YES, COMPLETE SECTIONS 18 AND 19.

3. LIST EACH COUNTY **IN PENNSYLVANIA** WHERE THIS ESTABLISHMENT IS CONDUCTING TAXABLE SALES ACTIVITY(IES).

COUNTY _____ COUNTY _____ COUNTY _____

COUNTY _____ COUNTY _____ COUNTY _____

ATTACH ADDITIONAL 8 1/2 X 11 SHEETS IF NECESSARY.

SECTION 9 – ESTABLISHMENT EMPLOYMENT INFORMATION

PART 1

1. ☐ YES ☐ NO DOES THIS ESTABLISHMENT EMPLOY INDIVIDUALS WHO **WORK IN PENNSYLVANIA?** IF YES, INDICATE:
   a. DATE WAGES FIRST **PAID** (MM/DD/YYYY) . . . . _____
   b. DATE WAGES RESUMED FOLLOWING A BREAK IN EMPLOYMENT . . . . ._____
   c. TOTAL NUMBER OF EMPLOYEES . . . . ._____
   d. NUMBER OF EMPLOYEES PRIMARILY WORKING IN NEW BUILDING OR INFRASTRUCTURE . . . . ._____
   e. NUMBER OF EMPLOYEES PRIMARILY WORKING IN REMODELING CONSTRUCTION ._____
   f. ESTIMATED GROSS WAGES PER QUARTER . . . .$ _____ .00
   g. NAME OF WORKERS' COMPENSATION INSURANCE COMPANY _____
      1. POLICY NUMBER _____ EFFECTIVE START DATE _____ END DATE _____
      2. AGENCY NAME _____ DAYTIME TELEPHONE NUMBER (___) _____
         MAILING ADDRESS _____ CITY/TOWN _____ STATE ____ ZIP CODE + 4 _____
      3. IF THIS ENTERPRISE DOES NOT HAVE WORKERS' COMPENSATION INSURANCE, CHECK ONE:
         a. THIS ESTABLISHMENT EMPLOYS ONLY EXCLUDED WORKERS . . . . _____ ☐
         b. THIS ESTABLISHMENT HAS ZERO EMPLOYEES . . . . _____ ☐
         c. THIS ESTABLISHMENT RECEIVED APPROVAL TO SELF-INSURE BY THE PA BUREAU OF
            WORKERS' COMPENSATION . . . . _____ ☐
            IF ITEM 3c. IS CHECKED, PROVIDE PA WORKERS' COMPENSATION BUREAU CODE _____

2. ☐ YES ☐ NO DOES THIS ESTABLISHMENT EMPLOY PA RESIDENTS WHO **WORK OUTSIDE OF PENNSYLVANIA?**
   IF YES, INDICATE:
      a. DATE WAGES FIRST **PAID** (MM/DD/YYYY) . . . . _____
      b. DATE WAGES RESUMED FOLLOWING A BREAK IN EMPLOYMENT . . . . ._____
      c. ESTIMATED GROSS WAGES PER QUARTER. . . . .$ _____ .00

3. ☐ YES ☐ NO DOES THIS ESTABLISHMENT PAY REMUNERATION FOR SERVICES TO PERSONS YOU DO NOT CONSIDER EMPLOYEES?
   IF YES, EXPLAIN THE SERVICES PERFORMED _____

PART 2

1. ☐ YES ☐ NO IS THIS REGISTRATION A RESULT OF A TAXABLE DISTRIBUTION FROM A BENEFIT TRUST, DEFERRED PAYMENT, OR RETIREMENT PLAN FOR PA RESIDENTS?
   IF YES, INDICATE:
      a. DATE BENEFITS FIRST **PAID** (MM/DD/YYYY) . . . . _____
      b. ESTIMATED BENEFITS PAID PER QUARTER . . . .$ _____ .00

SECTION 10 – BULK SALE/TRANSFER INFORMATION

IF ASSETS WERE ACQUIRED IN BULK FROM MORE THAN ONE ENTERPRISE, PHOTOCOPY THIS SECTION AND PROVIDE THE FOLLOWING INFORMATION ABOUT EACH SELLER/TRANSFEROR.

1. ☐ YES ☐ NO DID THE ENTERPRISE ACQUIRE 51% OR MORE OF **ANY CLASS** OF THE PA ASSETS OF ANOTHER ENTERPRISE? SEE THE CLASS OF ASSETS LISTED BELOW.

2. ☐ YES ☐ NO DID THE ENTERPRISE ACQUIRE 51% OR MORE OF THE **TOTAL ASSETS** OF ANOTHER ENTERPRISE?

IF THE ANSWER TO EITHER QUESTION IS YES, PROVIDE THE FOLLOWING INFORMATION ABOUT THE **SELLER/TRANSFEROR.**

3. SELLER/TRANSFEROR NAME

4. FEDERAL EIN

5. SELLER/TRANSFEROR STREET ADDRESS | CITY/TOWN | STATE | ZIP CODE + 4

6. DATE ASSETS ACQUIRED

7. ASSETS ACQUIRED:

☐ ACCOUNTS RECEIVABLE	☐ FIXTURES	☐ MACHINERY
☐ CONTRACTS	☐ FURNITURE	☐ NAME AND/OR GOODWILL
☐ CUSTOMERS/CLIENTS	☐ INVENTORY	☐ REAL ESTATE
☐ EQUIPMENT	☐ LEASES	☐ OTHER _____

IMPORTANT: IF, IN ADDITION TO ACQUIRING ASSETS IN BULK, THE ENTERPRISE ALSO ACQUIRED ALL OR PART OF A PREDECESSOR'S BUSINESS, SECTION 14 MUST BE COMPLETED.

PA-100 8-01

ENTERPRISE NAME

DEPARTMENT USE ONLY

SECTION 11 – CORPORATION INFORMATION

1. DATE OF INCORPORATION

2. STATE OF INCORPORATION

3. CERTIFICATE OF AUTHORITY DATE (NON-PA CORP.)

4. COUNTRY OF INCORPORATION

5. ☐ YES ☐ NO IS THIS CORPORATION'S STOCK PUBLICLY TRADED?

6. CHECK THE APPROPRIATE BOX(ES) TO DESCRIBE THIS CORPORATION:

CORPORATION: ☐ STOCK ☐ PROFESSIONAL BANK: ☐ STATE MUTUAL THRIFT: ☐ STATE INSURANCE ☐ PA
☐ NON-STOCK ☐ COOPERATIVE ☐ FEDERAL ☐ FEDERAL COMPANY: ☐ NON-PA
☐ MANAGEMENT ☐ STATUTORY CLOSE

7. S-CORPORATION: ☐ FEDERAL ☐ PENNSYLVANIA (REV-1640 MUST BE FILED TO ELECT PENNSYLVANIA S STATUS.)

SECTION 12 – REPORTING & PAYMENT METHODS

1. THE DEPARTMENT OF REVENUE REQUIRES THAT ANY ENTERPRISE THAT MEETS THE $20,000 PAYMENT THRESHOLD REMIT PAYMENTS VIA ELECTRONIC FUNDS TRANSFER (EFT). AN ENTERPRISE, REGARDLESS OF AMOUNT, MAY APPLY FOR EFT PAYMENT METHOD.

a. ☐ YES ☐ NO DOES THIS ENTERPRISE MEET THE DEPARTMENT OF REVENUE'S REQUIREMENTS FOR EFT?
b. ☐ YES ☐ NO DOES THIS ENTERPRISE WANT TO PARTICIPATE IN THE DEPARTMENT OF REVENUE'S EFT PROGRAM?

2. ☐ YES ☐ NO IF THIS ENTERPRISE IS A NON-PROFIT ORGANIZATION THAT IS EXEMPT UNDER IRS 501(c)(3), OR POLITICAL SUB-DIVISIONS, IS IT INTERESTED IN RECEIVING INFORMATION ABOUT THE DEPARTMENT OF LABOR & INDUSTRY'S OPTION OF FINANCING UC COSTS UNDER THE REIMBURSEMENT METHOD IN LIEU OF THE CONTRIBUTORY METHOD? FOR MORE DETAILS, REFER TO SECTION 12 INSTRUCTIONS.

3. THE DEPARTMENT OF LABOR & INDUSTRY REQUIRES THAT ANY ENTERPRISE WITH 250 OR MORE WAGE ENTRIES PER QUARTERLY REPORT, FILE THE WAGE INFORMATION VIA MAGNETIC MEDIA. AN ENTERPRISE, REGARDLESS OF SIZE, MAY APPLY TO FILE THEIR WAGE INFORMATION VIA MAGNETIC MEDIA.

a. ☐ YES ☐ NO DOES THIS ENTERPRISE MEET THE DEPARTMENT OF LABOR & INDUSTRY'S THRESHOLD FOR MAGNETIC MEDIA FILING?

b. ☐ YES ☐ NO DOES THIS ENTERPRISE WANT TO RECEIVE INFORMATION ABOUT THE MAGNETIC MEDIA FILING METHOD?

INFORMATION ABOUT INTERNET FILING OPTIONS FOR PENNSYLVANIA BUSINESS TAXES CAN BE FOUND ON THE E-TIDES HOME PAGE AT **www.etides.state.pa.us**

SECTION 13 – GOVERNMENT STRUCTURE

1. IS THE ENTERPRISE A:

☐ GOVERNMENT BODY ☐ GOVERNMENT OWNED ENTERPRISE ☐ GOVERNMENT & PRIVATE SECTOR OWNED ENTERPRISE

2. IS THE GOVERNMENT:

☐ DOMESTIC/USA ☐ FOREIGN/NON-USA ☐ MULTI-NATIONAL

3. IF DOMESTIC, IS THE GOVERNMENT:

☐ FEDERAL LOCAL: ☐ COUNTY ☐ BOROUGH
☐ STATE GOVERNOR'S JURISDICTION ☐ CITY ☐ SCHOOL DISTRICT
☐ STATE NON-GOVERNOR'S JURISDICTION ☐ TOWN ☐ OTHER _____
☐ TOWNSHIP

PA-100 8-01

ENTERPRISE NAME

SECTION 14 – PREDECESSOR/SUCCESSOR INFORMATION

COMPLETE THIS SECTION IF THE REGISTERING ENTERPRISE IS WHOLLY OR PARTIALLY SUCCEEDING A PREDECESSOR.
FOR ASSISTANCE, CONTACT THE NEAREST DEPARTMENT OF LABOR & INDUSTRY FIELD ACCOUNTING SERVICE OFFICE.

IF THE ENTERPRISE HAS MORE THAN ONE PREDECESSOR, PHOTOCOPY THIS PAGE TO PROVIDE THE FOLLOWING INFORMATION ABOUT EACH.

1. PREDECESSOR LEGAL NAME

2. PREDECESSOR PA UC ACCOUNT NUMBER

3. PREDECESSOR TRADE NAME

4. PREDECESSOR FEDERAL EIN

5. PREDECESSOR STREET ADDRESS | CITY/TOWN | STATE | ZIP CODE + 4

6. SPECIFY HOW THE BUSINESS OPERATION WAS ACQUIRED: ☐ ACQUISITION OF EXISTING OPERATION ☐ CHANGE IN LEGAL STRUCTURE
   ☐ CONSOLIDATION ☐ GIFT ☐ MERGER ☐ IRC SEC. 338 ELECTION ☐ OTHER (SPECIFY) _____

7. ☐ ACQUISITION DATE _____

8. PERCENTAGE OF THE PREDECESSOR'S TOTAL BUSINESS OPERATION (PA AND NON-PA) ACQUIRED _____ %

9. PERCENTAGE OF THE PREDECESSOR'S **PA** BUSINESS OPERATION ACQUIRED _____ %
   IF LESS THAN 100%, PROVIDE THE NAME(S) AND ADDRESS(ES) OF THE ESTABLISHMENT(S) THAT CONDUCTED OPERATIONS IN PA OR EMPLOYED PA RESIDENTS.
   ATTACH ADDITIONAL 8 1/2 X 11 SHEETS IF NECESSARY.

NAME OF ESTABLISHMENT(S) | ADDRESS(ES)

10. WHAT WAS THE PREDECESSOR'S BUSINESS ACTIVITY IN THE **PA** BUSINESS OPERATION THAT WAS ACQUIRED?

11. ASSETS ACQUIRED: ☐ ACCOUNTS RECEIVABLE ☐ FURNITURE AND FIXTURES ☐ MACHINERY AND EQUIPMENT ☐ OTHER (SPECIFY)
    ☐ CLIENTS/CUSTOMERS ☐ INVENTORIES ☐ NAME AND/OR GOODWILL _____
    ☐ CONTRACTS ☐ LEASES ☐ REAL ESTATE

12. ☐ YES ☐ NO HAS THE PREDECESSOR CEASED PAYING WAGES IN PA? IF YES, ENTER THE DATE PA WAGES CEASED,
    IF KNOWN. _____

13. ☐ YES ☐ NO HAS THE PREDECESSOR CEASED OPERATIONS IN PA? IF YES, ENTER THE DATE PA OPERATIONS CEASED,
    IF KNOWN. _____
    IF NO, DESCRIBE THE PREDECESSOR'S PRESENT PA BUSINESS ACTIVITY, IF KNOWN. _____

14. AT THE TIME OF TRANSFER FROM THE PREDECESSOR ENTERPRISE TO THE REGISTERING ENTERPRISE:

a. ☐ YES ☐ NO WERE ANY OF THE OWNERS, SHAREHOLDERS (5% OR GREATER), PARTNERS, OFFICERS, OR DIRECTORS OF THE PREDECESSOR
   OR OF ANY AFFILIATE, SUBSIDIARY OR PARENT CORPORATION OF THE PREDECESSOR ALSO OWNERS, SHAREHOLDERS (5% OR
   GREATER), PARTNERS, OFFICERS, OR DIRECTORS OF THE REGISTERING ENTERPRISE OR OF ANY AFFILIATE, SUBSIDIARY OR
   PARENT CORPORATION OF THE REGISTERING ENTERPRISE?

b. ☐ YES ☐ NO WAS THE PREDECESSOR, OR ANY AFFILIATE, SUBSIDIARY OR PARENT CORPORATION OF THE PREDECESSOR, AN OWNER,
   SHAREHOLDER (5% OR GREATER), OR PARTNER IN THE REGISTERING ENTERPRISE?

c. ☐ YES ☐ NO WAS THE REGISTERING ENTERPRISE, OR ANY AFFILIATE, SUBSIDIARY OR PARENT CORPORATION OF THE REGISTERING
   ENTERPRISE, AN OWNER, SHAREHOLDER (5% OR GREATER), OR PARTNER IN THE PREDECESSOR?

IF THE ANSWER TO ANY OF THE QUESTIONS IN 14 IS YES, PROVIDE THE FOLLOWING INFORMATION. ATTACH ADDITIONAL 8 1/2 X 11 SHEETS IF NECESSARY.

● IDENTIFY THOSE PERSONS AND ENTITIES BY THEIR FULL NAME;

● DESCRIBE THEIR RELATIONSHIP TO THE PREDECESSOR AND ANY AFFILIATE, SUBSIDIARY AND PARENT CORPORATION OF THE PREDECESSOR; AND

● DESCRIBE THEIR RELATIONSHIP TO THE REGISTERING ENTERPRISE AND ANY AFFILIATE, SUBSIDIARY AND PARENT CORPORATION OF THE REGISTERING ENTERPRISE.

THE REGISTERING ENTERPRISE MAY APPLY FOR A TRANSFER IN WHOLE OR IN PART OF THE PREDECESSOR'S UNEMPLOYMENT COMPENSATION (UC) EXPERIENCE RECORD AND RESERVE ACCOUNT BALANCE, IF THE REGISTERING ENTERPRISE IS CONTINUING ESSENTIALLY THE SAME BUSINESS ACTIVITY AS THE PREDECESSOR AND BOTH PROVIDED PA COVERED EMPLOYMENT. COMPLETE SECTION 15 AND, IF APPLICABLE, SECTION 16.

NOTE: A REGISTERING ENTERPRISE MAY APPLY THE UC TAXABLE WAGES PAID BY A PREDECESSOR TOWARD THE REGISTERING ENTERPRISE'S UC TAXABLE WAGE BASE FOR THE CALENDAR YEAR OF
       ACQUISITION WITHOUT TRANSFERRING THE PREDECESSOR'S EXPERIENCE RECORD AND RESERVE ACCOUNT BALANCE.

PA-100 8-01

ENTERPRISE NAME

DEPARTMENT USE ONLY

SECTION 15 – APPLICATION FOR PA UC EXPERIENCE RECORD AND RESERVE ACCOUNT BALANCE OF PREDECESSOR

A REGISTERING ENTERPRISE MAY APPLY THE UNEMPLOYMENT COMPENSATION (UC) TAXABLE WAGES PAID BY A PREDECESSOR TOWARD THE REGISTERING ENTERPRISE'S UC TAXABLE WAGE BASE FOR THE CALENDAR YEAR OF ACQUISITION WITHOUT TRANSFERRING THE PREDECESSOR'S EXPERIENCE RECORD AND RESERVE ACCOUNT BALANCE.

REFER TO THE INSTRUCTIONS TO DETERMINE IF IT IS ADVANTAGEOUS TO APPLY FOR A PREDECESSOR'S UC EXPERIENCE RECORD AND RESERVE ACCOUNT BALANCE.

IMPORTANT: THIS APPLICATION CANNOT BE CONSIDERED UNLESS IT IS SIGNED BY AN AUTHORIZED SIGNATORY OF BOTH THE PREDECESSOR AND THE REGISTERING ENTERPRISE. THE TRANSFER IN WHOLE OR IN PART OF THE EXPERIENCE RECORD AND RESERVE ACCOUNT BALANCE IS BINDING AND IRREVOCABLE ONCE IT HAS BEEN APPROVED BY THE DEPARTMENT OF LABOR AND INDUSTRY.

APPLICATION IS HEREBY MADE BY THE PREDECESSOR AND THE REGISTERING ENTERPRISE FOR A TRANSFER TO THE REGISTERING ENTERPRISE OF THE PENNSYLVANIA UNEMPLOYMENT COMPENSATION EXPERIENCE RECORD AND RESERVE ACCOUNT BALANCE OF THE PREDECESSOR WITH RESPECT TO THE TRANSFER.

WE HEREBY CERTIFY THAT THE TRANSFER REFERENCED IN SECTION 14 HAS OCCURRED AS DESCRIBED THEREIN AND THAT THE REGISTERING ENTERPRISE IS CONTINUING ESSENTIALLY THE SAME BUSINESS ACTIVITY AS THE PREDECESSOR.

COMPLETE THIS SECTION <u>ONLY</u> IF YOU WANT TO APPLY FOR THE PREDECESSOR'S EXPERIENCE RECORD AND RESERVE ACCOUNT BALANCE.

1. PREDECESSOR NAME		DATE
AUTHORIZED SIGNATURE	TYPE OR PRINT NAME	TITLE
2. REGISTERING ENTERPRISE NAME		DATE
AUTHORIZED SIGNATURE	TYPE OR PRINT NAME	TITLE

SECTION 16 – UNEMPLOYMENT COMPENSATION PARTIAL TRANSFER INFORMATION

COMPLETE THIS SECTION IF THE REGISTERING ENTERPRISE ACQUIRED ONLY PART OF THE PREDECESSOR'S PENNSYLVANIA (PA) BUSINESS OPERATION AND IS MAKING APPLICATION FOR THE TRANSFER OF A PORTION OF THE PREDECESSOR'S EXPERIENCE RECORD AND RESERVE ACCOUNT BALANCE.

COMPLETE REPLACEMENT UC-2A FOR PARTIAL TRANSFER (FORM UC-252). THE PREDECESSOR'S PA PAYROLL RECORDS FOR THE TWO YEARS PRIOR TO THE QUARTER OF THE TRANSFER AND/OR ACQUISITION MUST REMAIN AVAILABLE TO THE REGISTERING ENTERPRISE TO ENABLE THE REGISTERING ENTERPRISE TO PROVIDE REQUIRED INFORMATION REGARDING SEPARATED AND/OR TRANSFERRED EMPLOYEES.

UNEMPLOYMENT COMPENSATION (UC) TAXABLE WAGES ARE THOSE WAGES THAT DO NOT EXCEED THE UC TAXABLE WAGE BASE APPLICABLE TO A GIVEN CALENDAR YEAR.

1. DATE WAGES FIRST PAID BY PREDECESSOR OR PRE-PREDECESSOR(S) IN THE PART OF THE PA BUSINESS OPERATION TRANSFERRED (ACQUIRED) FOR WHICH CONTRIBUTIONS WERE PAID UNDER THE PROVISIONS OF THE PA UC LAW.

    DATE:

2. CHECKMARK THE CALENDAR QUARTERS IN THE YEAR OF TRANSFER AND IN THE PRECEDING FIVE CALENDAR YEARS IN WHICH PA UC CONTRIBUTIONS WERE **PAID IN THE PART OF THE PA BUSINESS OPERATION THAT WAS TRANSFERRED.** ENTER A ZERO IN EACH QUARTER WHEN NO CONTRIBUTION WAS DUE AND PAYABLE IN THE PART TRANSFERRED.

YEAR_____				YEAR_____				YEAR_____				YEAR_____				YEAR_____				YEAR_____ OF TRANSFER			
QUARTERS				QUARTERS				QUARTERS				QUARTERS				QUARTERS				QUARTERS			
1	2	3	4	1	2	3	4	1	2	3	4	1	2	3	4	1	2	3	4	1	2	3	4

3. CHECKMARK THE CALENDAR QUARTERS IN THE YEAR OF TRANSFER AND IN THE PRECEDING FIVE CALENDAR YEARS IN WHICH PA UC CONTRIBUTIONS WERE PAID IN THE **PART OF THE PA BUSINESS OPERATION THAT WAS <u>NOT</u> TRANSFERRED.** ENTER A ZERO IN EACH QUARTER WHEN NO CONTRIBUTION WAS DUE AND PAYABLE IN THE PART RETAINED.

YEAR_____				YEAR_____				YEAR_____				YEAR_____				YEAR_____				YEAR_____ OF TRANSFER			
QUARTERS				QUARTERS				QUARTERS				QUARTERS				QUARTERS				QUARTERS			
1	2	3	4	1	2	3	4	1	2	3	4	1	2	3	4	1	2	3	4	1	2	3	4

4a. PREDECESSOR'S PA UC **TAXABLE** PAYROLL IN THE **PART OF THE PA BUSINESS OPERATION TRANSFERRED FOR THE PERIOD OF THREE CALENDAR YEARS PRIOR TO THE YEAR OF TRANSFER (ACQUISITION).**

4b. IF THE **PART OF THE PA BUSINESS OPERATION TRANSFERRED** WAS NOT IN EXISTENCE FOR THREE CALENDAR YEARS PRIOR TO THE YEAR OF THE TRANSFER, ENTER THE PA **TAXABLE** PAYROLL **FOR THE PERIOD OF ITS EXISTENCE TO DATE OF TRANSFER .**

OR

$

$

5. PREDECESSOR'S ENTIRE PA UC **TAXABLE** PAYROLL FOR SAME PERIOD INDICATED IN ITEMS 4a OR 4b.

6. PREDECESSOR'S ENTIRE PA UC **TAXABLE** PAYROLL FOR THE PERIOD FROM THE BEGINNING OF THE QUARTER OF TRANSFER TO THE DATE OF TRANSFER.

$

$

PA-100 8-01

ENTERPRISE NAME	DEPARTMENT USE ONLY

SECTION 17 – MULTIPLE ESTABLISHMENT INFORMATION

COMPLETE THIS SECTION FOR EACH ADDITIONAL ESTABLISHMENT CONDUCTING BUSINESS IN PA OR EMPLOYING PA RESIDENTS. PHOTOCOPY THIS SECTION AS NECESSARY.

PART 1   ESTABLISHMENT INFORMATION

1. ESTABLISHMENT NAME (doing business as)		2. DATE OF FIRST OPERATIONS	3. TELEPHONE NUMBER ( )
4. STREET ADDRESS	CITY/TOWN	COUNTY	STATE	ZIP CODE + 4
5. SCHOOL DISTRICT		6. MUNICIPALITY	

PART 2   ESTABLISHMENT BUSINESS ACTIVITY INFORMATION

REFER TO THE INSTRUCTIONS TO COMPLETE THIS SECTION. COMPLETE SECTION 17 FOR MULTIPLE ESTABLISHMENTS.

1. ENTER THE PERCENTAGE THAT EACH **PA** BUSINESS ACTIVITY REPRESENTS OF THE TOTAL RECEIPTS OR REVENUES AT THIS ESTABLISHMENT. LIST ALL PRODUCTS OR SERVICES ASSOCIATED WITH EACH BUSINESS ACTIVITY. ENTER THE PERCENTAGE THAT THE PRODUCTS OR SERVICES REPRESENT OF THE TOTAL RECEIPTS OR REVENUES AT THIS ESTABLISHMENT.

PA BUSINESS ACTIVITY	%	PRODUCTS OR SERVICES	%	ADDITIONAL PRODUCTS OR SERVICES	%
Accommodation & Food Services					
Agriculture, Forestry, Fishing, & Hunting					
Art, Entertainment, & Recreation Services					
Communications/Information					
Construction (must complete question 3)					
Domestics (Private Households)					
Educational Services					
Finance					
Health Care Services					
Insurance					
Management of Companies & Enterprises					
Manufacturing					
Mining, Quarrying, & Oil/Gas Extraction					
Other Services					
Professional, Scientific, & Technical Services					
Public Administration					
Real Estate					
Retail Trade					
Sanitary Service					
Social Assistance Services					
Transportation					
Utilities					
Warehousing					
Wholesale Trade					
TOTAL	100%				

2. ENTER THE PERCENTAGE THAT THIS ESTABLISHMENT'S RECEIPTS OR REVENUES REPRESENT OF THE TOTAL PA RECEIPTS OR REVENUES OF THE ENTERPRISE.

_____ %

3. ESTABLISHMENTS ENGAGED IN CONSTRUCTION **MUST** ENTER THE PERCENTAGE OF CONSTRUCTION ACTIVITY THAT IS NEW AND/OR RENOVATIVE AND THE PERCENTAGE OF CONSTRUCTION ACTIVITY THAT IS RESIDENTIAL AND/OR COMMERCIAL.

_____ % NEW   +   _____ % RENOVATIVE = 100%

_____ % RESIDENTIAL   +   _____ % COMMERCIAL = 100%

PA-100 6-03

ENTERPRISE NAME	DEPARTMENT USE ONLY

PART 3 — ESTABLISHMENT SALES INFORMATION

1. ☐ YES ☐ NO IS THIS ESTABLISHMENT SELLING TAXABLE PRODUCTS OR OFFERING TAXABLE SERVICES TO CONSUMERS FROM A LOCATION **IN PENNSYLVANIA?** IF YES, COMPLETE SECTION 18.

2. ☐ YES ☐ NO IS THIS ESTABLISHMENT SELLING CIGARETTES **IN PENNSYLVANIA?** IF YES, COMPLETE SECTIONS 18 AND 19.

3. LIST EACH COUNTY **IN PENNSYLVANIA** WHERE THIS ESTABLISHMENT IS CONDUCTING TAXABLE SALES ACTIVITY(IES).

COUNTY _____   COUNTY _____   COUNTY _____

COUNTY _____   COUNTY _____   COUNTY _____

ATTACH ADDITIONAL 8 1/2 X 11 SHEETS IF NECESSARY.

PART 4a — ESTABLISHMENT EMPLOYMENT INFORMATION

1. ☐ YES ☐ NO DOES THIS ESTABLISHMENT EMPLOY INDIVIDUALS WHO **WORK IN PENNSYLVANIA?** IF YES, INDICATE:
   a. DATE WAGES FIRST **PAID** (MM/DD/YYYY) .... _____
   b. DATE WAGES RESUMED FOLLOWING A BREAK IN EMPLOYMENT .... _____
   c. TOTAL NUMBER OF EMPLOYEES .... _____
   d. NUMBER OF EMPLOYEES PRIMARILY WORKING IN NEW BUILDING OR INFRASTRUCTURE ... _____
   e. NUMBER OF EMPLOYEES PRIMARILY WORKING IN REMODELING CONSTRUCTION .... _____
   f. ESTIMATED GROSS WAGES PER QUARTER .... $ _____ .00

2. ☐ YES ☐ NO DOES THIS ESTABLISHMENT EMPLOY PA RESIDENTS WHO **WORK OUTSIDE OF PENNSYLVANIA?**
   IF YES, INDICATE:
   a. DATE WAGES FIRST **PAID** (MM/DD/YYYY) .... _____
   b. DATE WAGES RESUMED FOLLOWING A BREAK IN EMPLOYMENT .... _____
   c. ESTIMATED GROSS WAGES PER QUARTER. .... $ _____ .00

3. ☐ YES ☐ NO DOES THIS ESTABLISHMENT PAY REMUNERATION FOR SERVICES TO PERSONS YOU DO NOT CONSIDER EMPLOYEES?
   IF YES, EXPLAIN THE SERVICES PERFORMED _____

PART 4b

1. ☐ YES ☐ NO IS THIS REGISTRATION A RESULT OF A TAXABLE DISTRIBUTION FROM A BENEFIT TRUST, DEFERRED PAYMENT OR RETIREMENT PLAN FOR PA RESIDENTS? IF YES, INDICATE:
   a. DATE BENEFITS FIRST **PAID** (MM/DD/YYYY) .... _____
   b. ESTIMATED BENEFITS PAID PER QUARTER .... $ _____ .00

SECTION 6A – ADDITIONAL OWNERS, PARTNERS, SHAREHOLDERS, OFFICERS, AND RESPONSIBLE PARTY INFORMATION

PROVIDE THE FOLLOWING FOR **ALL** INDIVIDUAL AND/OR ENTERPRISE OWNERS, PARTNERS, SHAREHOLDERS, OFFICERS, AND RESPONSIBLE PARTIES. IF STOCK IS PUBLICLY TRADED, PROVIDE THE FOLLOWING FOR ANY SHAREHOLDER WITH AN EQUITY POSITION OF 5% OR MORE. *PHOTOCOPY IF ADDITIONAL SPACE IS NEEDED.*

1. NAME		2. SOCIAL SECURITY NUMBER	3. DATE OF BIRTH *	4. FEDERAL EIN
5. ☐ OWNER ☐ OFFICER ☐ PARTNER ☐ SHAREHOLDER ☐ RESPONSIBLE PARTY	6. TITLE	7. EFFECTIVE DATE OF TITLE	8. PERCENTAGE OF OWNERSHIP %	9. EFFECTIVE DATE OF OWNERSHIP
10. HOME ADDRESS (street)	CITY/TOWN	COUNTY	STATE	ZIP CODE + 4

11. THIS PERSON IS RESPONSIBLE TO REMIT/MAINTAIN: ☐ SALES TAX   ☐ EMPLOYER WITHHOLDING TAX   ☐ MOTOR FUEL TAXES   ☐ WORKERS' COMPENSATION COVERAGE

1. NAME		2. SOCIAL SECURITY NUMBER	3. DATE OF BIRTH *	4. FEDERAL EIN
5. ☐ OWNER ☐ OFFICER ☐ PARTNER ☐ SHAREHOLDER ☐ RESPONSIBLE PARTY	6. TITLE	7. EFFECTIVE DATE OF TITLE	8. PERCENTAGE OF OWNERSHIP %	9. EFFECTIVE DATE OF OWNERSHIP
10. HOME ADDRESS (street)	CITY/TOWN	COUNTY	STATE	ZIP CODE + 4

11. THIS PERSON IS RESPONSIBLE TO REMIT/MAINTAIN: ☐ SALES TAX   ☐ EMPLOYER WITHHOLDING TAX   ☐ MOTOR FUEL TAXES   ☐ WORKERS' COMPENSATION COVERAGE

* DATE OF BIRTH REQUIRED ONLY IF APPLYING FOR A CIGARETTE WHOLESALE DEALER'S LICENSE, A SMALL GAMES OF CHANCE DISTRIBUTOR LICENSE, OR A SMALL GAMES OF CHANCE MANUFACTURER CERTIFICATE.

11

PA-100 8-01

ENTERPRISE NAME

DEPARTMENT USE ONLY

SECTION 18 – SALES USE AND HOTEL OCCUPANCY TAX LICENSE, PUBLIC TRANSPORTATION ASSISTANCE TAX LICENSE, VEHICLE RENTAL TAX, TRANSIENT VENDOR CERTIFICATE, PROMOTER LICENSE, OR WHOLESALER CERTIFICATE

PART 1   SALES USE AND HOTEL OCCUPANCY TAX, PUBLIC TRANSPORTATION ASSISTANCE TAX, VEHICLE RENTAL TAX, OR WHOLESALER CERTIFICATE

ENTERPRISES APPLYING FOR A SALES, USE AND HOTEL OCCUPANCY TAX LICENSE, PUBLIC TRANSPORTATION ASSISTANCE TAX LICENSE, VEHICLE RENTAL TAX, AND/OR WHOLESALER CERTIFICATE.
COMPLETE PART 1. SALES TAX COLLECTED MUST BE SEGREGATED FROM OTHER FUNDS AND MUST REMAIN IN THE COMMONWEALTH OF PENNSYLVANIA UNTIL REMITTED TO THE DEPARTMENT OF REVENUE.

IF THE ENTERPRISE IS:

● SELLING TAXABLE PRODUCTS OR SERVICES TO CONSUMERS **IN PENNSYLVANIA,** ENTER DATE OF FIRST TAXABLE SALE _____

● PURCHASING TAXABLE PRODUCTS OR SERVICES FOR ITS OWN USE **IN PENNSYLVANIA** AND INCURRING NO SALES TAX, ENTER DATE OF FIRST PURCHASE _____

● SELLING NEW TIRES TO CONSUMERS **IN PENNSYLVANIA,** ENTER DATE OF FIRST SALE_____

● LEASING OR RENTING MOTOR VEHICLES, ENTER DATE OF FIRST LEASE OR RENTAL _____

● RENTING FIVE OR MORE MOTOR VEHICLES, ENTER DATE OF FIRST RENTAL _____

● CONDUCTING RETAIL SALES IN PENNSYLVANIA AND NOT MAINTAINING A PERMANENT LOCATION IN PA, ENTER DATE OF FIRST TAXABLE SALE _____ (COMPLETE PART 2)

● ACTIVELY PROMOTING SHOWS IN PENNSYLVANIA WHERE TAXABLE PRODUCTS WILL BE OFFERED FOR RETAIL SALE, ENTER DATE OF FIRST SHOW _____ . (COMPLETE PART 3)

● ENGAGED SOLELY IN THE SALE OF TANGIBLE PERSONAL PROPERTY AND/OR SERVICES FOR RESALE OR RENTAL. ENTER DATE OF FIRST PURCHASE. _____

PART 2   TRANSIENT VENDOR CERTIFICATE

IF THE ENTERPRISE PARTICIPATES IN ANY SHOWS OTHER THAN THOSE LISTED, PROVIDE THE NAME(S) OF THE SHOW(S) AND INFORMATION ABOUT THE SHOW(S) TO THE DEPARTMENT OF REVENUE AT LEAST 10 DAYS PRIOR TO THE SHOW.

PROVIDE THE FOLLOWING INFORMATION FOR **EACH SHOW:**

1. PROMOTER NUMBER	2. SHOW NAME		3. COUNTY	
4. SHOW ADDRESS (STREET, CITY, STATE, ZIP)			5. START DATE	6. END DATE
1. PROMOTER NUMBER	2. SHOW NAME		3. COUNTY	
4. SHOW ADDRESS (STREET, CITY, STATE, ZIP)			5. START DATE	6. END DATE

ATTACH ADDITIONAL 8 1/2 X 11 SHEETS IF NECESSARY.

PART 3   PROMOTER LICENSE

PROVIDE THE FOLLOWING INFORMATION FOR **EACH SHOW:**

1. SHOW NAME	2. TYPE OF SHOW	3. START DATE	4. END DATE
5. SHOW ADDRESS (STREET, CITY, STATE, ZIP)	6. COUNTY	7. NBR OF VENDORS	
1. SHOW NAME	2. TYPE OF SHOW	3. START DATE	4. END DATE
5. SHOW ADDRESS (STREET, CITY, STATE, ZIP)	6. COUNTY	7. NBR OF VENDORS	

ATTACH ADDITIONAL 8 1/2 X 11 SHEETS IF NECESSARY.

PA-100 8-01

ENTERPRISE NAME

DEPARTMENT USE ONLY

SECTION 19 – CIGARETTE DEALER'S LICENSE

PART 1   LICENSE TYPE

CHECK THE APPROPRIATE BOX(ES) TO INDICATE LICENSE TYPE REQUESTED. A SEPARATE LICENSE MUST BE OBTAINED FOR EACH ESTABLISHMENT THAT SELLS CIGARETTES (CSA, WHOLESALE, RETAIL, AND/OR VENDING). A SEPARATE DECAL MUST BE PURCHASED FOR EACH VENDING MACHINE LOCATION. A CHECK OR MONEY ORDER MUST BE SUBMITTED WITH THIS APPLICATION.

LICENSE TYPE	NUMBER	FEE	AMOUNT REMITTED
☐ RETAIL OVER-THE-COUNTER		@ $ 25 EACH LOCATION	$
☐ VENDING MACHINE (ATTACH A LIST OF LOCATIONS)		@ $ 25 EACH DECAL	$
☐ WHOLESALER		@ $ 500 EACH LICENSE	$
☐ CIGARETTE STAMPING AGENT AND WHOLESALER		@ $ 1,500 EACH LICENSE	$
		TOTAL AMOUNT REMITTED	$

MAKE CHECKS PAYABLE TO PA DEPARTMENT OF REVENUE

PART 2   CIGARETTE WHOLESALER

LIST CIGARETTE STORAGE LOCATION(S) (P.O. BOXES ARE NOT ACCEPTABLE).

1. STREET ADDRESS

CITY/TOWN	COUNTY	STATE	ZIP CODE + 4

2. ☐ YES   ☐ NO   HAS ANY OWNER, PARTNER, OFFICER, DIRECTOR, OR MAJOR STOCKHOLDER BEEN CONVICTED OF ANY VIOLATION OF THE PENNSYLVANIA CIGARETTE TAX ACT OR ANY MISDEMEANOR OR FELONY?

IF YES, LIST ALL CONVICTIONS WITHIN THE PREVIOUS 10 YEAR PERIOD. ATTACH ADDITIONAL 8 1/2 X 11 SHEETS IF NECESSARY.

3. THE APPLICANT HAS COMPLIED WITH ARTICLE II-A OF THE CIGARETTE SALES AND LICENSING ACT. UNDER PENALTY OF PERJURY, OF ADHERENCE TO STATE PRESUMPTIVE MINIMUM PRICES OR APPROVAL TO SELL AT A DIFFERENT PRICE, IN ACCORDANCE WITH THE ACT:

☐ CIGARETTES WILL BE SOLD AT OR ABOVE THE PRESUMPTIVE MINIMUM PRICE.

☐ CIGARETTES WILL BE SOLD AT AN APPROVED MINIMUM PRICE.

PART 3   CIGARETTE STAMPING AGENT

1. ☐ YES   ☐ NO   DOES THE ENTERPRISE PURCHASE OR SELL ANY CIGARETTES WHICH ARE NOT PA STAMPED?

IF YES, LIST STATES:

13

PA-100 8-01

ENTERPRISE NAME

SECTION 20 – SMALL GAMES OF CHANCE LICENSE/CERTIFICATE

PART 1   DISTRIBUTOR AND/OR MANUFACTURER

TO BE COMPLETED BY ALL APPLICANTS (DISTRIBUTOR AND/OR MANUFACTURER)

APPLICANTS MUST SUBMIT A COPY OF THE CERTIFICATE OF INCORPORATION, ARTICLES OF INCORPORATION, CERTIFICATE OF AUTHORITY (NON-PA CORPORATIONS), BY-LAWS, CONSTITUTION, OR FICTITIOUS NAME REGISTRATION.

APPLICANTS FOR A MANUFACTURER CERTIFICATE MUST SUBMIT A COPY OF THE COMPANY LOGO(S).

1.   CHECK APPROPRIATE BOX(ES) TO INDICATE TYPE OF LICENSE/CERTIFICATE REQUESTED

LICENSE/CERTIFICATE TYPE	FEE	AMOUNT REMITTED
☐ DISTRIBUTOR LICENSE	$ 1,000	$_____
☐ MANUFACTURER REGISTRATION CERTIFICATE	$ 2,000	$_____
☐ REPLACEMENT LICENSE	$ 100	$_____
☐ REPLACEMENT CERTIFICATE	$ 100	$_____
NUMBER OF BACKGROUND INVESTIGATIONS FOR OWNERS/OFFICERS, ETC. _____ @	$ 10	$_____
	TOTAL AMOUNT REMITTED	$_____

MAKE CHECKS PAYABLE TO PA DEPARTMENT OF REVENUE

IF THE DEPARTMENT DENIES AN APPLICATION, A $100 APPLICATION PROCESSING FEE SHALL BE RETAINED BY THE DEPARTMENT. NO PART OF THE REGISTRATION OR LICENSE FEE SHALL BE SUBJECT TO PRORATION. NO INVESTIGATION FEE SHALL BE REFUNDED.

2.   DISTRIBUTORS AND MANUFACTURERS - PROVIDE THE FOLLOWING INFORMATION FOR THE COMMONWEALTH OF PA RESIDENT DESIGNEE. THE INDIVIDUAL MUST HAVE PHYSICAL LOCATION WITHIN PA.

NAME

HOME ADDRESS (STREET)	CITY/TOWN	STATE	ZIP CODE + 4	TELEPHONE NBR. ( )

3.   DISTRIBUTORS AND MANUFACTURERS - PROVIDE THE FOLLOWING INFORMATION FOR ALL INDIVIDUALS RESPONSIBLE FOR TAKING ORDERS AND MAKING SALES OF SMALL GAMES OF CHANCE MERCHANDISE. IF AN INDIVIDUAL RESIDES IN PENNSYLVANIA, INDICATE IF COMMISSION OR NONCOMMISSION.

NAME	TITLE	☐ SELLS FOR DISTRIBUTOR ☐ SELLS FOR MANUFACTURER	☐ COMMISSION ☐ NONCOMMISSION
HOME ADDRESS (STREET)	CITY/TOWN	STATE ZIP CODE + 4	TELEPHONE NBR. ( )
NAME	TITLE	☐ SELLS FOR DISTRIBUTOR ☐ SELLS FOR MANUFACTURER	☐ COMMISSION ☐ NONCOMMISSION
HOME ADDRESS (STREET)	CITY/TOWN	STATE ZIP CODE + 4	TELEPHONE NBR. ( )

ATTACH ADDITIONAL 8 1/2 X 11 SHEETS IF NECESSARY

MANUFACTURERS ONLY MUST SUBMIT A CATALOG OF THE SMALL GAMES CHECKED BELOW. IF CATALOG IS UNAVAILABLE, PROVIDE NAME OF GAME(S) AND FORM NUMBER(S), NUMBER OF TICKETS PER DEAL, HIGHEST INDIVIDUAL PRIZE VALUE, AND PERCENTAGE OF PAYOUT.

4.   CHECK THE APPROPRIATE BOX(ES) TO INDICATE THE TYPES OF SMALL GAMES DISTRIBUTED OR MANUFACTURED.

☐ DAILY DRAWINGS   ☐ WEEKLY DRAWINGS   ☐ PULL-TABS   ☐ PUNCHBOARDS   ☐ RAFFLES   ☐ DISPENSING MACHINES

PART 2   DISTRIBUTOR

LIST ALL SMALL GAMES OF CHANCE MANUFACTURERS WITH WHOM THE DISTRIBUTOR DOES BUSINESS.

MANUFACTURER'S LEGAL NAME	MANUFACTURER'S CERTIFICATE NBR. M-	TELEPHONE NBR. ( )
STREET ADDRESS	CITY/TOWN	STATE ZIP CODE +4
MANUFACTURER'S LEGAL NAME	MANUFACTURER'S CERTIFICATE NBR. M-	TELEPHONE NBR. ( )
STREET ADDRESS	CITY/TOWN	STATE ZIP CODE +4

ATTACH ADDITIONAL 8 1/2 X 11 SHEETS IF NECESSARY

PART 3 SMALL GAMES OF CHANCE CERTIFICATION

MUST BE COMPLETED BY ALL SMALL GAMES OF CHANCE APPLICANTS.

I CERTIFY THAT THE FOLLOWING TAX STATEMENTS ARE TRUE AND CORRECT

- ALL PA STATE TAX REPORTS AND RETURNS HAVE BEEN FILED

- ALL PA STATE TAXES HAVE BEEN PAID

- ANY PA STATE TAXES OWED ARE SUBJECT TO TIMELY ADMINISTRATIVE OR JUDICIAL APPEAL; OR ANY DELINQUENT PA TAXES ARE SUBJECT TO DULY APPROVED DEFERRED PAYMENT PLAN (COPY ENCLOSED).

I CERTIFY THAT NO OWNER, PARTNER, OFFICER, DIRECTOR, OR OTHER PERSON IN A SUPERVISORY OR MANAGEMENT POSITION, OR EMPLOYEE ELIGIBLE TO MAKE SALES ON BEHALF OF THIS BUSINESS:

- HAS BEEN CONVICTED OF A FELONY IN A STATE OR FEDERAL COURT WITHIN THE PAST FIVE YEARS

- HAS BEEN CONVICTED WITHIN TEN YEARS OF THE DATE OF APPLICATION IN A STATE OR FEDERAL COURT OF A VIOLATION OF THE BINGO LAW OR OF THE LOCAL OPTION SMALL GAMES OF CHANCE ACT, OR A GAMBLING-RELATED OFFENSE UNDER TITLE 18 OF THE PENNSYLVANIA CONSOLIDATED STATUTES OR OTHER COMPARABLE STATE OR FEDERAL LAW

- HAS NOT BEEN REJECTED IN ANY STATE FOR A DISTRIBUTOR LICENSE OR MANUFACTURER REGISTRATION CERTIFICATE, OR EQUIVALENT THERETO.

I DECLARE THAT I HAVE EXAMINED THIS APPLICATION, INCLUDING ALL ACCOMPANYING STATEMENTS, AND TO THE BEST OF MY KNOWLEDGE AND BELIEF IT IS TRUE, CORRECT, AND COMPLETE.

NOTARY	AUTHORIZATION	
SWORN AND SUBSCRIBED TO BEFORE ME THIS		
_____ DAY OF _____ , 20___		
	_____	_____
	SIGNATURE OF AN OWNER, PARTNER, OFFICER, OR DIRECTOR	SOCIAL SECURITY NUMBER
_____	_____	_____
NOTARY PUBLIC	PRINT NAME	DATE
MY COMMISSION EXPIRES _____	_____	
	TITLE	
	(___) _____	
	TELEPHONE NUMBER	
_____		_____
NOTARY SEAL		CORPORATE SEAL

PA-100 8-01

ENTERPRISE NAME

DEPARTMENT USE ONLY

SECTION 21 – MOTOR CARRIER REGISTRATION & DECAL/MOTOR FUELS LICENSE & PERMIT

PART 1 — VEHICLE OPERATIONS

A DECAL IS REQUIRED IF AN ENTERPRISE IS OPERATING A QUALIFIED MOTOR VEHICLE, SEE PAGE 25, PART 1 - VEHICLE OPERATIONS.

CHECK THE APPROPRIATE BOX(ES) TO DESCRIBE THE ENTERPRISE OPERATIONS:

☐ COMMON CARRIER ☐ CONTRACT CARRIER ☐ FOR HIRE CARRIER ☐ PRIVATE CARRIER

INDICATE THE FUEL TYPES FOR PENNSYLVANIA BASED QUALIFIED MOTOR VEHICLES:

☐ DIESEL ☐ GASOLINE ☐ ETHANOL/GASOHOL ☐ LP GAS ☐ CNG/LNG

MOTOR CARRIER ROAD TAX/IFTA VEHICLE DECAL REQUESTS

COMPLETE THE FOLLOWING FOR EACH QUALIFIED MOTOR VEHICLE YOU INTEND TO OPERATE IN PENNSYLVANIA DURING THE ENSUING CALENDAR YEAR.

NOTE: DECALS ARE $5.00 PER SET OF TWO.

1. **IFTA** DECALS (NUMBER OF VEHICLES THAT TRAVEL IN PA AND OUT OF STATE) _____

2. **NON-IFTA** DECALS (NUMBER OF VEHICLES THAT TRAVEL IN PA EXCLUSIVELY) _____

3. TOTAL DECALS REQUESTED (ADD LINES 1 AND 2) _____

4. TOTAL AMOUNT DUE (MULTIPLY LINE 3 BY **$5**) $_____

REMITTANCE SUBMITTED:

5. AUTHORIZED ADJUSTMENT (ATTACH ORIGINAL CREDIT NOTICE) $_____

6. CHECK OR MONEY ORDER AMOUNT $_____

MAKE CHECKS PAYABLE TO PA DEPARTMENT OF REVENUE

CHECK THE APPROPRIATE BOX(ES) TO INDICATE THE JURISDICTION(S) WHERE:

COLUMN A – QUALIFIED MOTOR VEHICLES ARE OPERATED
COLUMN B – BULK STORAGE OF DIESEL FUEL IS MAINTAINED

COLUMN C – BULK STORAGE FOR GASOLINE IS MAINTAINED
COLUMN D – BULK STORAGE OF ANY OTHER MOTOR FUEL IS MAINTAINED

A B C D	A B C D	A B C D	A B C D
☐ ☐ ☐ ☐ AK – ALASKA	☐ ☐ ☐ ☐ ID – IDAHO	☐ ☐ ☐ ☐ MT – MONTANA	☐ ☐ ☐ ☐ RI – RHODE ISLAND
☐ ☐ ☐ ☐ AL – ALABAMA	☐ ☐ ☐ ☐ IL – ILLINOIS	☐ ☐ ☐ ☐ NC – NORTH CAROLINA	☐ ☐ ☐ ☐ SC – SOUTH CAROLINA
☐ ☐ ☐ ☐ AR – ARKANSAS	☐ ☐ ☐ ☐ IN – INDIANA	☐ ☐ ☐ ☐ ND – NORTH DAKOTA	☐ ☐ ☐ ☐ SD – SOUTH DAKOTA
☐ ☐ ☐ ☐ AZ – ARIZONA	☐ ☐ ☐ ☐ KS – KANSAS	☐ ☐ ☐ ☐ NE – NEBRASKA	☐ ☐ ☐ ☐ TN – TENNESSEE
☐ ☐ ☐ ☐ CA – CALIFORNIA	☐ ☐ ☐ ☐ KY – KENTUCKY	☐ ☐ ☐ ☐ NH – NEW HAMPSHIRE	☐ ☐ ☐ ☐ TX – TEXAS
☐ ☐ ☐ ☐ CO – COLORADO	☐ ☐ ☐ ☐ LA – LOUISIANA	☐ ☐ ☐ ☐ NJ – NEW JERSEY	☐ ☐ ☐ ☐ UT – UTAH
☐ ☐ ☐ ☐ CT – CONNECTICUT	☐ ☐ ☐ ☐ MA – MASSACHUSETTS	☐ ☐ ☐ ☐ NM – NEW MEXICO	☐ ☐ ☐ ☐ VA – VIRGINIA
☐ ☐ ☐ ☐ DC – DIST. OF COLUMBIA	☐ ☐ ☐ ☐ MD – MARYLAND	☐ ☐ ☐ ☐ NV – NEVADA	☐ ☐ ☐ ☐ VT – VERMONT
☐ ☐ ☐ ☐ DE – DELAWARE	☐ ☐ ☐ ☐ ME – MAINE	☐ ☐ ☐ ☐ NY – NEW YORK	☐ ☐ ☐ ☐ WA – WASHINGTON
☐ ☐ ☐ ☐ FL – FLORIDA	☐ ☐ ☐ ☐ MI – MICHIGAN	☐ ☐ ☐ ☐ OH – OHIO	☐ ☐ ☐ ☐ WI – WISCONSIN
☐ ☐ ☐ ☐ GA – GEORGIA	☐ ☐ ☐ ☐ MN – MINNESOTA	☐ ☐ ☐ ☐ OK – OKLAHOMA	☐ ☐ ☐ ☐ WV – WEST VIRGINIA
☐ ☐ ☐ ☐ HI – HAWAII	☐ ☐ ☐ ☐ MO – MISSOURI	☐ ☐ ☐ ☐ OR – OREGON	☐ ☐ ☐ ☐ WY – WYOMING
☐ ☐ ☐ ☐ IA – IOWA	☐ ☐ ☐ ☐ MS – MISSISSIPPI	☐ ☐ ☐ ☐ PA – PENNSYLVANIA	

A B C D	A B C D	A B C D	A B C D
☐ ☐ ☐ ☐ AB – ALBERTA	☐ ☐ ☐ ☐ NB – NEW BRUNSWICK	☐ ☐ ☐ ☐ NT – N W TERRITORY	☐ ☐ ☐ ☐ PQ – QUEBEC
☐ ☐ ☐ ☐ BC – BRITISH COLUMBIA	☐ ☐ ☐ ☐ NF – NEWFOUNDLAND	☐ ☐ ☐ ☐ ON – ONTARIO	☐ ☐ ☐ ☐ SK – SASKATCHEWAN
☐ ☐ ☐ ☐ MB – MANITOBA	☐ ☐ ☐ ☐ NS – NOVA SCOTIA	☐ ☐ ☐ ☐ PE – PRINCE EDWARD IS.	☐ ☐ ☐ ☐ YT - YUKON TERRITORY

PART 2 — FUELS

CHECK THE APPROPRIATE BOX(ES) IF THE ENTERPRISE WILL SELL, USE, OR TRANSPORT ANY FUELS IN PENNSYLVANIA.

☐ LIQUID FUELS AND FUELS TAX - YEARLY PERMIT REQUIRED BY WHOLESALE DISTRIBUTORS (E.G. ONE LICENSED TO HANDLE TAX-FREE LIQUID FUELS OR FUELS IN PA) OR AN IMPORTER OR EXPORTER OF LIQUID FUELS OR FUELS.
ESTIMATED DATE OF FIRST TAX-FREE LIQUID FUELS PURCHASE OR SALE _____

☐ ALTERNATIVE FUELS TAX - YEARLY PERMIT REQUIRED BY ALTERNATIVE FUEL DEALER-USERS FOR THE REMISSION OF TAX ON ALTERNATIVE FUELS (HIGHWAY FUELS OTHER THAN LIQUID FUELS OR FUELS) PLACED INTO THE SUPPLY TANK OF A MOTOR VEHICLE FOR USE ON PA HIGHWAYS.
ESTIMATED DATE OF FIRST FUELING OF VEHICLES _____

PROVIDE A LIST OF ALL PA LOCATIONS WHERE LIQUID FUELS OR FUELS WILL BE SOLD.

STREET ADDRESS	CITY/TOWN	COUNTY	STATE	ZIP CODE + 4
STREET ADDRESS	CITY/TOWN	COUNTY	STATE	ZIP CODE + 4

ATTACH ADDITIONAL 8 1/2 x 11 SHEETS IF NECESSARY

PA-100 8-01

| ENTERPRISE NAME | DEPARTMENT USE ONLY |

SECTION 22 – SALES TAX EXEMPT STATUS FOR CHARITABLE AND RELIGIOUS ORGANIZATIONS

PART 1

ACT 55 OF 1997, KNOWN AS THE INSTITUTIONS OF PURELY PUBLIC CHARITY ACT, WAS SIGNED INTO LAW ON NOVEMBER 26, 1997. THIS LAW HAS CODIFIED THE REQUIREMENTS AN INSTITUTION MUST MEET IN ORDER TO QUALIFY FOR EXEMPTION, OUTLINING FIVE CRITERIA THAT MUST BE MET. EACH INSTITUTION MUST: (1) ADVANCE A CHARITABLE PURPOSE; (2) DONATE OR RENDER GRATUITOUSLY A SUBSTANTIAL PORTION OF ITS SERVICES; (3) BENEFIT A SUBSTANTIAL AND INDEFINITE CLASS OF PERSONS WHO ARE LEGITIMATE SUBJECTS OF CHARITY; (4) RELIEVE THE GOVERNMENT OF SOME BURDEN; (5) OPERATE ENTIRELY FREE FROM PRIVATE PROFIT MOTIVE.

ORGANIZATIONS OF THE FOLLOWING TYPE DO NOT QUALIFY FOR EXEMPTION STATUS:

- AN ASSOCIATION OF EMPLOYEES, THE MEMBERSHIP OF WHICH IS LIMITED TO THE EMPLOYEES OF A DESIGNATED ENTERPRISE
- A LABOR ORGANIZATION
- AN AGRICULTURAL OR HORTICULTURAL ORGANIZATION
- A BUSINESS LEAGUE, CHAMBER OF COMMERCE, REAL ESTATE BOARD, BOARD OF TRADE, OR PROFESSIONAL SPORT LEAGUE
- A CLUB ORGANIZED FOR PLEASURE OR RECREATION
- A FRATERNAL BENEFICIARY SOCIETY, ORDER, OR ASSOCIATION.

TO APPLY OR RENEW SALES TAX EXEMPTION STATUS, A REV-72 APPLICATION **MUST** BE COMPLETED AND SUBMITTED ALONG WITH THE REQUIRED DOCUMENTATION. THIS APPLICATION CAN BE OBTAINED BY COMPLETING THE BELOW FORM OR CALL (717) 783-5473. SERVICE FOR CUSTOMERS WITH SPECIAL HEARING AND/OR SPEAKING NEEDS (TT ONLY) 1-800-447-3020.

IF THE ORGANIZATION CONDUCTS SALES ACTIVITIES AND IS NOT REGISTERED FOR COLLECTION OF PA SALES TAX, REFER TO SECTION 18 OF THIS BOOKLET.

PART 2   REQUEST FOR SALES TAX EXEMPT STATUS APPLICATION

NAME

| MAILING ADDRESS | CITY/TOWN | STATE | ZIP CODE + 4 |

TO REQUEST SALES TAX EXEMPT STATUS APPLICATION
COMPLETE THIS FORM AND RETURN TO:

PA DEPARTMENT OF REVENUE
BUREAU OF BUSINESS TRUST FUND TAXES
DEPT. 280909
HARRISBURG, PA 17128-0909

PA-100 8-01

SECTION 1 – REASON FOR THIS REGISTRATION

An enterprise may select more than one reason for registration.

1. **New Registration:** An enterprise never registered with the PA Department of Revenue or the PA Department of Labor & Industry must complete Sections 1 through 10 and additional sections as appropriate.

2. **Adding Tax(es) and Service(s):** A registered enterprise adding tax(es) and service(s) must complete Sections 1 through 4 and additional sections as appropriate.

3. **Reactivating Tax(es) and Service(s):** A registered enterprise reactivating tax(es) and service(s) must complete Sections 1 through 4 and additional sections as appropriate.

4. **Adding Establishment(s):** A registered enterprise adding establishment location(s) must complete Sections 1 through 4 and Section 17, Multiple Establishment Information.

5. **Information Update:** A registered enterprise providing changes in demographic or other information must complete Sections 1 through 4 and additional sections as appropriate.

6. **Did this Enterprise:**

   An enterprise acquiring the business operation of another enterprise in whole or in part must complete Section 14, Predecessor/Successor Information. The business operation can be acquired by consolidation, merger, gift, or change in legal structure. A stock acquisition _alone_ does not constitute a transfer of the business operation.

   Check the appropriate box to indicate the business operation of the enterprise. If yes:

   - A newly formed enterprise must complete Sections 1 through 10, Section 14 and additional sections as appropriate.

   - A previously registered enterprise must complete Sections 1 through 4, 10, 14 and additional sections as appropriate.

   - An enterprise requesting the PA Unemployment Compensation (UC) experience record and reserve account balance of a predecessor (prior owner) must also complete Section 15, Application for PA UC Experience Record and Reserve Account Balance of Predecessor.

SECTION 2 – ENTERPRISE INFORMATION

1. **Date of First Operations:** Enter the first date the enterprise conducted any activity. This includes start-up operations prior to opening for business.

2. **Date of First Operations in PA:** Enter the first date the enterprise conducted any activity in PA or employed PA residents. This includes start-up operations prior to opening for business.

3. **Enterprise Fiscal Year End:** Enter the month (January, February, etc.) used by the enterprise to designate the end of its accounting period.

4. **Enterprise Legal Name:** Enter the legal name of the enterprise.

IF THE BUSINESS STRUCTURE IS:	USE THE:
SOLE PROPRIETORSHIP	INDIVIDUAL OWNER'S NAME.
CORPORATION	NAME AS SHOWN IN THE ARTICLES OF INCORPORATION.
PARTNERSHIP	NAME AS SHOWN IN THE PARTNERSHIP AGREEMENT.
ASSOCIATION	NAME AS SHOWN IN THE ASSOCIATION AGREEMENT.
BUSINESS TRUST	NAME AS SHOWN IN THE TRUST AGREEMENT.
ESTATE	LEGAL NAME OF THE ESTATE.
TRUST	NAME AS SHOWN IN THE TRUST AGREEMENT.
LIMITED LIABILITY COMPANY	NAME AS SHOWN IN THE ARTICLES OF ORGANIZATION.
RESTRICTED PROFESSIONAL COMPANY	NAME AS SHOWN IN THE ARTICLES OF ORGANIZATION.
GOVERNMENT	OFFICIAL/LEGAL NAME OF THE ORGANIZATION.

5. **Federal EIN:** Enter the Federal Employer Identification Number (EIN) assigned to the enterprise by the Internal Revenue Service. If the enterprise does not have an EIN, enter "N/A". If the enterprise has made application for an EIN, enter "Applied For".

6. **Enterprise Trade Name:** Enter the name by which the enterprise is commonly known (doing business as, trading as, also known as), if it is a name other than the legal name. If the enterprise has a fictitious name registered with the PA Department of State, enter it here. If the trade name is the same as the legal name, enter "Same".

7. **Enterprise Telephone Number:** Enter the telephone number for the enterprise.

8. **Enterprise Street Address:** Enter the physical location of the enterprise. **A post office box is not acceptable.**

9. **Enterprise Mailing Address:** Enter the address where the enterprise prefers to receive mail, if at an address other than the enterprise street address. A post office box is acceptable. If the mailing address is the same as the enterprise street address, enter "Same".

   To indicate multiple mailing addresses and the purposes, attach a separate 8 1/2 X 11 sheet and identify the purpose of each.

   For example, an enterprise may want tax forms or licenses mailed to the enterprise address, but payroll-related forms such as Employer Withholding and Unemployment Compensation Returns mailed to the address of a particular payroll service.

10. **Location of Enterprise Records:** Enter the street address where the enterprise records are kept. A post office box is not acceptable. If the records are kept at the enterprise street address, enter "Same".

11. **Establishment Name:** Enter the name by which the establishment is known to the public; for example, the name on the front of the store. If the same as the enterprise legal name, enter "Same".

12. **Number of Establishments:** Enter the number of establishments. If the enterprise has more than one establishment conducting business in PA or employing PA residents, refer to the instructions and complete Section 17, Multiple Establishment Information.

13. **School District:** Enter the school district where the establishment is located. If not a PA school district, enter "N/A".

14. **Municipality:** Enter the municipality (borough, city, town, or township) where the establishment is located. The municipality may be different from the city/town used for postal delivery. If not a PA municipality, enter "N/A".

SECTION 3 – TAXES AND SERVICES

Indicate the tax(es) and service(s) requested. Descriptions, additional requirements and sections to complete are on page(s) 2 and 3. Enter the previous account number(s) when reactivating tax(es) and service(s).

SECTION 4 – AUTHORIZED SIGNATURE

Authorized Signature: Owner, general partner, officer, or agent signature is required. Enter the title and daytime phone number of the person who signed the form. Attach Power of Attorney document, if applicable.

Type or Print Name: Type or print the name of the person who signed the document, enter their e-mail address, and the date it was signed.

Type or Print Name: Type or print the name of the preparer, the title of the person who prepared the form, if other than the owner, partner or officer. Enter the preparer's daytime telephone number, e-mail address, and the date the form was prepared.

SECTION 5 – BUSINESS STRUCTURE

1. Check the box to select the form of organization that applies to the enterprise.

   - A sole proprietor is one individual owner and indicates 100 percent ownership.

   - Two or more individuals listed as owners constitute a partnership and will be registered as one. Registrants for Unemployment Compensation should attach a copy of the partnership agreement, if available.

   - Limited liability companies and restricted professional companies must enter the state/province where chartered.

   The following forms of organization require the completion of additional sections:

   - Corporation - Complete Section 11, Corporation Information.

   - Government - Complete Section 13, Government Information.

2. Check the box to indicate if the enterprise is profit or non-profit.

3. If an enterprise is exempt under Section 501(c)(3) of the Internal Revenue Code, and is also subject to the contribution provisions of the Pennsylvania Unemployment Compensation (UC) Law, it has the option to elect to finance UC costs under the reimbursement method in lieu of the contributory method.

See page 22 of the instructions for further explanations regarding contributory and reimbursement methods of making payments to the Unemployment Compensation Fund.

SECTION 6 – OWNERS, PARTNERS, SHAREHOLDERS, OFFICERS, AND RESPONSIBLE PARTY INFORMATION

Identify and provide information on the following:

- The sole proprietor who is 100 percent owner. A sole proprietor must be one individual.

- All general partners and all limited partners who are involved in the daily operation of the business.

- All shareholders (both individuals and enterprises) owning stock. If the stock is publicly traded, identify any shareholder with an equity position of 5 percent or more.

- All officers of the corporation, association, or business trust.

- All individuals responsible for remitting trust fund taxes or maintaining Workers' Compensation Coverage.

1. **Name:** Enter the name(s) of the owner, partner, shareholder, officer, or responsible party of the enterprise. If the owner is another enterprise, enter the legal name of the enterprise.

2. **Social Security Number:** Enter the Social Security Number of the owner, partner, shareholder, officer, or responsible party.

3. **Date of Birth:** Enter the individual's date of birth if applying for a Cigarette Wholesale Dealer's License, a Small Games of Chance Distributor License, or Manufacturer Certificate.

4. **Federal EIN:** Enter the Federal Employer Identification Number (EIN) if the owner, partner, or shareholder is another enterprise.

5. **Type of Ownership/Position:** Check the box(es) to designate if an owner, partner, officer, shareholder, or responsible party.

6-9. **Title, Effective Dates, Percentage of Ownership:** Enter the title, effective dates, and percentage of ownership as indicated.

10. **Home Address:** Enter the home street address of the owner, partner, shareholder, officer, or responsible party. If the owner, partner, or shareholder is another enterprise, enter the street address of the enterprise. **A post office box is not acceptable.**

11. **Person Responsible to Remit/Maintain:** Check the appropriate box(es) to indicate the Taxes/Services for which this individual is responsible.

Responsible Party: Please identify the person(s) responsible for remitting Sales Tax, Employer Withholding Tax, Liquid Fuels and Fuels Taxes, or maintaining Workers' Compensation Coverage. Under PA law, a proprietor, a general partner, a corporation's chief operating officer(s), and/or a chief financial officer is responsible for ensuring that collected trust fund taxes are remitted on a timely basis and workers' compensation coverage is maintained when required. Other individuals may also be responsible if their duties, position, or authority over financial matters and decision-making put them in a position to influence the payment of these taxes or maintaining business operation. Failure to remit these taxes in a timely manner or to maintain ongoing workers' compensation coverage when required may result in the personal assessment of a responsible party, together with the possibility of criminal sanctions, if warranted.

Space for additional information of owners, partners, shareholders, officers, and/or responsible parties can be found on page 11. Attach additional 8 1/2 X 11 sheets if necessary.

SECTION 7 – ESTABLISHMENT BUSINESS ACTIVITY INFORMATION

ENTER THE PERCENTAGE THE PA BUSINESS ACTIVITY REPRESENTS OF THE TOTAL RECEIPTS OR REVENUES AT THIS ESTABLISHMENT. SPECIFY THE PRODUCTS AND/OR SERVICES PROVIDED AT THIS ESTABLISHMENT AND ENTER THE PERCENTAGE EACH REPRESENTS OF THE TOTAL RECEIPTS OR REVENUES AT THIS ESTABLISHMENT.

EXAMPLE

PA BUSINESS ACTIVITY	%	PRODUCTS OR SERVICES	%	ADDITIONAL PRODUCTS OR SERVICES	%
CONSTRUCTION	70	BUILDING SINGLE FAMILY HOMES	40	BUILDING APARTMENT BUILDINGS	30
MANUFACTURING					
RETAIL TRADE					
WHOLESALE TRADE	30	WOOD PANELING	30		

PA BUSINESS ACTIVITIES AND TYPICAL PRODUCTS OR SERVICES EXAMPLES.
THIS SECTION IS NOT FOR DETERMINING THE TAXABILITY OF PRODUCTS OR SERVICES, ONLY THE CLASSIFICATION OF PRODUCTS AND SERVICES.

PA BUSINESS ACTIVITY	TYPICAL PRODUCTS OR SERVICES
ACCOMMODATION AND FOOD SERVICES ESTABLISHMENTS ENGAGED IN ACTIVITIES OF THIS SECTOR PROVIDE CUSTOMERS WITH LODGING AND/OR PREPARE MEALS, SNACKS, AND BEVERAGES FOR IMMEDIATE CONSUMPTION.	SPECIFY THE TYPE OF FACILITY WHERE ACTIVITY TAKES PLACE. *FOR EXAMPLE:* HOTELS / MOTELS / RV PARKS AND CAMPGROUNDS / VACATION CAMPS / FULL/LIMITED SERVICE RESTAURANTS / MOBILE FOOD SERVICES AND CATERERS
AGRICULTURE, FORESTRY, FISHING, AND HUNTING ESTABLISHMENTS ENGAGED IN ACTIVITIES OF THIS SECTOR ARE INVOLVED IN GROWING CROPS, RAISING ANIMALS, HARVESTING FISH AND OTHER ANIMALS FROM FARMS, RANCHES, OR ANIMALS' NATURAL HABITATS.	SPECIFY THE TYPE OF CROP GROWN, LIVESTOCK RAISED, FISH CAUGHT, AND FORESTRY WORK. *FOR EXAMPLE:* CROPS (CORN, WHEAT, APPLE) AND WHETHER UNDER COVER / NURSERY/TREE PRODUCTIONS / CATTLE RANCHING / DAIRY CATTLE AND MILK PRODUCTION / CHICKEN (EGG OR MEAT TYPE) / TIMBER TRACTS, LOGGING / COMMERCIAL FISHING / HUNTING AND TRAPPING / SUPPORT ACTIVITIES FOR CROP PRODUCTION/ FORESTRY (AERIAL DUSTING, CULTIVATING SERVICES, FOREST FIRE FIGHTING, PEST CONTROL)
ART, ENTERTAINMENT, AND RECREATION SERVICES ESTABLISHMENTS ENGAGED IN ACTIVITIES OF THIS SECTOR ARE OPERATING OR PROVIDING SERVICES TO MEET VARIED CULTURAL, ENTERTAINMENT, AND RECREATIONAL INTERESTS OF THEIR PATRONS.	SPECIFY THE TYPE OF ART, ENTERTAINMENT, AND/OR RECREATION PROVIDED. *FOR EXAMPLE:* THEATER COMPANIES / DANCE COMPANIES / MUSICAL GROUPS AND ARTISTS / SPORTS TEAMS AND CLUBS / RACETRACKS / AGENTS AND MANAGERS / INDEPENDENT ARTISTS, WRITERS, AND PERFORMERS / CASINOS / AMUSEMENT AND THEME PARKS / RIDING STABLES
COMMUNICATIONS/INFORMATION ESTABLISHMENTS ENGAGED IN ACTIVITIES OF THIS SECTOR ARE DISTRIBUTING INFORMATION AND CULTURAL PRODUCTS, PROVIDING THE MEANS TO TRANSMIT OR DISTRIBUTE THESE PRODUCTS AS DATA OR COMMUNICATIONS, AND PROCESSING DATA.	SPECIFY THE TYPE OF COMMUNICATION/INFORMATION ACTIVITY PERFORMED. *FOR EXAMPLE:* PUBLISHING (NEWSPAPER, DATABASE, SOFTWARE) / MOTION PICTURE/VIDEO PRODUCTION / RADIO/TELEVISION BROADCASTING / CABLE / WIRED/WIRELESS TELECOMMUNICATIONS / PAGING / ON-LINE INFORMATION SERVICES / LIBRARIES AND ARCHIVES
CONSTRUCTION ESTABLISHMENTS ENGAGED IN ACTIVITIES OF THIS SECTOR ARE PRIMARILY ENGAGED IN THE CONSTRUCTION OF BUILDINGS OR ENGINEERING PROJECTS (E.G. HIGHWAYS AND UTILITY SYSTEMS) INCLUDING SITE PREPARATION FOR NEW CONSTRUCTION AND SUBDIVIDING LAND FOR SALE AS BUILDING SITES. ACTIVITIES MAY INCLUDE RESIDENTIAL/COMMERCIAL NEW WORK, ADDITIONS, ALTERATIONS, OR MAINTENANCE AND REPAIRS.	SPECIFY THE TYPE OF CONSTRUCTION. *FOR EXAMPLE:* GENERAL OR OPERATIVE BUILDERS (RESIDENTIAL OR NONRESIDENTIAL) / COMMERCIAL / INDUSTRIAL / HEAVY (BRIDGES, HIGHWAYS, STREETS) / PLUMBING / ELECTRIC / EXCAVATION
DOMESTICS ESTABLISHMENTS ENGAGED IN ACTIVITIES OF THIS SECTOR ARE COMPRISED OF PRIVATE HOUSEHOLDS ENGAGED IN EMPLOYING WORKERS ON OR ABOUT THE PREMISES IN ACTIVITIES PRIMARILY CONCERNED WITH THE OPERATION OF THE HOUSEHOLD.	SPECIFY THE TYPE OF SERVICE. *FOR EXAMPLE:* COOKS / MAIDS / NANNIES / BUTLERS / GARDENERS / CARETAKERS, AND OTHER MAINTENANCE WORKERS
EDUCATIONAL SERVICES ESTABLISHMENTS ENGAGED IN ACTIVITIES OF THIS SECTOR ARE PROVIDING INSTRUCTION AND TRAINING IN A WIDE VARIETY OF SUBJECTS.	SPECIFY THE TYPE OF TRAINING FACILITY. *FOR EXAMPLE:* SCHOOLS / COLLEGES / UNIVERSITIES / BUSINESS/SECRETARIAL SCHOOLS / TRAINING CENTERS (COMPUTER, FLIGHT, TECHNICAL AND TRADE, APPRENTICESHIP, COSMETOLOGY AND BARBER SCHOOLS)
FINANCE ESTABLISHMENTS ENGAGED IN ACTIVITIES OF THIS SECTOR INVOLVE THE CREATION, LIQUIDATION, OR CHANGE IN OWNERSHIP OF FINANCIAL ASSETS (FINANCIAL TRANSACTIONS) AND/OR FACILITATING FINANCIAL TRANSACTIONS.	SPECIFY THE TYPE OF FINANCIAL INSTITUTION, CHARTER, AND TYPE OF FINANCIAL PRODUCTS AND SERVICES OFFERED. *FOR EXAMPLE:* COMMERCIAL BANKS / CREDIT UNIONS / SALES FINANCING / REAL ESTATE LENDING / INVESTMENT BANKING AND SECURITIES DEALING
HEALTH CARE SERVICES ESTABLISHMENTS ENGAGED IN ACTIVITIES OF THIS SECTOR ARE PROVIDING HEALTH CARE FOR INDIVIDUALS.	SPECIFY THE TYPE OF SERVICE PERFORMED. *FOR EXAMPLE:* AMBULATORY HEALTH CARE / PHYSICIANS / DENTISTS / OPTOMETRISTS / MENTAL HEALTH PRACTITIONERS / PODIATRISTS / OUTPATIENT CARE CENTERS / HMO MEDICAL CENTERS / KIDNEY DIALYSIS CENTERS / MEDICAL AND DIAGNOSTIC LABORATORIES / HOME HEALTH CARE SERVICES
INSURANCE ESTABLISHMENTS ENGAGED IN ACTIVITIES OF THIS SECTOR ARE PRIMARILY ENGAGED IN UNDERWRITING ANNUITIES AND INSURANCE POLICIES, OR FACILITATING SUCH UNDERWRITING BY SELLING INSURANCE POLICIES, AND BY PROVIDING OTHER INSURANCE AND EMPLOYEE-BENEFIT RELATED SERVICES.	SPECIFY THE TYPE OF INSURANCE SOLD, AND SPECIFY IF THE INSURANCE IS UNDERWRITTEN BY THE SAME ENTERPRISE. *FOR EXAMPLE:* DIRECT LIFE / HEALTH AND MEDICAL / INSURANCE CARRIERS / PROPERTY AND CASUALTY / TITLE / REINSURANCE / CLAIMS ADJUSTING / FUNDS AND TRUSTS
MANAGEMENT OF COMPANIES AND ENTERPRISES ESTABLISHMENTS ENGAGED IN ACTIVITIES OF THIS SECTOR ARE HOLDING SECURITIES OF COMPANIES AND ENTERPRISES, FOR THE PURPOSE OF OWNING CONTROLLING INTEREST OR INFLUENCING THEIR MANAGEMENT DECISION, OR ADMINISTERING, OVERSEEING, AND MANAGING OTHER ESTABLISHMENTS OF THE SAME COMPANY OR ENTERPRISE AND NORMALLY UNDERTAKING THE STRATEGIC OR ORGANIZATIONAL PLANNING AND DECISION MAKING OF THE COMPANY OR ENTERPRISE.	SPECIFY TYPE OF OFFICE. *FOR EXAMPLE:* OFFICES OF BANK HOLDING COMPANIES / OFFICES OF OTHER HOLDING COMPANIES / CENTRALIZED ADMINISTRATIVE OFFICE / CORPORATE OFFICE / DISTRICT AND REGIONAL OFFICES / HEAD OFFICE / HOLDING COMPANY THAT MANAGES, OR SUBSIDIARY MANAGEMENT OFFICES / PROFESSIONAL EMPLOYEE ORGAINZATION

PA BUSINESS ACTIVITY	TYPICAL PRODUCTS OR SERVICES		
MANUFACTURING ESTABLISHMENTS ENGAGED IN ACTIVITIES OF THIS SECTOR ARE INVOLVED IN THE MECHANICAL, PHYSICAL, OR CHEMICAL TRANSFORMATION OF MATERIAL, SUBSTANCES, OR COMPONENTS INTO NEW PRODUCTS.	SPECIFY THE PRODUCTS MANUFACTURED AND/OR TYPE OF PLANT & PRINCIPAL PROCESS USED. *FOR EXAMPLE:* FOOD (FROZEN OR UNFROZEN, CANNED) TEXTILES CLOTHING/FOOTWEAR (MEN'S, BOY'S, WOMEN'S, GIRL'S)	WOOD PRODUCTS (PALLETS, DOORS, WINDOWS) PULP, PAPER, AND PAPER-BOARD PRINTING (LITHOGRAPH	FLEXOGRAPHIC, GRAVURE QUICK, SCREEN, OR DIGITAL) CHEMICAL METAL (FERROUS, NONFER-ROUS, FABRICATED, FORGED, OR STAMPED)
MINING, QUARRYING, OIL/GAS EXTRACTION ESTABLISHMENTS ENGAGED IN ACTIVITIES OF THIS SECTOR ARE EXTRACTING NATURALLY OCCURRING MINERAL SOLIDS, SUCH AS COAL AND ORE; LIQUID MINERALS, SUCH AS CRUDE PETROLEUM; AND GASES, SUCH AS NATURAL GAS. THE TERM MINING IS USED IN THE BROAD SENSE TO INCLUDE QUARRYING, WELL OPERATIONS, BENEFICIATING (E.G., CRUSHING, SCREENING, WASHING, AND FLOTATION), AND OTHER PREPARATION CUSTOMARILY PERFORMED AT THE MINE SITE, OR AS PART OF MINING ACTIVITY.	SPECIFY EACH MINERAL OR PRODUCT EXTRACTED, IF SERVICES, DESCRIBE SERVICE AND MINERAL INVOLVED. *FOR EXAMPLE:* OPERATING AND/OR DEVELOP-ING OIL AND GAS FIELDS OR CRUDE PETROLEUM AND NAT-URAL GAS EXTRACTION EXPLORATION FOR CRUDE PETROLEUM, BITUMINOUS, OR	ANTHRACITE COAL MINING (SURFACE OR UNDERGROUND) METAL/NON- METAL ORES GOLD, SILVER, STONE, SAND, REFRACTORY	SUPPORT ACTIVITY, EXCAVAT-ING SLUSH PITS, GEOLOGICAL OBSERVATIONS, GRADING AND BUILDING FOUNDATIONS AT WELL LOCATIONS
OTHER SERVICES (EXCEPT PUBLIC ADMINISTRATION) ESTABLISHMENTS ENGAGED IN ACTIVITIES OF THIS SECTOR ARE PROVIDING SERVICES NOT ELSEWHERE SPECIFIED, INCLUDING REPAIRS, RELIGIOUS ACTIVITIES, GRANT MAKING, ADVOCACY, LAUNDRY, PERSONAL CARE, DEATH CARE, AND OTHER PERSONAL SERVICES.	SPECIFY THE TYPE OF SERVICE PROVIDED. *FOR EXAMPLE:* AUTOMOTIVE ELECTRONIC COMPUTER	COMMUNICATION COMMERCIAL AND INDUSTRIAL MACHINERY REPAIRS	BARBER BEAUTY AND NAIL SALONS PET CARE (GROOMING, AND/OR BOARDING)
PROFESSIONAL, SCIENTIFIC, AND TECHNICAL SERVICES ESTABLISHMENTS ENGAGED IN ACTIVITIES OF THIS SECTOR ARE PERFORMING PROFESSIONAL, SCIENTIFIC, AND TECHNICAL SERVICES FOR THE OPERATIONS OF OTHER ORGANIZATIONS.	SPECIFY THE TYPE OF SERVICE PROVIDED. *FOR EXAMPLE:* LEGAL ADVICE AND REPRE-SENTATION ACCOUNTING BOOKKEEPING PAYROLL SERVICES	ARCHITECTURAL ENGINEERING COMPUTER SERVICES CONSULTING RESEARCH	ADVERTISING PHOTOGRAPHIC TRANSLATION AND INTERPRE-TATION VETERINARY SERVICES
PUBLIC ADMINISTRATION ESTABLISHMENTS ENGAGED IN ACTIVITIES OF THIS SECTOR ARE ADMINISTRATION, MANAGEMENT, AND OVERSIGHT OF PUBLIC PROGRAMS BY FEDERAL, STATE, AND LOCAL GOVERNMENTS.	SPECIFY OFFICE. *FOR EXAMPLE:* EXECUTIVE OFFICES OF PRESIDENT GOVERNORS AND MAYORS IN ADDITION TO EXECUTIVE ADVISORY COMMISSIONS	ZONING BOARDS AND COM-MISSIONS (PUBLIC ADMINISTRATION) GOVERNMENT URBAN PLANNING COMMISSIONS	CIVILIAN COURTS OF LAW COURTS OF LAW AND SHERIFFS OFFICES CONDUCT-ING COURT FUNCTIONS ONLY
REAL ESTATE ESTABLISHMENTS ENGAGED IN ACTIVITIES OF THIS SECTOR ARE RENTING, LEASING, OR OTHERWISE ALLOWING THE USE OF TANGIBLE OR INTANGIBLE ASSETS (EXCEPT COPYRIGHTED WORKS), AND PROVIDING RELATED SERVICES.	SPECIFY THE TYPE OF REAL ESTATE ACTIVITY. *FOR EXAMPLE:* SELF-STORAGE RENTAL, REAL ESTATE AGENTS/BROKERS CAR RENTAL/LEASING	CONSUMER GOODS COMMERCIAL AND INDUSTRIAL MACHINERY/EQUIPMENT	PATENTS TRADEMARKS BRAND NAMES, AND/OR FRAN-CHISE AGREEMENT
RETAIL TRADE ESTABLISHMENTS ENGAGED IN ACTIVITIES OF THIS SECTOR RETAIL MERCHANDISE, GENERALLY IN SMALL QUANTITIES, TO THE GENERAL PUBLIC, AND PROVIDE SERVICES INCIDENTAL TO THE SALE OF THE MERCHANDISE.	SPECIFY THE DIFFERENT TYPES OF RETAIL STORES. *FOR EXAMPLE:* DEPARTMENT STORES FURNITURE STORES	CLOTHING AND GROCERY IN-HOME DEMONSTRATION, INFOMERCIALS	VENDING MACHINES AND STREET VENDORS (EXCEPT FOOD)
SANITARY SERVICE ESTABLISHMENTS ENGAGED IN ACTIVITIES IN THIS SECTOR ARE INVOLVED IN THE COLLECTION, TREATMENT, AND DISPOSAL OF WASTE MATERIALS NOT THROUGH SEWER SYSTEMS OR SEWAGE TREATMENT FACILITIES.	SPECIFY THE TYPE OF SERVICE PROVIDED. *FOR EXAMPLE:* LOCAL HAULING OF WASTE MATERIALS REMEDIATION SERVICES	SEPTIC PUMPING HAZARDOUS AND NON-HAZARDOUS WASTE TRANSFER STATIONS	SOLID WASTE LANDFILLS COMBUSTORS AND INCINERATORS
SOCIAL ASSISTANCE SERVICE ESTABLISHMENTS ENGAGED IN ACTIVITIES OF THIS SECTOR PROVIDE A WIDE VARIETY OF SOCIAL ASSISTANCE SERVICES DIRECTLY TO THEIR CLIENTS. THESE SERVICES DO NOT INCLUDE RESIDENTIAL OR ACCOMMODATION SERVICES, EXCEPT ON A SHORT STAY BASIS.	SPECIFY THE TYPE OF SERVICE PROVIDED. *FOR EXAMPLE:* YOUTH CENTERS ADOPTION AGENCIES	TEMPORARY SHELTERS SERVICES FOR ELDERLY AND PERSONS WITH DISABILITIES	CHILD DAY CARE
TRANSPORTATION ESTABLISHMENTS ENGAGED IN ACTIVITIES OF THIS SECTOR PROVIDE TRANSPORTA-TION OF PASSENGERS AND CARGO, SCENIC AND SIGHTSEEING TRANSPORTATION, AND SUPPORT ACTIVITIES RELATED TO MODES OF TRANSPORTATION.	SPECIFY THE TYPE OF TRANSPORTATION MODE. *FOR EXAMPLE:* AIR (SPECIFY SCHEDULED OR NONSCHEDULED; PASSENGER OR FREIGHT) RAIL, DEEP SEA, COASTAL,	AND GREAT LAKES TRUCKING (GENERAL OR SPE-CIALIZED LONG-DISTANCE OR LOCAL)	BUS TAXI SCHOOL BUS LIMOUSINE
UTILITIES ESTABLISHMENTS ENGAGED IN ACTIVITIES OF THIS SECTOR PROVIDE ELECTRIC POWER, NATURAL GAS, STEAM SUPPLY, WATER SUPPLY, AND SEWAGE REMOVAL. THE SPECIFIC ACTIVITIES ASSOCIATED WITH THE UTILITY SERVICES PROVIDED VARY BY UTILITY: ELECTRIC POWER INCLUDES GENERATION, TRANSMISSION, AND DISTRIBU-TION; NATURAL GAS INCLUDES DISTRIBUTION; STEAM SUPPLY INCLUDES PROVISION AND/OR DISTRIBUTION; WATER SUPPLY INCLUDES TREATMENT AND DISTRIBUTION; AND SEWAGE REMOVAL INCLUDES COLLECTION, TREATMENT, AND DISPOSAL OF WASTE THROUGH SEWER SYSTEMS AND SEWAGE TREATMENT FACILITIES.	SPECIFY THE TYPE OF SERVICE. *FOR EXAMPLE:* ELECTRIC HYDROELECTRIC NUCLEAR FOSSIL FUEL TRANSMISSION	DISTRIBUTION WATER TREATMENT AND/OR WATER SUPPLY SYSTEMS SEWAGE TREATMENT FACILITIES	
WAREHOUSING ESTABLISHMENTS ENGAGED IN ACTIVITIES OF THIS SECTOR ARE PRIMARILY ENGAGED IN OPERATING WAREHOUSE AND STORAGE FACILITIES FOR GENERAL MERCHANDISE, REFRIGERATED GOODS, AND OTHER WAREHOUSE PRODUCTS, WHICH MAY INCLUDE LOGISTICS.	SPECIFY THE TYPE OF STORAGE. *FOR EXAMPLE:* GENERAL WAREHOUSING	REFRIGERATED FARM PRODUCTS	EXCLUDED ARE RENTING AND LEASING SPACE FOR SELF-STORAGE – SEE REAL ESTATE
WHOLESALE TRADE ESTABLISHMENTS ENGAGED IN ACTIVITIES OF THIS SECTOR COMPRISE TWO MAIN TYPES OF ENTERPRISES SELLING OR ARRANGING FOR THE PURCHASE OR SALE OF GOODS FOR RESALE; CAPITAL OR DURABLE NON-CONSUMER GOODS; AND RAW AND INTERMEDIATE MATERIALS AND SUPPLIES USED IN PRODUCTION, AND PROVIDING SERVICES INCIDENTAL TO THE SALE OF THE MERCHANDISE.	SPECIFY THE DIFFERENT TYPES OF TRADERS. *FOR EXAMPLE:* MERCHANT WHOLESALERS (DISTRIBUTORS, JOBBERS, DROP SHIPPERS, AND IMPORT/EXPORT MERCHANTS)	BUSINESS TO BUSINESS ELEC-TRONIC MARKETS	AGENTS, AND BROKERS ARRANGING SALES AND PUR-CHASES FOR OTHERS ON A FEE OR COMMISSION BASIS

2. **Percentage:** Enter the percentage that this ESTABLISHMENT'S receipts or revenues represent of the total PA receipts or revenues of the enterprise.

3. Establishments involved in construction business activity must enter the percentages of each type; residential and/or commercial; new and/or renovative. Each set of percentage types should equal 100 percent of the construction activity at this establishment.

SECTION 8 – ESTABLISHMENT SALES INFORMATION

1. Check the appropriate box to indicate if the establishment is selling products or services subject to Sales Tax **in PA**. Products and services include the sale and/or repair to tangible personal property, prepared food, rental and leasing of motor vehicles, and rental and leasing of equipment. Complete Section 18 to apply for a PA Sales Tax License.

2. Check the appropriate box to indicate if cigarettes are sold over-the-counter or at vending machine locations. Complete Section 18 to apply for a Sales Tax License and Section 19 to apply for a Cigarette Tax License.

3. List each county **in PA** where taxable sales and/or services are offered or supplied.

SECTION 9 – ESTABLISHMENT EMPLOYMENT INFORMATION

PART 1

1. **a – g** Complete if the establishment employs individuals working **in PA**. If the principal business activity is not construction, enter "N/A" in items d and e.

   Check the appropriate box in g-3 if the establishment is not required to have workers' compensation coverage and provide bureau code.

2. **a – c** Complete if the establishment employs **PA residents working outside of PA**.

3. Check the appropriate box. If yes, explain the services performed and why you do not consider the individual(s) to be employee(s).

PART 2

1. **a – b** Complete if registering for withholding on **taxable benefits paid from a benefit trust, deferred payment, or retirement plan for PA residents.**

SECTION 10 – BULK SALE/TRANSFER INFORMATION

A separate copy of Section 10 must be completed for each transferor from which assets were acquired.

Assets include, but are not limited to, any stock of goods, wares, or merchandise of any kind, fixtures, machinery, equipment, buildings or real estate, name and/or goodwill. Refer to the form for the class of assets.

1. Indicate if the enterprise has acquired "IN BULK" 51 percent or more of **any class of PA assets** of another enterprise.

2. Indicate if the enterprise has acquired "IN BULK" 51 percent or more of the **total assets** of another enterprise.

3-7. Complete if the answer to question 1 or 2 is "Yes".

SECTION 11 – CORPORATION INFORMATION

All corporations must register with the PA Department of State to secure corporate name clearance and register for corporation tax purposes. To register a new corporation via the Internet or to download the necessary forms, visit www.paopenforbusiness.state.pa.us, or call the PA Department of State at (717) 787-1057.

1-6. Describe the corporation.

7. Check the appropriate box if the corporation is a federal "S" corporation. If so, check the box to indicate if the corporation is also a PA "S" corporation. **Note:** This does **not** constitute a PA "S" election. To elect PA "S" status, a REV-1640, Election and Shareholder's Consent Form must be submitted. To complete this form on-line visit www.paopenforbusiness.state.pa.us, or call the PA De-partment of Revenue at (717) 787-1064.

SECTION 12 – REPORTING & PAYMENT METHODS

1. Payments equal to or greater than $20,000 to the Department of Revenue must be remitted via an approved EFT method. If a payment of $20,000 or more is not made via an approved EFT method, the account is subject to a $500.00 penalty. Taxpayers must register with the PA Department of Revenue to remit payments via EFT.

   The enterprise may participate voluntarily in the Department of Revenue's EFT Program.

2. The Unemployment Compensation Contribution Methods are: **Contributory Method:** Under the contributory method, the amount of employer contributions due is based on a specified percentage of taxable wages. The maximum amount of taxable wages subject to the employer contribution may change from year to year.

   For-profit enterprises must pay under the contributory method.

   Reimbursement Method: Non-profit enterprises exempt under Section 501(c)(3) of the Internal Revenue Code and political subdivisions of PA who elect the reimbursement method are required to reimburse the UC Fund for all regular benefits paid which are attributable to service with the enterprise. Non-profit enterprises must pay for one-half of any extended benefits, while political subdivisions must pay the full amount of any extended benefits.

   An enterprise will be assigned the contributory method of payment unless they file an election for reimbursement coverage with the PA Department of Labor & Industry.

   UC Employee Withholding Contributions: Enterprises are required to report gross wages paid to employees, regardless of the method used to finance UC costs (contributory or reimbursement). Enterprises may be required to withhold and remit employee contributions according to Section 301.4(a) of the PA UC Law. The amount of employee contributions due is based on a specified percentage of gross wages. Employee contributions are not credited to an enterprise's reserve account balance, nor are they considered to be contributions for federal certification purposes under the Federal Unemployment Tax Act.

   Payments for UC should be made payable to the PA Unemployment Compensation Fund.

   Additional information is available by contacting the nearest Department of Labor & Industry Field Accounting Service Office.

3. Enterprises with 250 or more wage entries are required to report quarterly Unemployment Compensation wages to the Department of Labor & Industry via magnetic media. Non-compliance may result in penalty charges. Enterprises may also voluntarily report individuals' wages to the Department of Labor & Industry in the same media. Any magnetic reporting file must be submitted for compatibility with the Department of Labor & Industry's format. Contact the Magnetic Media Reporting Unit at (717) 783-5802 for more information.

   The Commonwealth's Electronic Tax Information and Data Exchange System (E-TIDES) is an Internet based filing and payment system that can be used to simplify reporting requirements for Unemployment Compensation, Employer Withholding Tax and Sales and Use Tax. Using E-TIDES will help your enterprise reduce the costs and delays associated with processing paper tax returns. To learn more about E-TIDES, visit the home page at **www.etides.state.pa.us.**

SECTION 13 – GOVERNMENT STRUCTURE

Complete this section if the enterprise is a political subdivision of the Commonwealth of PA, or if the enterprise exercises political authority as a government organization.

1. Check the appropriate box to describe the enterprise.

2. Check the appropriate box to further describe the type of government.

3. If the enterprise is a Domestic/USA form of government, check the appropriate box.

If an enterprise is a political subdivision of the Commonwealth of PA and is also subject to the contribution provisions of the PA Unemployment Compensation (UC) Law, it has the option to elect to finance UC costs under the reimbursement method in lieu of the contributory method. A state government organization will be assigned the reimbursement method.

See page 22 of the instructions for further explanations regarding contributory and reimbursement methods of making payments to the Unemployment Compensation Fund.

SECTION 14 – PREDECESSOR/SUCCESSOR INFORMATION

Complete this section if the registering enterprise is succeeding a predecessor (prior owner) in whole or in part. For assistance in completing Sections 14, 15, and 16, contact the nearest Department of Labor & Industry Field Accounting Service Office.

Predecessor: An enterprise that transfers all or part of its organization, trade, or business to another enterprise.

Successor: An enterprise that acquires by transfer all or part of the organization, trade, or business from another enterprise.

The registering enterprise may apply for the Unemployment Compensation (UC) experience record and reserve account balance of the predecessor by completing Section 15, Application for PA UC Experience Record & Reserve Account Balance of Predecessor.

The Department of Labor & Industry may determine that a transfer of experience from a predecessor to the registering enterprise will be mandatory provided there is common ownership or control, either directly or indirectly between the predecessor and the registering enterprise.

1-5. Provide predecessor information as requested on the form.

6. Check the appropriate box to indicate how the predecessor's business operation was acquired.

   Acquisition of an Existing Enterprise: Occurs when operations are continued by a new owner; for example, a purchase of all or part of the enterprise.

   Change in Legal Structure: Occurs when the form of organization changes; for example, when a sole proprietorship incorporates, or forms a partnership.

   Consolidation: Occurs when a new corporation is formed by combining two or more corporations which then cease to exist.

   Gift: Occurs when the title to the property is transferred without consideration.

   Merger: Occurs when one corporation is absorbed by another. One corporation preserves its original charter or identity and continues to exist and the other corporate existence terminates.

   IRC Section 338 Election: Occurs when a stock purchase is treated as an asset purchase under the Internal Revenue Code Section 338.

7. Enter the date the business operation was acquired.

8. Enter the percentage of the predecessor's total business operation acquired. Total business operation is defined as all activities reportable under a single Federal Employer Identification Number (FEIN) including any activities occurring outside of PA.

9. Enter the percentage of the predecessor's PA business operation acquired. If less than 100 percent, provide the additional information as requested on the form.

10. Describe the PA business activity(ies) that the registering enterprise acquired from the predecessor.

11. Check the appropriate box(es) to indicate the type(s) of assets acquired from the predecessor.

12. Enter the date the predecessor last paid wages in PA, if applicable.

13. Enter the date the predecessor ceased operations in PA, if applicable. If operations have not ceased, describe the predecessor's ongoing business activity in PA.

14. Check the appropriate box(es). If "Yes", provide the information requested on the form. Attach additional sheets if necessary.

SECTION 15 – APPLICATION FOR PA UC EXPERIENCE RECORD & RESERVE ACCOUNT BALANCE OF PREDECESSOR

If the registering enterprise is continuing essentially the same business activity as the predecessor, the registering enterprise may apply for a transfer in whole or in part of the predecessor's Unemployment Compensation (UC) experience record and reserve account balance, provided that:

- The registering enterprise is continuing essentially the same business activity as the predecessor; _and_

- The registering enterprise's risk of unemployment is related to the employment experience of the predecessor based upon the following factors:

  - Nature of the business activity of each enterprise
  - Number of individuals employed by each enterprise
  - Wages paid to the employees by each enterprise.

It is important to consider more than the predecessor's existing rate. The benefit charges attributed to the business acquired from the predecessor may have an adverse effect on future rate calculations.

The basic contribution rate for a newly liable non-construction employer is 3.5 percent (.0350). The basic contribution rate for newly liable employers involved in the performance of a contract or sub-contract for the construction of new roads, bridges, highways, buildings, factories, housing developments, or other construction projects is 9.7 percent (.0970).

For any given calendar year, newly liable contribution rates are subject to a positive or negative surcharge according to Sections 301.5 and 301.7 of the PA UC Law.

To be considered timely, an Application for the Transfer of the Experience Record & Reserve Account Balance of a Predecessor must be filed prior to the end of the calendar year immediately following the year in which the transfer occurred.

1-2. Complete only to apply for the predecessor's experience record and reserve account balance. The authorized signature should be that of the owner, general partner, or officer of the predecessor and the registering enterprise. Attach Power of Attorney document, if applicable. If the predecessor's signature is unavailable, contact the nearest Department of Labor & Industry Field Accounting Service Office for additional information.

SECTION 16 – UNEMPLOYMENT COMPENSATION PARTIAL TRANSFER INFORMATION

Complete this section if the registering enterprise acquired only part of the predecessor's PA business operation and is making application for the transfer of a portion of the predecessor's experience record and reserve account balance.

Contact the nearest Department of Labor & Industry Field Accounting Service Office for Replacement UC-2A for Partial Transfer (Form UC-252) or for more information on the Unemployment Compensation (UC) taxable wage base for a specific year. Refer to page 27 for a list of offices.

If the Department of Labor & Industry determines that a transfer of experience is mandatory, the registering enterprise will be required to complete this section and Form UC-252.

1. Enter the exact date wages were first paid in the part of the predecessor's PA business operation that was transferred. This date must include any wages paid by known pre-predecessors; that is, any previous owners of the part transferred who had transferred their experience and reserve account balance to any successors, the last of which would be the current predecessor.

2. Identify the year(s) and calendar quarters in which contributions were payable to the PA UC Fund for **taxable wages** applicable to the part of the predecessor's PA business operation that was transferred. Include any quarters applicable to known pre-predecessors.

3. Identify the year(s) and calendar quarters in which contributions were payable to the PA UC Fund for **taxable wages** applicable to any part of the predecessor's PA business operation that was retained. Include any quarters applicable to known pre-predecessors.

4. For the three calendar year period prior to the year of transfer (4a) or for a lesser period (4b) from the date wages were first paid to the actual date of transfer (acquisition), enter the total amount of **taxable wages** applicable to the part of the predecessor's PA business operation that was transferred.

5. Enter the total amount of **taxable wages** applicable to the predecessor's entire PA business operation for the period that directly corresponds to the same period in item 4a or 4b.

6. Enter the total amount of **taxable wages** applicable to the predecessor's entire PA business operation for the period from the beginning of the quarter the transfer occurred to the actual date of transfer.

SECTION 17 – MULTIPLE ESTABLISHMENT INFORMATION

When an enterprise has more than one establishment conducting business in PA or employing PA residents, Section 17, Parts 1 through 4 must be completed. Photocopy this section as necessary.

PART 1 - ESTABLISHMENT INFORMATION

1. **Establishment Name:** Enter the name by which this establishment is known to the public; for example, the name on the front of the store.

2. **Date of First Operations:** Enter the first date this establishment conducted any activity in PA or employed PA residents. This includes start-up operations prior to opening for business.

3. **Telephone Number:** Enter the telephone number for this establishment.

4. **Street Address:** Enter the physical location of this establishment. **A post office box is not acceptable.**

5. **School District:** Enter the school district where this establishment is located. If not a PA school district enter "N/A".

6. **Municipality:** Enter the municipality (borough, city, town or township) where this establishment is located. The municipality may be different from the city/town used for postal delivery. If not a PA municipality, enter "N/A".

PART 2 - ESTABLISHMENT BUSINESS ACTIVITY INFORMATION

Refer to the instructions for Establishment Business Activity Information (Section 7).

PART 3 - ESTABLISHMENT SALES INFORMATION

Refer to the instructions for Establishment Sales Information (Section 8).

PART 4a & b - ESTABLISHMENT EMPLOYMENT INFORMATION

Refer to the instructions for Establishment Employment Information (Section 9).

SECTION 6A – ADDITIONAL OWNERS, PARTNERS, SHAREHOLDERS, OFFICERS, AND RESPONSIBLE PARTY INFORMATION

Refer to the instructions for Owners, Partners, Shareholders, Officers, and Responsible Party Information (Section 6).

SECTION 18 – SALES USE AND HOTEL OCCUPANCY TAX LICENSE, PUBLIC TRANSPORTATION ASSISTANCE TAX LICENSE, VEHICLE RENTAL TAX, TRANSIENT VENDOR CERTIFICATE, PROMOTER LICENSE, OR WHOLESALER CERTIFICATE

PART 1 - SALES, USE AND HOTEL OCCUPANCY TAX, PUBLIC TRANSPORTATION ASSISTANCE TAX, VEHICLE RENTAL TAX, OR WHOLESALER CERTIFICATE

Complete Part 1 to apply for a PA Sales and Use Tax License or a Public Transportation Assistance Tax License that will authorize the enterprise to do any of the functions listed below. Applications for a Wholesale Certificate will only authorize the enterprise to do the function listed in bullet four:

● Collect State and Local **Sales Tax** on taxable sales made within PA. Local Sales and Use Tax is collected in those counties where required by statute.

● Remit State and Local **Use Tax** incurred on property or services used within Pennsylvania where no Sales Tax has been paid to a vendor.

● Collect taxes and fees on leases of motor vehicles, sales of new tires, and rentals of motor vehicles.

● Purchase tangible personal property and/or services for resale or rental in the normal course of business sales tax-free.

PART 2 - TRANSIENT VENDOR CERTIFICATE

Complete Parts 1 and 2 to apply for a Transient Vendor Certificate. The certificate will authorize the enterprise to collect and remit Sales Tax on taxable sales made within PA.

Only enterprises whose business structure is a sole proprietorship or a partnership may apply for a transient vendor certificate.

A Transient Vendor Certificate is needed if the enterprise:

● Does not have a permanent Sales & Use Tax License.

● Brings into PA, by automobile, truck or other means of transportation, or purchases in PA, tangible personal property that is subject to Sales Tax, or comes into PA to perform services that are subject to PA Sales Tax.

- Offers or intends to offer tangible personal property for retail sale in PA.

- Does not maintain an established office, distribution house, sales house, warehouse, service enterprise or residence where business is conducted in PA.

The term "transient vendor" does not include an enterprise that does one of the following:

- Delivers tangible personal property solicited or placed by mail or telephone order.

- Makes handcrafted items for sale at special events (e.g. fairs, carnivals, festivals, art and craft shows, and other celebrations within Pennsylvania).

A Show is any event that involves the display or exhibition of any tangible personal property or services for sale. It may include, but is not limited to, a flea market, antique show, coin show, stamp show, comic book show, hobby show, automobile show, fair, or any similar show, if held regularly or temporarily where more than one vendor displays for sale or sells tangible personal property or services subject to Sales Tax.

The Transient Vendor Certificate is renewable on a yearly basis beginning February 1 of each year.

PART 3 - PROMOTER LICENSE

Complete Parts 1 and 3 to apply for a Promoter License. A Promoter is a person or enterprise who either directly or indirectly rents, leases, or otherwise operates or grants permission to any person to use space at a show for the display for sale or for the sale of tangible personal property or services subject to tax.

The Promoter's License is renewable on a yearly basis beginning February 1 of each year.

This application must be completed and returned to the Department of Revenue at least 30 days prior to the opening of the first show.

SECTION 19 - CIGARETTE DEALER'S LICENSE

PART 1 - LICENSE TYPE

Complete Section 19, Part 1 to apply for a Cigarette Dealer's License. A separate license must be obtained for each location where retail sale of cigarettes, cigarette wholesale activity, or cigarette tax stamping will occur.

A Cigarette Dealer's License is **not** transferable.

If the enterprise is applying for a Cigarette Vending Machine License, a list of machine locations must be attached to the registration form. Provide the name of the establishment, street address, city, and county where each machine is located.

Note: The Department of Revenue will allow the purchase of extra vending machine decals for machines to be placed at new locations (up to 10 percent or 10 extra decals, whichever is greater) without submitting actual locations. Within 30 days, licensees must advise the Department of the date an additional vending machine decal is affixed and the location of the machine.

All Cigarette Dealer's Licenses expire on the last day of February and are renewable on a yearly basis. License fees are not prorated.

PART 2 - CIGARETTE WHOLESALER

Complete Parts 1 and 2 to apply for a Cigarette Wholesaler License.

All applicants for a Cigarette Wholesaler or Cigarette Stamping Agent License will be subject to a criminal background investiga-

tion prior to the issuance of a license. This investigation will be completed within 60 days of receipt of the completed application.

PART 3 - CIGARETTE STAMPING AGENT

Complete Parts 1, 2, and 3 to apply for a Cigarette Stamping Agent License.

SECTION 20 - SMALL GAMES OF CHANCE LICENSE/CERTIFICATE

Complete Parts 1, 2, and 3 to apply for a Distributor License.

Complete Parts 1 and 3 to apply for a Manufacturer Registration Certificate.

Questions may be directed to (717) 787-8275.

PART 1 - DISTRIBUTOR AND/OR MANUFACTURER

The following items must be enclosed with the registration form.

- Corporations must submit a copy of the Certificate of Incorporation, Articles of Incorporation, Certificate of Authority (non-PA corporations), By-laws or Constitution. If doing business using a fictitious name, submit a copy of the fictitious name registration.

- The logo(s) used by the Manufacturer.

- The fee for the Distributor License or the Manufacturer Registration Certificate as listed on the registration form.

- A $10 nonrefundable background investigation fee for each owner, partner, officer, director, and shareholder controlling 10 percent or more of outstanding stock.

- Distributors and/or Manufacturers must identify an agent and a physical location within Pennsylvania as a designee for purposes of service of process.

A Distributor License expires on April 30 and is renewable on a yearly basis.

A Manufacturer Registration Certificate expires on March 31 and is renewable on a yearly basis.

PART 2 - DISTRIBUTOR

Complete this section to apply for a Distributor License only.

PART 3 - SMALL GAMES OF CHANCE CERTIFICATION

Certification must be **signed and notarized** by all Small Games of Chance applicants.

SECTION 21 - MOTOR CARRIER REGISTRATION & DECAL/MOTOR FUELS LICENSE & PERMIT

All enterprises applying for a Motor Carrier Road Tax (MCRT)/ International Fuel Tax Agreement (IFTA) Decal must complete Part 1.

The applicant's authorized signature in Section 4 of the form indicates applicant agrees to comply with the reporting, payment, record keeping, and license display requirements as specified in MCRT and/or the IFTA.

PART 1 - VEHICLE OPERATIONS

A qualified motor vehicle is a motor vehicle used, designed, or maintained for the transportation of persons or property which has: (a) two axles and a gross or registered gross weight greater than 26,000 pounds, (b) three axles or more regardless of weight, or (c) a combination weight greater than 26,000 pounds.

MOTOR CARRIER ROAD TAX

Common Carrier: Any motor carrier which holds itself out of the general public to engage in the transportation by motor vehicle of passengers or property for compensation.

Contract Carrier: Any motor carrier transporting persons or property for compensation or hire under contract to a particular person, firm, or corporation.

For-Hire Carrier: An enterprise providing transportation of passengers or property by motor vehicle using the public utility commission rights of another carrier.

Private Carrier: A person, firm, or corporation which utilizes its own trucks to transport its own freight.

Truck: Every motor vehicle designed, used, or maintained primarily for the transportation of property.

Truck Tractor: A motor vehicle designed and used primarily for drawing other vehicles but so constructed as to carry a load other than a part of the weight of the vehicle and load so drawn.

Combination: A power unit used in combination with trailers and semi-trailers.

Exemptions Include: Vehicles operated by the U.S. Government, the Commonwealth of PA and its political subdivisions, other states publicly-owned vehicles, volunteer fire, rescue and ambulance associations, farm vehicles, implements of husbandry, tow truck (not roll-backs), special mobile equipment, unladen vehicles being operated with a repair facility certificate from a PA repair facility, carriers who obtain permission from the PA State Police for emergency repair, and carriers operating on dealer or similar tags and operating vehicle incidental to their sale, demonstration, or repossession.

IFTA Decals: Request IFTA Decals for PA-qualified vehicles that travel in and outside of PA. An IFTA License must be carried in each vehicle and the vehicle must display decals on both sides of the cab.

Carriers purchasing IFTA credentials must file Quarterly IFTA Fuel Tax reports.

Non-IFTA Decals: For PA-qualified vehicles that travel exclusively in PA, request non-IFTA Decals. Carriers from non-IFTA states operating qualified motor vehicles exclusively in PA must likewise display non-IFTA Decals. A Road Tax Cab Card must be carried in each vehicle and the vehicle must display decals on both sides of the cab. As of January 1, 2001, the only U.S. and Canadian jurisdictions not participating in IFTA are: Alaska, Hawaii, District of Columbia, Northwest Territories, and the Yukon Territory.

Carriers purchasing non-IFTA credentials must maintain operational records; however, quarterly Motor Carrier Road Tax reports are **not required.**

If a carrier is based in a non-IFTA jurisdiction and intends to operate qualified motor vehicles based in that state and travel in PA, complete this application to order non-IFTA Decals.

ALL DECALS ARE VALID FOR ONE CALENDAR YEAR.

Make checks or money orders payable to the PA Department of Revenue. Allow two or three weeks for delivery of the decals. **Do not send cash.** If a decal is purchased, quarterly tax reports will be required.

For IFTA, decal, and tax information, contact the PA Department of Revenue, Bureau of Motor Fuel Taxes at (1-800) 482-IFTA (4382) or (717) 787-5355, TT# 1-800-447-3020 (Service for Customers with special hearing and/or speaking needs only).

PART 2 - FUELS

Before the issuance of a Liquid Fuels and Fuel Tax Permit, an on-site inspection contact will be made by the PA Department of Revenue, Enforcement Division.

A surety bond is required for Liquid Fuels and Fuel Tax. The enterprise will be contacted by the PA Department of Revenue, Bureau of Motor Fuel Taxes, Enforcement Division, regarding the surety bond requirements.

SECTION 22 – SALES TAX EXEMPT STATUS FOR CHARITABLE AND RELIGIOUS ORGANIZATIONS

Charitable, religious, non-profit educational institutions, and volunteer fire companies may be eligible for Sales Tax exempt status.

Act 55 of 1997, known as the Institutions of Purely Public Charity Act, changes the procedure and filing requirements for organizations seeking to qualify or renew Sales and Use Tax exemption status.

To apply, a separate application (REV-72) must be completed. See Section 22, page 17 for more details. In addition to completing the REV-72, the following documents are required and must be attached to the application:

- A copy of the Articles of Incorporation, By-laws, Constitution, or other governing legal document specifically including:
  * Aims and purpose of the institution;
  * A provision that expressly prohibits the use of any surplus funds for private inurement to any person in the event of a sale or dissolution of the institution.

- The most current financial statement (new organizations may substitute a proposed budget) including:
  * All income and expenses listed by source and category;
  * A list of the beneficiaries (individual, general public, other organizations, etc.) of the institution's activities and how those beneficiaries are selected; and
  * A list of sales activities (gift shop, bookstore, social club, etc.) used to raise funds. The institution must apply for a Sales Tax License if engaging in sales activities.

- If the institution has tax exempt status with the Internal Revenue Service, a copy of the approval letter must be submitted.

- If the institution has voluntary agreements with political subdivisions, enclose copy of same.

- If the institution files Form 990, provide a copy of the most recently completed form.

CONTACT US

DEPARTMENT OF REVENUE	LABOR & INDUSTRY		PROGRAM QUESTIONS	
General Information 1-888-PATAXES	Unemployment Compensation (UC)	717-787-7679	UC Benefit Charges	717-787-4677
(728-2937)	Workers' Compensation (WC)	717-783-5421	WC Employer Help Line	717-772-3702
E-mail:	**E-mail:**		WC Self-Insurance Division	717-783-4476
www.revenue.state.pa.us	**UC-news@state.pa.us**		WC Compliance Section	717-787-3567

Forms and information for both Departments are available at: **www.paopenforbusiness.state.pa.us**

The location of these offices may change.
To verify the location of an office, please call Monday through Friday 8:30 AM to 5:00 PM (EST) at the number listed for that office.

REVENUE DISTRICT OFFICES
LOCATIONS AND COUNTIES SERVED

Altoona
(Blair, Centre, Fulton, Huntingdon,and Mifflin)
Cricket Field Plz.
Ste. 204
615 Howard Ave.
Altoona, PA 16601-4867
(814) 946-7310

Bethlehem
(Lehigh and Northampton)
44 E. Broad St.
Bethlehem, PA 18018-5998
(610) 861-2000

Bradford
(Cameron, Elk, Forest, McKean, Potter, and Warren)
Ste. 2
600 Chestnut St.
Bradford, PA 16701-2011
(814) 368-7113

Doylestown
(Bucks)
Ste. 104
600 Louis Dr.
Warminster, PA 18974-2847
(215) 443-2990

Erie
(Erie and Crawford)
448 W. 11th St.
Erie, PA 16501-1501
(814) 871-4491

Greensburg
(Westmoreland)
Second Fl.
15 W. Third St.
Greensburg, PA 15601-3003
(724) 832-5386

Harrisburg
(Cumberland, Dauphin, and Perry)
Lobby
Strawberry Sq.
Harrisburg, PA 17128-0101
(717) 783-1405

Indiana
(Armstrong, Clarion, Indiana, and Jefferson)
Canterbury Office Stes.
2263 Philadelphia St.
Indiana, PA 15701-1595
(724) 357-7600

Johnstown
(Bedford, Cambria, Clearfield, and Somerset)
Third Fl.
345 Main St.
Johnstown, PA 15901-1614
(814) 533-2495

Lancaster
(Lancaster and Lebanon)
Ste. 201
315 W. James St.
Lancaster, PA 17603-2911
(717) 299-7581

New Castle
(Beaver, Butler, Lawrence, Mercer, and Venango)
103 S. Mercer St.
New Castle, PA 16101-3849
(724) 656-3203

Newtown Square
(Chester and Delaware)
Ste. 1
90 S. Newtown St. Rd.
(Route 252)
Newtown Square, PA 19073-4090
(610) 353-4051

Norristown
(Montgomery)
Second Fl.
Stoney Creek Office Center
151 W. Marshall St.
Norristown, PA 19401-4739
(610) 270-1780

Philadelphia
(Philadelphia)
Rm. 201
State Office Bldg.
1400 W. Spring Garden St.
Philadelphia, PA 19130-4088
(215) 560-2056

Pittsburgh
(Allegheny)
Ste. 104
State Office Bldg.
300 Liberty Ave.
Pittsburgh, PA 15222-1210
(412) 565-7540

Pottsville
(Carbon and Schuylkill)
115 S. Centre St.
Pottsville, PA 17901-3047
(570) 621-3175

Reading
(Berks)
Rm. 239
625 Cherry St.
Reading, PA 19602-1186
(610) 378-4401

Scranton
(Lackawanna, Monroe, Pike, Susquehanna, and Wayne)
Rm. 305
Samters Bldg.
101 Penn Ave.
Scranton, PA 18503-1970
(570) 963-4585

Sunbury
(Columbia, Juniata, Montour, Northumberland, Snyder, and Union)
535 Chestnut St.
Sunbury, PA 17801-3404
(570) 988-2834

Washington
(Fayette, Greene, and Washington)
Ste. 145 UL
Millcraft Center.
90 W. Chestnut St.
Washington, PA 15301-4963
(724) 223-4550

Wilkes-Barre
(Luzerne and Wyoming)
Ste. 201
Thomas C. Thomas Bldg.
100 E. Union St.
Wilkes-Barre, PA 18701-3200
(570) 826-2466

Williamsport
(Bradford, Clinton, Lycoming, Sullivan, and Tioga)
440 Little League Blvd.
Williamsport, PA 17701-5055
(570) 327-3475

York
(Adams, Franklin, and York)
140 N. Duke St.
York, PA 17401-1110
(717) 845-6661

LABOR & INDUSTRY FIELD ACCOUNTING SERVICE OFFICES
LOCATIONS AND COUNTIES SERVED

Allentown
1 S. Second St., Ste. 400
Allentown, PA 18102-4901
(610) 821-6559
Lehigh
Northampton

Altoona
3303 Pleasant Valley Blvd.
Altoona, PA 16602-4311
(814) 946-6991
Bedford
Blair
Centre
Huntingdon

Beaver Falls
2103 Ninth Ave.
Beaver Falls, PA 15010-3957
(724) 846-8803
Beaver
Lawrence

Bristol
1242 New Rodgers Rd.
Bristol, PA 19007-2591
(215) 781-3217
Bucks

Carlisle
1 Alexandra Ct.
Carlisle, PA 17013-7667
(717) 249-8211
Cumberland

Chambersburg
600 Norland Ave., Ste. 7
Chambersburg, PA 17201
(717) 264-7192
Franklin
Fulton

Chester
2nd Fl., Ste. D
701 Crosby St.
Chester, PA 19013-6089
(610) 447-3290
Delaware

Clearfield
501 E Market St., Ste. 6
Clearfield, PA 16830
(814) 765-0572
Cameron
Clearfield
Elk
Forest
Jefferson
McKean
Warren

Erie
1309 French St.
Erie, PA 16501-1999
(814) 871-4381
Crawford
Erie

Greensburg
593 Sells Ln.
Greensburg, PA 15601-4458
(724) 832-5275
Westmoreland

Harrisburg
1171 S. Cameron St., Rm. 311
Harrisburg, PA 17104-2591
(717) 787-1700
Dauphin
Juniata
Lebanon
Mifflin
Perry

Johnstown
200 Lincoln St.
Johnstown, PA 15901-1592
(814) 533-2371
Armstrong
Cambria
Indiana
Somerset

Lancaster
1016 N. Charlotte St., Ste. 109
Lancaster, PA 17603
(717) 299-7606
Lancaster

Malvern
Century Plz., 2nd Fl.
72 Lancaster Ave.
Malvern, PA 19355-2160
(610) 647-3799
Chester

Mercer
114 W. South St.
Mercer, PA 16137-1549
(724) 662-4007
Butler
Clarion
Mercer
Venango

Nanticoke
40 E. Main St.
Nanticoke, PA 18634
(570) 740-2440
Carbon
Luzerne
Sullivan

Norristown East/West
1885 New Hope St.
Norristown, PA 19401-3146
(610) 270-1316 - East
(610) 270-3450 - West
Montgomery

Philadelphia
444 N. Third St., Ste. 3B
Philadelphia, PA 19123-4190
(215) 560-3136/1828
Philadelphia

Pittsburgh
933 Penn Ave., 2nd Fl.
Pittsburgh, PA 15222-3815
(412) 565-2400
Allegheny

Reading
625 Cherry St., Rm. 250
Reading, PA 19602-1184
(610) 378-4395
Berks

Scranton
135 Franklin Ave.
Scranton, PA 18503-1935
(570) 963-4686
Bradford
Lackawanna
Susquehanna
Wayne
Wyoming

Shamokin
2 E. Arch St.
P.O. Box 279
Shamokin, PA 17872-0279
(570) 644-3415
Columbia
Montour
North-umberland
Schuylkill
Snyder
Union

Tannersville
Rt. 611 Merchants Plz.
P.O. Box 789
Tannersville, PA 18372-0789
(570) 620-2870
Monroe
Pike

Uniontown
140 N. Beeson Ave., Ste. 403
Uniontown, PA 15401-2937
(724) 439-7230
Fayette
Greene

Washington
Millcraft Center, Ste. 120UL
90 W. Chestnut St.
Washington, PA 15301
(724) 223-4530
Washington

Williamsport
208 W. Third St., Ste. 301
Williamsport, PA 17701-6477
(570) 327-3525
Clinton
Lycoming
Potter
Tioga

York
841 Vogelsong Rd.
York, PA 17404-1397
(717) 767-7620
Adams
York

Out-of-State
L & I Bldg., Rm. 703
Seventh & Forster Sts.
Harrisburg, PA 17121-0001
(717) 787-5939
Those enterprises not having a PA location.

For the hearing impaired only
(717) 783-3545

PA-100 (6-03)

COMMONWEALTH OF PENNSYLVANIA
DEPARTMENT OF REVENUE
BUREAU OF BUSINESS TRUST FUND TAXES
DEPT. 280901
HARRISBURG, PA 17128-0901

Go Paperless . . .
REGISTER ON THE INTERNET
www.paopenforbusiness.state.pa.us

PENNSYLVANIA
ENTERPRISE
REGISTRATION
FORM AND INSTRUCTIONS

DETACH AND MAIL COMPLETED REGISTRATION FORM TO:

COMMONWEALTH OF PA · DEPARTMENT OF REVENUE · BUREAU OF BUSINESS TRUST FUND TAXES · DEPT. 280901 · HARRISBURG, PA 17128-0901

PENNSYLVANIA ENTERPRISE REGISTRATION

The Pennsylvania Enterprise Registration Form (PA-100) must be completed by enterprises to register for certain taxes and services administered by the PA Department of Revenue and the PA Department of Labor & Industry. The form is also designed to be used by previously registered enterprises to register for additional taxes and services, reactivate a tax or service, or notify both Departments that additional establishment locations have been added. The form is also used to request the Unemployment Compensation Experience Record and Reserve Account Balance of a Predecessor.

For registration assistance, contact:
(717) 787-1064, Monday through Friday 8:00 AM to 4:30 PM (EST); Service for Customers with special hearing and/or speaking needs (TT only) 1-800-447-3020.

What is an enterprise?

An enterprise is any individual or organization, sole-proprietorship, partnership, corporation, government organization, business trust, association, etc., which is subject to the laws of the Commonwealth of Pennsylvania and performs at least one of the following:

- Pays wages to employees
- Offers products for sale to others
- Offers services for sale to others
- Collects donations
- Collects taxes
- Is allocated use of tax dollars
- Has a name which is intended for use and, by that name, is to be recognized as an organization engaged in economic activity.

What is an establishment?

An establishment is an economic unit, generally at a single physical location where:

- Business is conducted inside PA
- Business is conducted outside PA with reporting requirements to PA
- PA residents are employed, inside or outside of PA.

The enterprise and the establishment may have the same physical location.

Multiple establishments exist if the following apply:

- Business is conducted at multiple locations.
- Distinct and separate economic activities involving separate employees are performed at a single location. Each activity may be treated as a separate establishment as long as separate reports can be prepared for the number of employees, wages and salaries, or sales and receipts.

How to complete the registration form:

- **New registrants** must complete every item in Sections 1 through 10 and additional sections as indicated.
- **Registered enterprises** must complete every item in Sections 1 through 4 and additional sections as indicated.
- Section 5 has indicators to direct the registrant to additional sections.
- To determine the registration requirements for a specific tax service and/or license, see pages 2 and 3.
- Type or print legibly using black ink.
- Enter all dates in MM/DD/YYYY format (E.G. 10/22/2001).
- Retain a copy of the completed registration form for your records.

How to avoid delays in processing:

- Review the registration form and accompanying sections to be sure that every item is complete. The preparer will be contacted to supply information if required sections are not completed.
- Enclose payment for license or registration fees, payable to **PA Department of Revenue.**
- If a quarterly UC Report/payment is submitted, attach a separate check payable to **PA Unemployment Compensation Fund.**
- Sign the registration form.
- Remove completed pages from the booklet, arrange in sequential order, and mail to the PA Department of Revenue.

It is your responsibility to **notify the Bureau of Business Trust Fund Taxes** in writing within 30 days of any change to the information provided on the registration form.

Completing this form will NOT fulfill the requirement to register for corporate taxes. Registering corporations must also contact the PA Department of State to secure corporate name clearance and register for corporation tax purposes. Contact the PA Department of State at (717) 787-1057, or visit www.paopenforbusiness.state.pa.us.

TABLE OF CONTENTS

THE FOLLOWING CHART WILL HELP DETERMINE THE SECTIONS OF THIS BOOKLET THAT SHOULD BE COMPLETED FOR VARIOUS TAX TYPES.

COMPLETE THE SECTIONS THAT APPLY TO YOUR ENTERPRISE.

- New registrants should complete sections 1 through 10 plus the sections indicated.
- Previous registrants should complete sections 1 through 4 plus the additional sections indicated.

TAXES AND SERVICES	REQUIREMENTS	SECTIONS TO COMPLETE
CIGARETTE TAX IS AN EXCISE TAX IMPOSED ON THE SALE OR POSSESSION OF CIGARETTES. A DEALER IS ANY CIGARETTE STAMPING AGENT, WHOLESALER, OR RETAILER.	• CIGARETTE DEALER'S LICENSE • SALES TAX LICENSE (RETAILER)	• SECTION 19 • SECTION 18
CORPORATION TAXES ARE IMPOSED ON DOMESTIC AND FOREIGN CORPORATIONS, CERTAIN BUSINESS TRUSTS, AND LIMITED LIABILITY COMPANIES WHICH ARE REGISTERED AND/OR TRANSACTING BUSINESS WITHIN THE COMMONWEALTH OF PENNSYLVANIA. SUBJECTIVITY TO SPECIFIC CORPORATION TAXES IS DETERMINED BY THE TYPE OF CORPORATE ORGANIZATION AND THE ACTIVITY CONDUCTED.	• REGISTRATION WITH PA DEPARTMENT OF STATE • FORMS MUST BE OBTAINED FROM PA DEPARTMENT OF STATE	• SECTION 11
• **FINANCIAL INSTITUTIONS TAXES:** THE BANK AND TRUST COMPANY SHARES TAX IS IMPOSED ON EVERY BANK AND TRUST COMPANY HAVING CAPITAL STOCK AND CONDUCTING BUSINESS IN PENNSYLVANIA. DOMESTIC TITLE INSURANCE COMPANIES ARE SUBJECT TO THE TITLE INSURANCE COMPANY SHARES TAX. THE MUTUAL THRIFT INSTITUTIONS TAX IS IMPOSED ON SAVINGS INSTITUTIONS, SAVINGS BANKS, SAVINGS AND LOAN ASSOCIATIONS, AND BUILDING AND LOAN ASSOCIATIONS CONDUCTING BUSINESS IN PENNSYLVANIA. CREDIT UNIONS ARE NOT SUBJECT TO TAX.	• REGISTRATION WITH FEDERAL OR STATE AUTHORITY THAT GRANTED CHARTER	
• **GROSS PREMIUMS TAX** IS LEVIED ON DOMESTIC AND FOREIGN INSURANCE COMPANIES. THE YEARLY GROSS PREMIUMS RECEIVED FORM THE TAX BASE. GROSS PREMIUMS ARE PREMIUMS, PREMIUM DEPOSITS, OR ASSESSMENTS, FOR BUSINESS TRANSACTED IN PENNSYLVANIA.	• REGISTRATION WITH PA DEPARTMENT OF INSURANCE	
• **GROSS RECEIPTS TAX** IS LEVIED ON PIPELINE, CONDUIT, WATER NAVIGATION AND TRANSPORTATION COMPANIES; TELEPHONE AND TELEGRAPH COMPANIES; ELECTRIC LIGHT, WATER POWER AND HYDROELECTRIC COMPANIES; AND FREIGHT AND OIL TRANSPORTATION COMPANIES. THE TAX IS BASED ON GROSS RECEIPTS FROM PASSENGERS, BAGGAGE AND FREIGHT TRANSPORTED WITHIN PENNSYLVANIA; TELEGRAPH AND TELEPHONE MESSAGES TRANSMITTED WITHIN PENNSYLVANIA; AND SALES OF ELECTRICITY IN PENNSYLVANIA.	• REGISTRATION WITH PA PUBLIC UTILITY COMMISSION	
• **PUBLIC UTILITY REALTY TAX** IS LEVIED AGAINST CERTAIN ENTITIES FURNISHING UTILITY SERVICES. PENNSYLVANIA IMPOSES THIS TAX ON PUBLIC UTILITY REALTY IN LIEU OF LOCAL REAL ESTATE TAXES AND DISTRIBUTES THE LOCAL REALTY TAX EQUIVALENT TO LOCAL TAXING AUTHORITIES.	• REGISTRATION WITH PA PUBLIC UTILITY COMMISSION	
• **OTHER CORPORATION TAXES:** THIS GROUP IS COMPOSED PRIMARILY OF THE CORPORATE LOANS TAX, THE COOPERATIVE AGRICULTURAL ASSOCIATION AND ELECTRIC COOPERATIVE CORPORATION TAXES.	• REGISTRATION WITH PA DEPARTMENT OF STATE	
EMPLOYER WITHHOLDING IS THE WITHHOLDING OF PENNSYLVANIA PERSONAL INCOME TAX BY EMPLOYERS FROM COMPENSATION PAID TO PENNSYLVANIA RESIDENT EMPLOYEES FOR WORK PERFORMED INSIDE OR OUTSIDE OF PENNSYLVANIA AND NONRESIDENT EMPLOYEES FOR WORK PERFORMED INSIDE PENNSYLVANIA. (SEE UNEMPLOYMENT COMPENSATION DEFINITION)		• SECTION 9
LIQUID FUELS AND FUELS TAX IS AN EXCISE TAX IMPOSED ON ALL LIQUID FUELS AND FUELS USED OR SOLD AND DELIVERED BY DISTRIBUTORS WITHIN PENNSYLVANIA, EXCEPT THOSE DELIVERED TO EXEMPT PURCHASERS. LIQUID FUELS INCLUDE GASOLINE, GASOHOL, JET FUEL, AND AVIATION GASOLINE. FUELS INCLUDE CLEAR DIESEL FUEL AND KEROSENE. ADDITIONALLY, THE LIQUID FUELS AND FUELS TAX ACT TAXES ALTERNATIVE FUELS (i.e. HIGHWAY FUELS OTHER THAN LIQUID FUELS OR FUELS) AT A RETAIL/USE TAX LEVEL.	• LIQUID FUELS AND FUELS TAX PERMIT	• SECTION 21
MOTOR CARRIERS ROAD TAX IS IMPOSED ON MOTOR CARRIERS ENGAGED IN OPERATIONS ON PENNSYLVANIA HIGHWAYS. A MOTOR CARRIER IS ANY PERSON OR ENTERPRISE OPERATING A QUALIFIED MOTOR VEHICLE USED, DESIGNED, OR MAINTAINED FOR THE TRANSPORTATION OF PERSONS OR PROPERTY WHERE (A) THE POWER UNIT HAS TWO AXLES AND A GROSS OR REGISTERED GROSS WEIGHT GREATER THAN 26,000 POUNDS, (B) THE POWER UNIT HAS THREE AXLES OR MORE REGARDLESS OF WEIGHT, OR (C) VEHICLES ARE USED IN COMBINATION AND THE DECLARED COMBINATION WEIGHT EXCEEDS 26,000 POUNDS OR THE GROSS WEIGHT OF THE VEHICLES EXCEEDS 26,000 POUNDS.	• IFTA LICENSE AND IFTA DECALS • PA NON-IFTA VEHICLE REGISTRATION AND PA NON-IFTA DECALS	• SECTION 21

PROMOTER IS ANY ENTERPRISE ENGAGED IN RENTING, LEASING, OR GRANTING PERMISSION TO ANY PERSON TO USE SPACE AT A SHOW FOR THE DISPLAY OR FOR THE SALE OF TANGIBLE PERSONAL PROPERTY OR SERVICES.	• PROMOTER LICENSE	• SECTION 18
PUBLIC TRANSPORTATION ASSISTANCE TAX IS A TAX OR FEE IMPOSED ON EACH SALE IN PENNSYLVANIA OF NEW TIRES FOR HIGHWAY USE, ON THE LEASE OF MOTOR VEHICLES, AND ON THE RENTAL OF MOTOR VEHICLES. THE TAX IS ALSO LEVIED ON THE STATE TAXABLE VALUE OF UTILITY REALTY OF ENTERPRISES SUBJECT TO THE PUBLIC UTILITY REALTY TAX AND ON PETROLEUM REVENUE OF OIL COMPANIES.	• SALES USE AND HOTEL OCCUPANCY TAX LICENSE • PUBLIC TRANSPORTATION ASSISTANCE TAX LICENSE	• SECTION 18
REPORTING AND PAYMENT METHODS OFFER THE TAXPAYER THE ABILITY TO FILE CERTAIN TAXES THROUGH ELECTRONIC DATA INTERCHANGE (EDI) AND TO MAKE PAYMENT THROUGH ELECTRONIC FUNDS TRANSFER (EFT). UNEMPLOYMENT COMPENSATION (UC) WAGES MAY BE REPORTED VIA A MAGNETIC MEDIUM. IN CERTAIN INSTANCES, AN ENTERPRISE MAY ELECT TO FINANCE UC COSTS UNDER A REIMBURSEMENT METHOD RATHER THAN THE CONTRIBUTORY METHOD.	• AUTHORIZATION AGREEMENT	• SECTION 12
SALES TAX IS AN EXCISE TAX IMPOSED ON THE RETAIL SALE OR LEASE OF TAX-ABLE, TANGIBLE PERSONAL PROPERTY, AND ON SPECIFIED SERVICES.	• SALES USE AND HOTEL OCCUPANCY TAX LICENSE	• SECTION 18
• **HOTEL OCCUPANCY TAX** IS AN EXCISE TAX IMPOSED ON EVERY HOTEL OR MOTEL ROOM OCCUPANCY LESS THAN THIRTY (30) CONSECUTIVE DAYS.	• SALES USE AND HOTEL OCCUPANCY TAX LICENSE	• SECTION 18
• **LOCAL SALES TAX** MAY BE IMPOSED, IN ADDITION TO THE STATE SALES AND USE TAX, ON THE RETAIL SALE OR USE OF TANGIBLE PERSONAL PROPERTY AND SERVICES AND ON HOTEL/MOTEL OCCUPANCIES IN COUNTIES THAT HAVE ENACTED SUCH ORDINANCES.	• SALES USE AND HOTEL OCCUPANCY TAX LICENSE	• SECTION 18
SALES TAX EXEMPT STATUS FOR CHARITABLE AND RELIGIOUS ORGANIZATIONS IS THE QUALIFICATION OF AN INSTITUTION OF PURELY PUBLIC CHARITY TO BE EXEMPT FROM SALES AND USE TAX ON THE PURCHASE OF TANGIBLE PERSONAL PROPERTY OR SERVICES FOR USE IN CHARITABLE ACTIVITY.	• CERTIFICATE OF EXEMPT SALES TAX STATUS	• SECTION 22
SMALL GAMES OF CHANCE IS THE REGULATION OF LIMITED GAMES OF CHANCE THAT QUALIFIED CHARITABLE AND NON-PROFIT ORGANIZATIONS CAN OPERATE IN PENNSYLVANIA.	• SMALL GAMES OF CHANCE DISTRIBUTOR LICENSE AND/OR • MANUFACTURER REGISTRATION CERTIFICATE	• SECTION 20
TRANSIENT VENDOR IS ANY ENTERPRISE WHOSE BUSINESS STRUCTURE IS SOLE PROPRIETOR OR PARTNERSHIP, NOT HAVING A PERMANENT PHYSICAL BUSINESS LOCATION IN PENNSYLVANIA, WHICH SELLS TAXABLE, TANGIBLE PERSONAL PROPERTY OR PERFORMS TAXABLE SERVICES IN PENNSYLVANIA.	• TRANSIENT VENDOR CERTIFICATE	• SECTION 18
UNEMPLOYMENT COMPENSATION (UC) PROVIDES A FUND FROM WHICH COMPENSATION IS PAID TO WORKERS WHO HAVE BECOME UNEMPLOYED THROUGH NO FAULT OF THEIR OWN. CONTRIBUTIONS ARE REQUIRED TO BE MADE BY ALL EMPLOYERS WHO PAY WAGES TO INDIVIDUALS WORKING IN PA AND WHOSE SERVICES ARE COVERED UNDER THE UC LAW. THIS TAX MAY INCLUDE EMPLOYEE CONTRIBUTIONS WITHHELD BY EMPLOYERS FROM EACH EMPLOYEE'S GROSS WAGES. (SEE EMPLOYER WITHHOLDING DEFINITION)		• SECTIONS 7, 9, IF APPLICABLE 10 AND 14
• **APPLICATION FOR PA UC EXPERIENCE RECORD AND RESERVE ACCOUNT BALANCE** ENABLES THE REGISTERING ENTERPRISE TO BENEFIT FROM A PREDECESSOR'S REPORTING HISTORY. REFER TO THE INSTRUCTIONS TO DETERMINE IF THIS IS ADVANTAGEOUS.	• APPLICATION FOR EXPERIENCE RECORD AND RESERVE ACCOUNT BALANCE OF PREDECESSOR	• SECTIONS 14, 15 IF APPLICABLE, 16
USE TAX IS AN EXCISE TAX IMPOSED ON PROPERTY USED IN PENNSYLVANIA ON WHICH SALES TAX HAS NOT BEEN PAID.	• USE TAX ACCOUNT	• SECTION 18
VEHICLE RENTAL TAX IS IMPOSED ON RENTAL CONTRACTS BY ENTERPRISES HAVING AVAILABLE FOR RENTAL: (1) 5 OR MORE MOTOR VEHICLES DESIGNED TO CARRY 15 OR LESS PASSENGERS, OR (2) TRUCKS, TRAILERS, OR SEMI-TRAILERS USED IN THE TRANSPORTATION OF PROPERTY. A RENTAL CONTRACT IS FOR A PERIOD OF 29 DAYS OR LESS.	• SALES USE AND HOTEL OCCUPANCY TAX LICENSE • PTA LICENSE	• SECTION 18
WHOLESALER CERTIFICATE PERMITS AN ENTERPRISE SOLELY ENGAGED IN SELLING TANGIBLE PERSONAL PROPERTY AND/OR SERVICES FOR RESALE OR RENTAL. TO PURCHASE TANGIBLE PERSONAL PROPERTY OR SERVICES FOR RESALE OR RENTAL SALES TAX-FREE WHEN USED IN THE NORMAL COURSE OF THE ENTERPRISE'S BUSINESS.	• WHOLESALER CERTIFICATE	• SECTION 18
WORKERS' COMPENSATION COVERAGE IS MANDATORY AND PROTECTS EMPLOYERS FROM LIABILITY FOR WAGE LOSS AND MEDICAL BENEFITS INCURRED AS A RESULT OF EMPLOYEES' JOB RELATED INJURIES OR DISEASES. ENTERPRISES WHO EMPLOY AT LEAST ONE EMPLOYEE WHO COULD BE INJURED OR DEVELOP A WORK RELATED DISEASE IN PA OR OUTSIDE OF PA WHILE UNDER A CONTRACT OF HIRE MADE IN PA, IF THE EMPLOYMENT IS PRINCIPALLY LOCALIZED IN PA, NOT PRINCIPALLY LOCALIZED IN ANY STATE, OR PRINCIPALLY LOCALIZED IN ANY STATE WHOSE WORKERS' COMPENSATION LAWS DO NOT APPLY, MUST INSURE THEIR WORKERS' COMPENSATION LIABILITY BY PURCHASING A WORKERS' COMPENSATION POLICY THROUGH AN INSURANCE COMPANY OR BY SECURING THE AUTHORITY TO SELF-INSURE. ENTERPRISES ARE EXCLUDED FROM THE REQUIREMENT TO INSURE THEIR WORKERS' COMPENSATION LIABILITY IF **ALL** WORKERS EMPLOYED BY IT FALL INTO ONE OR MORE OF THE EXEMPT CATEGORIES.	• WORKERS' COMPENSATION COVERAGE	• SECTION 9

Index

C

D

E

Internet Corporation for Assigned Names and Numbers (ICANN), 75
interstate commerce, 22, 86, 111, 154
interviews, 96, 103
inventory, 3, 40, 69, 164
investors, 24, 26, 28, 41, 42

J

jurisdiction, 51, 81, 82

L

labeling, 21, 87, 127, 138, 150, 154, 156, 157
lease, 45, 46, 47, 93
  renewal, 46
liability, 7, 8, 10, 11, 12, 13, 19, 20, 67, 68, 69, 70, 82, 83, 84, 92, 109, 112, 121, 163, 168
libel, 82
licenses, 7, 12, 13, 49, 50, 51, 53, 54, 56, 58, 177
limited liability company (LLC), 7, 11, 12, 13, 30, 84, 163
limited liability partnership, 12, 13
limited partnership, 7, 10, 11, 13
Loan Interest and Protection Law, 146
loans, 37, 39, 40, 42, 54, 146, 187

M

management, 2, 3, 26, 28, 34, 54, 69, 102

manufacturing, 26, 27, 28, 45, 57, 81, 89, 93, 128, 139
marketing, 3, 25, 26, 27, 28, 30, 31, 35, 42, 46, 79, 87, 91, 131, 148, 151, 160
Medicare, 99, 100, 165, 169, 170, 171
merchant status, 143
meta tags, 78
minimum wage, 111

N

nonprofit corporation, 9, 10

O

Occupational Safety and Health Administration (OSHA), 89, 90, 92, 186
off the books employment, 121
officers, 9, 10, 13, 168

P

partnership, 2, 7, 8, 9, 10, 11, 12, 13, 41, 163, 167, 168, 170
Patent and Trademark Office (PTO), 16, 20, 21, 149, 150
patents, 16, 20, 21, 149, 150, 151
Pennsylvania Enterprise Registration, 175, 176, 179
Pennsylvania Exemption Certificate, 176, 177
Pennsylvania Human Relations Act, 109
pension plans, 101, 102, 113, 115, 116

R

S

T

U

Uniform Commercial Code (UCC), 147
unions, 110, 122
Universal Accessibility Act (UAA), 107
usury, 146

V

Veteran's Preference Act (VPA), 123
visas, 120

W

Wage Payment and Collection Law, 112,
    113
warehouse, 45
websites, 16, 29, 31, 54, 73, 74, 75, 76, 77,
    78, 79, 80, 81, 82, 84, 85, 86, 88, 90, 91,
    103, 106, 120, 123, 149, 157, 172, 176
    designer, 85
weights, 138, 139
wholesale, 3, 127, 177
withholding, 100, 166, 168, 169, 170, 171,
    178
workers' compensation, 57, 67, 68, 101,
    104

Z

zoning, 45, 47, 49, 50, 93